The information you ne[barcode] regarding the issues affecting you. . . your w[barcode]d your world. Subscribe to

P9-DKE-296

THE ANNALS

Subscription Order Form

	Individual			Institution		
	One Year	Two Years	Three Years	One Year	Two Years	Three Years
Hardcover	☐ $60	☐ $120	☐ $180	☐ $156	☐ $312	☐ $468
Softcover	☐ $42	☐ $84	☐ $126	☐ $132	☐ $264	☐ $396

Name / Institution _____

Address _____

_____

City _____ State _____ Zip _____ Country _____

☐ My check or credit card information is enclosed. ☐ Bill me.

Charge my: ☐ MasterCard ☐ Visa Exp. Date _____

Account # _____ Signature _____

Prices effective through December 31, 1993. Make checks payable to Sage Publications. Institutional checks for personal orders cannot be accepted. In Canada, add 7% GST (#R129786448). On subscriptions outside the United States, add $9 per year for foreign postage. All foreign orders must be paid in U.S. funds.

Ⓢ **SAGE Publications, Inc.** • P.O. Box 5084 • Newbury Park, CA 91359 • (805) 499-0721 **T3627**

THE ANNALS

Gift Order Form

Please send **THE ANNALS** as my gift, preceded by a gift announcement in my name, to:

	Individual			Institution		
	One Year	Two Years	Three Years	One Year	Two Years	Three Years
Hardcover	☐ $60	☐ $120	☐ $180	☐ $156	☐ $312	☐ $468
Softcover	☐ $42	☐ $84	☐ $126	☐ $132	☐ $264	☐ $396

My Name _____ Gift To _____

Address _____ Address _____

City _____ State _____ City _____ State _____

Zip _____ Country _____ Zip _____ Country _____

☐ My check or credit card information is enclosed. ☐ Bill me.

Charge my: ☐ MasterCard ☐ Visa Exp. Date _____

Account # _____ Signature _____

Prices effective through December 31, 1993. Make checks payable to Sage Publications. Institutional checks for personal orders cannot be accepted. In Canada, add 7% GST (#R129786448). On subscriptions outside the United States, add $9 per year for foreign postage. All foreign orders must be paid in U.S. funds.

Ⓢ **SAGE Publications, Inc.** • P.O. Box 5084 • Newbury Park, CA 91359 • (805) 499-0721

T3627

VOLUME 527   MAY 1993

THE ANNALS

of The American Academy *of* Political
and Social Science

RICHARD D. LAMBERT, *Editor*
ALAN W. HESTON, *Associate Editor*

RELIGION IN THE NINETIES

Special Editor of this Volume

WADE CLARK ROOF

University of California
Santa Barbara

Ⓢ SAGE PERIODICALS PRESS   *NEWBURY PARK   LONDON   NEW DELHI*

27996390

THE ANNALS

© 1993 *by* The American Academy *of* Political *and* Social Science

Editorial Office: 3937 Chestnut Street, Philadelphia, PA 19104.

For information about membership* (individuals only) and subscriptions (institutions), address:

SAGE PUBLICATIONS, INC.
2455 Teller Road
Newbury Park, CA 91320

From India and South Asia, write to:
SAGE PUBLICATIONS INDIA Pvt. Ltd.
P.O. Box 4215
New Delhi 110 048
INDIA

From the UK, Europe, the Middle East and Africa, write to:
SAGE PUBLICATIONS LTD
6 Bonhill Street
London EC2A 4PU
UNITED KINGDOM

SAGE Production Staff: LINDA GRAY, LIANN LECH, and JANELLE LeMASTER
*Please note that members of The Academy receive THE ANNALS with their membership.
Library of Congress Catalog Card Number 93-83086
International Standard Serial Number ISSN 0002-7162
International Standard Book Number ISBN 0-8039-4894-8 (Vol. 527, 1993 paper)
International Standard Book Number ISBN 0-8039-4893-X (Vol. 527, 1993 cloth)
Manufactured in the United States of America. First printing, May 1993.

The articles appearing in THE ANNALS are indexed in *Book Review Index, Public Affairs Information Service Bulletin, Social Sciences Index, Current Contents, General Periodicals Index, Academic Index, Pro-Views,* and *Combined Retrospective Index Sets.* They are also abstracted and indexed in *ABC Pol Sci, Historical Abstracts, Human Resources Abstracts, Social Sciences Citation Index, United States Political Science Documents, Social Work Research & Abstracts, Sage Urban Studies Abstracts, International Political Science Abstracts, America: History and Life, Sociological Abstracts, Managing Abstracts, Social Planning/Policy & Development Abstracts, Automatic Subject Citation Alert, Book Review Digest, Work Related Abstracts, Periodica Islamica,* and/or *Family Resources Database,* and are available on microfilm from University Microfilms, Ann Arbor, Michigan.

Information about membership rates, institutional subscriptions, and back issue prices may be found on the facing page.

Advertising. Current rates and specifications may be obtained by writing to THE ANNALS Advertising and Promotion Manager at the Newbury Park office (address above).

Claims. Claims for undelivered copies must be made no later than three months following month of publication. The publisher will supply missing copies when losses have been sustained in transit and when the reserve stock will permit.

Change of Address. Six weeks' advance notice must be given when notifying of change of address to ensure proper identification. Please specify name of journal. Send address changes to: THE ANNALS, c/o Sage Publications, Inc., 2455 Teller Road, Newbury Park, CA 91320.

The American Academy of Political and Social Science

3937 Chestnut Street   Philadelphia, Pennsylvania 19104

Origin and Purpose. The Academy was organized December 14, 1889, to promote the progress of political and social science, especially through publications and meetings. The Academy does not take sides in controverted questions, but seeks to gather and present reliable information to assist the public in forming an intelligent and accurate judgment.

Meetings. The Academy occasionally holds a meeting in the spring extending over two days.

Publications. THE ANNALS is the bimonthly publication of The Academy. Each issue contains articles on some prominent social or political problem, written at the invitation of the editors. Also, monographs are published from time to time, numbers of which are distributed to pertinent professional organizations. These volumes constitute important reference works on the topics with which they deal, and they are extensively cited by authorities throughout the United States and abroad. The papers presented at the meetings of The Academy are included in THE ANNALS.

Membership. Each member of The Academy receives THE ANNALS and may attend the meetings of The Academy. Membership is open only to individuals. Annual dues: $42.00 for the regular paperbound edition (clothbound, $60.00). Add $9.00 per year for membership outside the U.S.A. Members may also purchase single issues of THE ANNALS for $13.00 each (clothbound, $18.00). Add $1.50 for shipping and handling on all prepaid orders.

Subscriptions. THE ANNALS (ISSN 0002-7162) is published six times annually—in January, March, May, July, September, and November. Institutions may subscribe to THE ANNALS at the annual rate: $132.00 (clothbound, $156.00). California institutions: $141.57 paperbound, $167.31 clothbound. Add $9.00 per year for subscriptions outside the U.S.A. Institutional rates for single issues: $24.00 each (clothbound, $29.00). California institutions: $25.74 paperbound, $31.10 clothbound.

Second class postage paid at Thousand Oaks, California, and additional offices.

Single issues of THE ANNALS may be obtained by individuals who are not members of The Academy for $17.00 each (clothbound, $26.00). California residents: $18.23 paperbound, $27.89 clothbound. Add $1.50 for shipping and handling on all prepaid orders. Single issues of THE ANNALS have proven to be excellent supplementary texts for classroom use. Direct inquiries regarding adoptions to THE ANNALS c/o Sage Publications (address below).

All correspondence concerning membership in The Academy, dues renewals, inquiries about membership status, and/or purchase of single issues of THE ANNALS should be sent to THE ANNALS c/o Sage Publications, Inc., 2455 Teller Road, Newbury Park, CA 91320. Telephone: (805) 499-0721; FAX/Order line: (805) 499-0871. *Please note that orders under $30 must be prepaid.* Sage affiliates in London and India will assist institutional subscribers abroad with regard to orders, claims, and inquiries for both subscriptions and single issues.

Printed on recycled, acid-free paper

THE ANNALS

of The American Academy *of* Political
and Social Science

RICHARD D. LAMBERT, *Editor*
ALAN W. HESTON, *Associate Editor*

———————— **FORTHCOMING** ————————

CITIZENS, PROTEST, AND DEMOCRACY
Special Editor: Russell J. Dalton

Volume 528   July 1993

RURAL AMERICA:
BLUEPRINT FOR TOMORROW
Special Editor: William Gahr

Volume 529   September 1993

INTERMINORITY AFFAIRS IN THE U.S. TODAY:
A TATTERED COAT OF MANY COLORS
Special Editor: Peter I. Rose

Volume 530   November 1993

See page 3 for information on Academy membership and
purchase of single volumes of **The Annals.**

CONTENTS

BOOK DEPARTMENT CONTENTS

PREFACE

Anyone trying to figure out what is happening religiously in the United States in the 1990s is struck by a mix of disparate and sometimes confusing trends: declining institutions yet continuing religious vitality, a weak public religious presence yet strong personal and spiritual energies, dissolution of older cultures and support structures yet rediscoveries of mythical unities. It is a time not of celebrated establishments but of reformulations and grass-roots ferment. It is a time when, in fact, we may appreciate anew what Tocqueville observed 150 years ago, that in a country where the spirit of religion and the spirit of freedom march together in common cause, religious life tends to be in flux, ever changing and taking on new forms.

But some times are more in flux than others, and the 1990s stand out in this respect. Martin E. Marty's lead article captures the flavor of the period. Drawing off William James's notion of "habitual centres of energy," Marty writes of energies flowing as follows: the personal, private, and autonomous at the expense of the communal, the public, and the derivative; emphasis on meaning rather than on inherited patterns of belonging; attention to the local rather than the cosmopolitan; concern for the practical and affective life instead of the devotional and intellectual; the feminist as opposed to the male dominated; commitment to separate causes rather than to larger, encompassing purposes. He points out that these shifts in the centers of energy have been under way for some time in this country, and he challenges us (see his footnote 3) to look at these broader historical changes by comparing trends as reported in special issues on religion by *The Annals* in 1948, 1960, 1985, and 1993.

Those who take up Marty's challenge should find the articles in the present volume helpful. Several themes surface in the collection that give us a clearer sense of the direction of religious changes. Without any prodding on my part as special editor in shaping the content of what people wrote—beyond assigning general topics—it is remarkable how well the articles dovetail with one another in pointing to current trends and in their characterization of the American religious context in these waning years of the twentieth century. In what follows, I shall comment briefly on what I take to be the more important themes.

One theme is the source of religion's continuing vitality. Roger Finke and Laurence R. Iannaccone point to the importance of supply-side factors historically in America's religious life: innovative religious leaders, popular forms of organizations, and how judicial and governmental regulations affect the religious marketplace. Colonial revivalists, Asian cult leaders, and contemporary televangelists, they observe, all flourished when regulatory changes gave them freer access to the American people. In the 1960s and 1970s, a time of declining religious establishments, major changes were in the direction of opening up religious opportunities; however, judicial decisions now threaten to restrict the supply of religious innovation. Edward A. Tiryakian takes up the well-known argument about "American exceptionalism" but goes beyond the usual interpretation about religious activism to show how religious elements continue to be infused in popular moral causes, including poverty, civil rights, smoking, dieting, and physical fitness and, abroad, campaigns against "the evil empire" and Saddam Hussein. This phenomenon of mobilization, he notes, is a continuing feature of the country's diffused religion and heritage of "this-worldly activism," to borrow Max Weber's term.

A second theme is the broad social changes affecting organized religion, many of which have been under way for a long time but are now better understood. Phillip E. Hammond and Kee Warner explore the changing patterns of religion and ethnicity. Given trends toward greater individual choice in American culture, both religion and ethnicity are less inheritable than in the past. Assimilation and secularization are correlated, but both processes, they note, occur at a slower pace for ethnic groups regarded as minorities and who have experienced discrimination. Other changes such as declines in anti-Semitism and racial prejudice, new roles for women, and liberalization of attitudes toward sexual practices are singled out by Charles Y. Glock as crucial for the mainline churches. All the major Protestant denominations plus the Roman Catholic Church are caught up in fierce controversies over issues of gender, life-style, and sexual abuse today. Glock speaks of an "enigmatic" future for these churches, given the great divisions within them over how to respond to such social changes and over fundamental articles of faith, including how scripture is to be read and understood.

A third theme, especially prominent in the 1990s, is realignment and reassessment. Across domains as diverse as theological education, new religious movements, and televangelism, this is a time of thinking things through once again. In the case of theological education, Barbara G. Wheeler discusses how the premises of theological study—views of clerical tasks, conceptions of theory and practice—are today being challenged. The unity of theology and its deeply personal character are threatened in an age when theory is divorced from practice and disciplines of clergy education are themselves highly specialized. Consequently, there are increasing calls among educators for a unifying theological focus despite countertrends in seminaries in the direction of greater program diversification.

Since the 1960s, the new religious movements have attracted a great deal of attention. But according to J. Gordon Melton, we need to revise our views of these movements. He suggests that they are not as marginal or ephemeral as we often think and proposes that they are best viewed not as cults but as products of the massive diffusion of the world's religions globally. Such movements will continue to grow as a result of a change in immigration laws in the mid-1960s. Likewise, televangelism was one of the most visible features of the American religious scene during the late 1970s and much of the 1980s. Jeffrey K. Hadden traces the rise of the televangelists and their involvement in politics and their subsequent fall as a result of financial and sexual scandals and changing religious market conditions. He assesses the prospects for the future of religious broadcasting and of new televangelist empires.

A fourth theme, picked up in the last set of articles, centers on spiritual renewal. Catherine L. Albanese looks at the New Age as an expression of American nature religion stemming from the nineteenth century. This "old" New Age, as she puts it, "conflated material and spiritual worlds," resulting in a great emphasis upon harmony with nature and healing. Today's new spirituality is an offshoot of this older heritage, which, combined with additional psychological and religious motifs, makes for a strong holistic approach to life. She sees this spirituality as having a social ethic capable of engaging public discourse on topics such as environmentalism and hints at its having a stronger public presence in the future than either the mainline churches or civil religion. Meredith B. McGuire looks at health and healing as metaphors for salvation and holiness. She explores nonmedical approaches to health and healing, underscoring that these are holistic in the belief that spiritual, emotional, and physical aspects of well-being are all connected. A powerful thrust in these spiritual movements is the rediscovery of the body along with concern more generally at overcoming many of the dualisms— such as mind-body—of our culture. In the final essay, I explore what I judge to be some new, embryonic forms of religion. Three reconstructions of religious space are described. The new immigrant religions created by a global political economy are reshaping America's central cities and forging a new religious consciousness among many groups. New family and life-style patterns are another domain where spiritual energies today find growing expression. For members of the baby-boom generation generally, there are signs of a reinvigorated spiritual quest, of a concern both for sacred and expressive values and for greater balance between pursuit of individual needs and social responsibilities.

To all the contributors, my great appreciation for what I believe to be a provocative set of articles.

WADE CLARK ROOF

ANNALS, *AAPSS*, **527**, May 1993

Where the Energies Go

By MARTIN E. MARTY

ABSTRACT: American religious energies neither disappear nor flow through fixed channels. What William James called "the habitual centres of energy" in an individual have cultural counterparts. In recent decades the centers of energy have increasingly sought channels such as these: the personal, private, and autonomous at the expense of the communal, the public, and the derivative; the accent on meaning at the expense of inherited patterns of belonging; concentration on the local and particular more than the cosmopolitan or ecumenical; concern for practical and affective life accompanied by less devotion to the devotional and intellectual expressions; the feminist as opposed to the male dominated; and attention to separate causes more than to overarching civil commitments. These contrasts are themselves neither absolute nor final; the less stressed center of energy in each case survives but is not currently prevailing or coming to prevail.

Martin E. Marty, Ph.D., is the Fairfax M. Cone Distinguished Service Professor at the University of Chicago and senior editor of The Christian Century. *His most recent books are* Modern American Religion, *volume 2,* The Noise of Conflict, 1919-1941 *and, with R. Scott Appleby,* The Power and the Glory: The Fundamentalist Challenge to the Modern World.

I N *The Varieties of Religious Experience,* William James located energy in the "hot place" of a person's consciousness. James, our greatest philosopher-psychologist of religion, called the "group of ideas to which [a person] devotes himself, and from which he works, . . . *the habitual centre of his personal energy.*" Thus when someone is "converted" it means that "religious aims form the habitual centre of his energy."[1]

Individuals with their energies together make up cultures, societies, and nations like the United States. The mass of their religious ideas, devotions, and aims also makes for communal "hot places" and "habitual centres" of energy. When a couple hundred million people devote their lives to ideas that help them make sense of their world, when they respond to the sacred or seek the transcendent or find God, when they undertake the rites of passage through life with religious ceremonies, as most of them do, they are expending and exuding energies. Virtually every thoughtful foreign observer who has written about American ideas, devotions, and aims has pointed to these religious energies and notes where some of them go.

The channels and outlets for religious energies constantly change. For example, through most of human history until 1789 in the new United States, people routed their spiritual energies through institutions connected with ruling powers. As the United States was born, citizens came to find ways to direct these energies into voluntarily supported institutions or individual outlets. The processes by which they made this adaptation have been subject to constant change as citizens abandoned or revised the old ways and invented or adopted new ones.

The Founders and the citizens saw to it, said political scientist Walter Berns as he observed the move toward constitutionalism, that "religion was subordinated through relegation to the private realm, where everyone is free to believe [with Thomas Jefferson] that there is one god or twenty gods or no god at all." Berns added to this judgment the observation of Alexis de Tocqueville that such subordination represented a wise move. To the surprise of many who could not picture religion apart from regime, the new situation did not mean the end of religion. " 'The whole nation,' " according to the French visitor, held religion " 'to be indispensable to the maintenance of republican institutions.' "[2] The whole nation, at least the vast majority of its citizens when polled, still holds religion to be indispensable, or at least highly salutary. But ever since religion was relegated to "the private realm," it has tended to be overlooked in the barterings of power within the worlds of the academy, media, government, and commerce. Therefore, in order to answer the question about where religious energies have increasingly flowed, one must borrow

1. William James, *The Varieties of Religious Experience* (Cambridge, MA: Harvard University Press, 1985), p. 162. This classic first appeared in 1902.

2. Walter Berns, *The First Amendment and the Future of American Democracy* (New York: Basic Books, 1976), pp. 30, 32. Berns cited Alexis de Tocqueville, *Democracy in America* (New York: Vintage, 1945), 1:316.

the spectacles of people like James, Jefferson, and Tocqueville. Observers of recent[3] changes in the "habitual centres" of cultural energies and their outlets tend to concur in locating a number of directions or emphases, about which I shall generalize and which I shall name in headings.

PERSONAL RELIGIOUS PREOCCUPATION MORE THAN THE COMMUNAL

First, these emphases come to focus in personal religious preoccupation more than the communal.

3. "Recent" here means, approximately, the period since two reports in this journal on religion in America, reports dating from a period that started just before a postwar "revival of interest in religion" first began to appear (1948) and at about the time it peaked (1960). See *The Annals* of the American Academy of Political and Social Science, 256:1-172 (Mar. 1948); ibid., 332:1-155 (Nov. 1960). The former was called *Organized Religion in the United States*. Ten articles dealt with "religious institutions," and five others with "churches" or "religious bodies." Only two dealt with "religion" in a generic and noninstitutional sense. The editors' choice of accent was appropriate to the situation in 1948, when organized or institutional religion preoccupied the concern of scholars and the public. By 1960, the accent had begun to shift, as reflected in the Nov. 1960 issue, *Religion in American Society*. Now more articles dealt generically with "religious interest," "revival," "laity," and broad-based themes such as "religion and education," "religion and politics," and "religion among ethnic and racial minorities." Only three or four articles concentrated on institutions of religion as such. By the time of a third concentration in *The Annals* (480:9-174 [July 1985]), almost all the articles dealt with "isms" such as "pluralism," "Protestantism," and the like, the accent having shifted even more from attention to formal denominational life. It would be instructive for readers to disinter the 1948 and 1960 volumes to provide contrast with the trends reported in 1985 and 1993.

That the focus of "the habitual centre of [one's] personal energy" has always been individualized or personal is a tautology made ever more evident through the passage of the years. Thomas Jefferson helped patent for the nineteenth century the notion of the individual as the center. With other Enlightenment figures, he averred that his own mind was his temple. William James enhanced this with his classic but somewhat exaggerated exclusion of the communal or institutional dimension from religious experience. Religion in his context, a context that became ever more privileged through the course of the twentieth century, was "the feelings, acts, and experiences of individual men in their solitude, so far as they apprehend themselves to stand in relation to whatever they may consider the divine."[4] Ordinary people have not needed a Jefferson or a James to provide a formula for them. From the born-again Christian who has all but forgotten New Testament communalism when he or she asked, "Have you accepted Jesus Christ as your personal savior?" to the New Age entrepreneur who has found God in the isolation of his or her "inner self," this modern countenance that religion wears has become ever more noteworthy.

To look for drastic sea changes in American religion, however, would be to miss the force of inertia. Better to compare religious change to the slower and more gradual movement of the glacier. Thus, paradoxically, the communal, social, and institutional expressions have not disap-

4. James, *Varieties of Religious Experience*, p. 34.

peared through the movement of religion into the voluntary zone. The most vivid evidence for this claim is the ever expanding section marked "Churches and Synagogues" in the Yellow Pages of any telephone book. A small city of 50,000 people may easily display notice of fifty denominations and hundreds of places of worship. Where their traditional congregations do not satisfy, clienteles and constituencies for putatively noninstitutional but still group religion develop and attract citizen energies to degrees that astonish those who compare the United States with other industrialized nations. Religion was supposed to have disappeared in a modern, secular era; instead, in America, it simply found new channels for citizen energies.

In most accounting for the combination of individualized faith concurrent with the survival of religious institutions, this trend gets noticed: whereas, once, inherited loyalties to a particular ecclesiastical tradition—for example, Catholic, Quaker, Orthodox Jewish—prevailed, increasingly, people have come to adopt a more arbitrary, pick-and-choose approach to communal expressions of faith. An individual chooses a spiritual trajectory and then, so long as and insofar as an institution matches his or her course, the institution is favored—often only to be later dropped more casually than it might have been in the past.

PRIVATE SPHERE
OVER THE PUBLIC SPHERE

This combination of increasingly individualized faith and surviving communal routing of energies has been accompanied by a corollary phenomenon. The "habitual centre of . . . energy" deals more with the private sphere than with the public.

Noting the dialectic between the private and the public coursing of religious energies has been part of the classic observations. This dialectic was also reinforced by the decisions that Americans made in their constitutional period, to relegate religion administratively to the private realm. The trends of modernity, which lead to increasing differentiation and specialization—in colloquial terms, the chopping up of life—left religion to be segregated largely in the private zone. After mid-century, social critics developed a full-fledged polemic against what sociologist Peter Berger called "the privatization of religion" as a " 'solution' to the religious problem of modern society." Religion consequently had to " 'evacuate' one area after another in the public sphere," while it "successfully maintained itself as an expression of private meaning."[5] Church and synagogue were consequently identified with leisure, residential and family life, and suburban isolation. The public realm existed independently of them.

This relegation of religion to the private zone manifestly promoted civil peace and generated a mixed spiritual and secular climate that most Americans appreciate. They demonstrate this by their consistently negative views of militant religion in the public order elsewhere.

5. Peter L. Berger, Brigitte Berger, and Hansfried Kellner, *The Homeless Mind: Modernization and Consciousness* (New York: Random House, 1973), pp. 80, 186.

They see the negation of their patterns in Shi'ite and Sunni Islamic regimes or where religion is an element in tribal warfare, from Northern Ireland through Israel to India. The premium put on extreme individualism and the market orientation of religion in America, where faith becomes the subject of competition for best-selling books, for the most highly rated televangelism broadcasts, the most successful megachurches, and the most credible ideologies that would encourage people to "do their own thing" or "do it their way," encourages further privatization of faith.

The change to the private has not been total, and there are countertrends. Again, apparently paradoxically, we have seen some sustained and even new attention devoted to agencies of religion in the public order. While in private life many have been pursuing their "spiritual journeys," they have also seen the perduring power of African American churches in metropolitan elections. Other examples include the endeavors of the Roman Catholic bishops to address the public order; intense fundamentalist-inspired activities in respect to so-called social issues such as abortion; synagogue support for national policies favoring Israel; evangelical intrusions into the political scene that the religious conservatives had earlier abandoned; and the continuing efforts of mainstream Protestants to address public issues. What had become manifestly different from past public expressions was the increasing need of religionists to amass constituencies instead of to speak for them. Thus

whenever the National Council of Churches or the leadership of a Protestant denomination issued pronouncements on the social order, the pronouncements were not viewed as being automatically expressive of the private views of their constituents. However, when a televangelist produced evidence that millions were donating to his cause and supporting his public and political positions, the political leadership had to reckon with it in fresh ways. But for most citizens, the individual and the private modes predominated over the communal and public expressions.

INDIVIDUAL AUTONOMY OVER INHERITED AUTHORITY

Another way to put the first two emphases is to say that "habitual centres" of cultural energy lead believers to engage in expressions of individual autonomy over inherited authority. The passion for asserting expressive individualism, the growth of an educated laity, and the enhancement of choice in a free market of religion have together made for a buyer's market. The individual seeker and chooser has come increasingly to be in control. This enhancement of a long-term trend reaches back for precedents at least to the 1740s and the Great Awakening. Back then, believers began to be able freely to reject the established faith of a region or polity. They could go on then to seek and find a new, independent, and probably heated-up faith. This has all meant a shift in the understandings of religious authority. This authority comes to be challenged whenever leaders attempt to run other people's spiritual lives.

Once upon a time, to use colloquial terms, the faithful might say, "What the pope says, goes" or "What the bishop, or priest, or rabbi, or minister, or theologian says, goes." Not that people longer ago refrained from crossing their fingers as they professed loyalty or did not engage in creative foot-dragging when called upon to follow. But in the premodern world and even in the recent modern past, most believers showed signs of being content with inherited and automatic loyalty to those who happened to wield religious power. In recent times, across the denominational board, assertions of individualism have led to decline in respect for coercive authority. It is hard for the pope to make the case for banning or excommunicating dissident priests or to gain support for efforts to do such disciplining. Similarly, let a leader try to discipline a Protestant, and in response the subject of discipline will simply move on and find a home in another Protestant body.

Assertion of authority has not disappeared, however, so much as it has found new outlets and modes. To use one grand sweep of a phrase, it has moved from the coercive to the persuasive realm. It might be said that when a religious leader, by making a variety of charismatic, courageous, or clarified moves, attracts a followership, he or she cannot fail to be compelling. If, however, he or she fails to persuade and then falls back on coercion, the followers will lose heart or disappear. For example, according to the evidence of polls, American Catholics by and large agree with their leaders' position against abortion, so they tend to follow. All the polls show that they disagree on birth control, and almost no one even makes a show of following the authorities. While followership is now more complicated than before— one minister rued, "You are only as good as your last act"—in this circumstance some purifying goes on. Therefore, some good things should be said for the newer construct. When religion appears, it would seem to be more authentically expressed than when it was voiced only in assent to coercive authority or unquestioned dogma and interpretation. When people simply belonged to an inherited religious tradition and went about interpreting it, authoritative and authoritarian leadership possessed strategic advantages. But they would not be of much help when "the habitual centre" of a culture's religious energies are directed more to personal meaning than to the act of belonging.

PERSONAL MEANING OVER THE ACT OF BELONGING

From primordial times to the modern, religion certainly provided meaning in the lives of adherents, but it was more natural for them to satisfy that search for meaning through their membership in a group that provided them with an identity. After the onset of anything that can credibly be termed modernity and especially in modern America, individuals came to be left more to their own devices as they sought interpretations of meaning in life. Contemporarily, in many places in the world, religious identification dominates, and it provides believers with what we might call a prefabricated meaning system. This is demonstrably the case in the various assertive fundamentalist movements that follow what I call tribal or national lines. In America, however, most can easily violate the boundaries of their racial or ethnic group, the expectations of class, and even the constraints of family to follow their chosen spiritual trajectories.

In this period, however, there has not been simple or total displacement of one channel of energies by another; continuities with past patterns remain. It would again be melodramatic and unscientific to suggest that the trend follows the lines of a metaphoric sea change instead of a glacial movement. While one is free to violate inherited cultural bonds and instinctive social boundaries, there is a continuing use of religion to define who one is, to what one belongs, and whom one can trust.

In the 1970s, America saw a revival of interest in ethnicity as an element in religious expression; race also continues to help define expectations in religious choice. One expects an African American to be Baptist, Methodist, or Pentecostal; Americans of Polish, Italian, or Irish descent are as likely to be identified with Catholicism as Scandinavians are with Lutheranism or Scots with Presbyterianism. For many, denominational inheritance or choice therefore does remain some sort of a factor in providing identity. Therefore, to be integrated into a system of meaning still, despite what Jefferson and James contended or to what they gave priority, is accompanied by integration into some system of belonging.

The evident accent on meaning in recent decades results from the desperate urgency imposed on the individual by modern life, where automatic support for one's outlook does not come from a single and obvious set of surrounding institutions. But the concept and experience of belonging survive as attractions, albeit in changed ways. The notion of belonging to something remote and inclusive—for example, the "one holy catholic and apostolic church" or "the people of God"—is an elusive possibility in a world of very defined and concrete expressions. Close to home, this means that the "habitual centre" of cultural energies finds a home more in the local, which predominates over the cosmopolitan.

THE LOCAL OVER THE COSMOPOLITAN

Virtually every American denomination has fallen on fiscal hard times, but not because there are fewer members or because members have become more miserly and poorer stewards. The flow of money—an approved indicator of where American energies go!—remains constant, but it is diverted into or contained predominantly in local congregations, in parachurches over which the donors have more control, or in caucuses and causes of their choice. Visitors to America who are familiar with the financing of religion elsewhere consistently express astonishment at the relative generosity of American religious donors. Well over half the billions of dollars donated by citizens to various causes each year are routed through religious institutions. Despite inflation, the figure keeps growing. Fragmentary evidence from 42 denominations suggests, for instance, that, from 1961 to 1988, giving by the average church member grew, in current dollars, from $69.00 to $376.04 or, in constant dollars, from $77.01 to $106.14. The latter growth is an increase of 37.8 percent, or slightly less than 1.4 percent a year on average. This figure alarms denominational leadership, which sees it as low, but awes many nonreligious observers, who are astounded to see such devotion.[6]

Where financial energies are, there are the heart and imagination as well. Most religions aspire to articulate universalizing messages. Much of the major news made by America's predominant complex, Christianity in its broadest sense, has occurred outside America in recent years. The greatest Christian growth has been in sub-Saharan Africa; great change is occurring and intra-Christian conflict is developing in increasingly Protestantized, formerly Catholic, Latin America; the prime religious drama has been seen in Eastern Orthodox and Catholic adjustments to life in Eastern Europe after the demise of communism. Yet editors of religious magazines report that they ordinarily chronicle news of such places out of a sense of responsibility; the stories do not attract subscribers' attention the way those that feature America and its familiar and particular places do.

Around the world there seems to be a massive revolt against bureaucracy, remoteness, and the unfamil-

6. Constant H. Jacquet, Jr., ed., *Yearbook of American and Canadian Churches 1990* (Nashville, TN: Abingdon, 1990), p. 270.

iar in religion; this pattern is accompanied not by a loss of interest in religion itself but by a residual and perhaps increasing devotion to the local. Bureaucracy was modernity's instrument for giving people connections with what was remote. Twentieth-century religious ideology has often promoted familiarity with the previously unfamiliar and stressed the cosmopolitan reach of the religions. But while there may still be generalized or lip service to cosmopolitanism in an age when access to the distant and the larger world has been made easy, through high-speed travel, or made instantaneous, through electronic communication, most religious energies go into what can be controlled locally, rendered malleable to individual initiative, and tested empirically by ordinary people. However much one's ideology or ethos may lead to a criticism of the failure of cosmopolitanism fully to develop, the passion for the local is itself impressive evidence of religion's power, if now in altered channels. A corollary of this local-cosmopolitan dialectic is another: the "habitual centre" of the culture's energies moves more through the particular rather than the ecumenical forms.

THE PARTICULAR,
NOT THE ECUMENICAL

At mid-century, an ecumenical vision still prevailed, and lovers of the particular were on the defensive. This, many had prophesied, was the ecumenical century; for Christians, ecumenism was what Anglican Archbishop William Temple called "the great new fact of our era." The interfaith movement, especially Christian-Jewish, concurrently received public acclaim. For moderates and liberals, the time-honored moves toward proselytization or religious conquest were being modified to accommodate an appreciation for other religions, with which one's own might interact. The World and National Council of Churches aspired to inclusiveness, and the Second Vatican Council of 1962-65 was ecumenical not only in name but also in aspiration. There was a United Nations; there were United World Federalists; a typical major photographic exhibit stressed "the family of man"; inhabitants of the world were featured as living in a "global village" or on "spaceship Earth."

That mid-century vision changed in the last third of this century. There developed in America, after the rise of the generalizing ecumenical movement, a set of revivals of ethnicity and ethnic religious ties, or identifications of God with one's race—black, Native American, Jewish, Hispanic—or gender. Theology became particularized: black theology, womanchurch, African liberation, and the like came into favor. The decisive separations in the majority (in America) Christian world did not follow denominational lines so much as lines of gender, class, race, ethnicity, cause, or ideology and political preference. The God witnessed to by some was now seen as black, or red, or female—or, said some critics, God remained the preserve of white males who reinforced male imagery for the divine. The denomination as a coordinating institution was in trouble, as sound book-length chronicles re-

vealed.[7] Ecumenism as an institutionalizing movement also came to be seen as compromised, ignored, or disdained.

However, here, as so often happens, the rechanneling of energies did not mean the drying up of all old channels. The denomination survived in the form of revised centers for loyalty and to fulfill altering functions. Evidence of that was present in the passions devoted to control of denominational machinery in some battles of the 1970s and 1980s—for example, in large Protestant bodies like the Southern Baptist Convention and the Lutheran Church-Missouri Synod. Both of these saw conflict and division that was being virtually matched in Roman Catholic polarities, mainstream Protestant church conflicts, and even within the clearly defined and intense fundamentalist, evangelical, and Pentecostal bodies. After almost a century of ecumenical endeavor, there are not fewer denominations in the *Yearbook*.[8] While certain denominational families have set their divided confessional houses in partial order—through mergers of Lutherans, United Methodists, United Presbyterians, and more—there have been only one or two true mergers across familial lines, such as the United Church of Christ in 1957. It cannot fairly be said, even by its partisans, that a movement called the Church of Christ Uniting caught and held public attention or the devotion of

7. For example, in Robert Wuthnow, *The Restructuring of American Religion* (Princeton, NJ: Princeton University Press, 1988).

8. Jacquet, ed., *Yearbook of American and Canadian Churches 1990*.

its potential members, who remained within divided denominations.

The denomination by and large was no longer the definer of doctrine for members or outsiders. It was undercut by parachurch movements, localism, and the privatization of religion, to which I have already pointed. Yet the denomination survived, to serve some remaining functions—for example, administering ministerial pension plans—some altered ones, and some new ones. Thus, in the very midst of modern individualism and differentiation, the denomination represented for some converts and many traditional members some sort of religious family and familial expression. For all its weaknesses, the denomination attracted fiscal and other devotion of a sort the ecumenical movement could not summon.

Ecumenism, however, also did not disappear. Its leadership made some adjustments and set out to attract different sets of energies. The movement grew more complex as Christian-Jewish and a variety of Western approaches to "world religious pluralism" developed, for these made even the huge Christian ecumenical endeavor look somewhat chummy and self-enclosed. Nonetheless, the involvement of Eastern Orthodoxy in ecumenical expressions such as the National Council of Churches and the open but still limited embrace by Roman Catholicism of other churches after Vatican II; the vitality of evangelical Protestantisms not associated with World and National Councils; the general revolt against bureaucracy and remoteness already referred to—all these led to the loss of luster by traditional ecumenical

organizations. Most historians date the founding of these from a meeting at Edinburgh in 1910 through the Second Vatican Council, which ended in 1965.

The ecumenical spirit, however, survived this decline of interest in religious institutions. The principle of picking and choosing among faiths seemed increasingly to prevail. For example, on a certain issue, members of one wing of United Methodism found more congenial spiritual and practical bonds with those in a corollary wing of Catholicism, Episcopalianism, or Mennonitism than each of these parties found with other fellow members in their own Methodist, Catholic, Episcopal, and Mennonite churches. On another issue, there might well be different coalescences. Before ecumenical breakthroughs signaled by the Second Vatican Council, it had been widely assumed that the laity of one church were and would remain hostile to those in all others. Instead, it was revealed that there were enormous reservoirs of goodwill and pent-up ecumenical energies waiting to be expressed. But these were not accompanied by a corollary interest in the machinery and mechanics of the very organized ecumenical movements that made their expression possible.

What has resulted is what I call a criss-cross pattern of ecumenism as opposed to a rigid, formal patterning. The same situation is seen as well in Christian-Jewish relations. One set of Christians relates positively to Jews on one set of issues: an example is evangelical premillennialists who are ardent supporters of Israel while many liberal ecumenists have been more reluctant advocates or have even been desirous of finding a balance that includes pro-Palestinian sentiment. On another issue, liberal Catholics and Protestants side with Jews on many theological and domestic social causes while evangelicals stay at a distance, dismissing the liberalism of both. The ecumenical spirit in American religions has in any case been strong enough to produce a contrast between religious tolerance in their nation over against more belligerent religious articulation elsewhere. From all this, one can conclude that in the United States the "habitual centre" of cultural energy in religion is evident in action devoted to healing more than to creating conflict or killing.

HEALING OVER CONFLICT OR KILLING

The healing in this polarity is literal; the killing is generally metaphoric. American religious conflict produces few dead bodies.[9] Ameri-

cans take for granted that religion as such should not produce killing; perhaps they overlook the religious justifications in their own religious pasts for the genocide and removal of Native Americans or the religious symbolization of both sides in the devastating Civil War. But religion has as often been associated with killing as with healing throughout history and certainly in the headlines of recent decades. The Inquisition, the Crusades, the Thirty Years War, and persecutions or martyrdoms in the European Christian past are today matched by Sikh, Hindu, Islamic, Jewish, and Christian lethality in the Middle East, North Africa, the Asian subcontinent, increasingly in Latin America, Northern Ireland, and elsewhere. Americans look on at these in bemusement: how can religion produce such violence, a violence that seems only to be increasing after the Cold War, in the postcolonial era, and during religious resurgences on other continents?

In the United States, deaths involving extreme right-wing movements occur only very occasionally, usually where white extremists invoke religious symbols. Now and then a child dies because of medical practices, or their absence, in what the public calls a cult. Religious motivation led some civil rights workers to martyr's deaths, and religious motivation may also well have been a

9. On this subject, see Martin E. Marty, *Modern American Religion*, vol. 2, *The Noise of Conflict, 1919-1941* (Chicago: University of Chicago Press, 1990). This book chronicles a period of intense religious conflict: "original-stock Protestants vs. everyone else; 100 percent Americans vs. Communists and Slavs in the Red Scare; old-stock Anglo-Saxons vs. Catholic or Jewish or Asian immigrants; the Ku Klux Klan vs. the same, plus liberals and blacks; white Christians vs. black Christians; conventional black churches vs. 'Back to Africa' movements; Zionists vs. anti-Zionists; pro-labor Catholics vs. antilabor Catholics; Protestant Fundamentalists vs. Modernists; pro-Peace Pact movements vs. anti-League of Nations sorts; pro-Repeal wets vs. anti-Repeal drys; Protestants against a Catholic president vs. Catholics for a Catholic president; supporters of birth control vs. enemies of birth control; Depression demagogues of the Right vs. left-wing firebrands; Protestant liberals vs. Protestant realists; Catholic Workers vs. capitalists; pro-New Deal religionists vs. anti-New Dealers; pacifists vs. 'preparedness for war' partisans, and more." Yet there was "a virtual absence of dead bodies as a result of these intense conflicts." Ibid., pp. 3-4.

part of the killers' justifications. There were deaths two decades ago in violence associated with battles over evolution and religion in West Virginia. But most American violence has been of a verbal sort. Again, the criss-cross patternings of American life once envisioned by James Madison in the Tenth and Fifty-First Federalist Papers contribute to the diminution of religion's powers to kill and the limitation of the effects even of rhetorical violence.

A new trend sees the increasing visibility of religion's energies directed to healing. Most religions, certainly Judaism and Christianity among them, were born if not as healing cults then as movements whose leaders and pioneers offered healing in their ministry. The post-Enlightenment period, with the devotion of its leaders to scientific medicine and the professionalization of medical healing within institutions specializing in healing arts, for a time obscured from view the healing concerns of religion. These had always remained manifest among many of the laity who in prayer if not also in overt practices—the use of healing oils, sacred herbs, miracle-producing shrines—and in the quiet ministries of priest and minister, rabbi and chaplain, engaged in consolatory and therapeutic ventures. With some more recent questioning of technical medicine and some compromising of the Enlightenment Project, accompanied by some decline in the belief in progress or in mastery realized through science, there has grown a new attachment to religion for its healing promise.

This attachment takes many forms. One sees the uses of the congregation as a place of healing; the development of religiously generated and motivated 12-step programs and support ministries for those addicted; New Age and Asian healing projects; recoveries of healing ministries in Pentecostal, charismatic, and some mainstream churches that are attentive to rites and beliefs about healing; theological justifications for religious care and the interpretation of suffering; the rise of centers of medical ethics informed by faith; huge industries devoted to pastoral counseling and clinical pastoral education. Taken together, these movements sometimes seem to acquire an aura of promise and independence that leads them to qualify as autonomous religions or quasi religions. These movements and expressions typically appear more as counsels for mere practice, without a summoning of fully developed theological justifications. When such appearances occur, they are in line with a long-term American religious genre, heightened in our time. It sees the "habitual centre" of cultural energies in religion to be practical more than mystical.

PRACTICAL MORE
THAN MYSTICAL

One of the two terms in this duality comes from Charles Peguy, who averred that "everything begins in mysticism and ends in politics." Most scholars who observe genres of Euro-American religion—more than African, Asian, or Native American—have readily generalized about the busyness of the American pious. Citizens have excelled in praxis. They have been productive: of effects, institutions, results, causes, policies—usually at the expense of what most people have claimed religion was about. This tendency has not diminished in recent decades. Thus the spiritual side of Alcoholics Anonymous and so many other 12-step and support movements usually results in devotion and altered ways of life. But there has been little theological explication of what goes on, and the unquestionably spiritual undergirding of such movements resists clarification, often upon the impulse of the leaders, who do not wish to become mired in the inevitable controversy that would accompany such explication or clarification.

Americans remain great volunteers for activity in the public realm. As was the case with volunteer dollars, well over half of all volunteer hours issue through religious causes and depend on religious motivations. The generalizations about American religionists as doers need little justification; tests for them are manifold. But one must note also the recent rise of a strong subsidiary or complementary strand: the devotion to what Peguy called the mystical but what most Americans call the spiritual. Here, there has been some shifting of attention in recent years. As late as the mid-1960s, in a time when many Protestants spoke of a secular theology, during the civil rights movement, in the presence of Catholic activism after the Second Vatican Council, assertive African American causes, Jewish devotion to Israel,

and the like, the spiritual was downvalued to the point that the very term was suspect or seen as doomed.

Twenty-five years later, the spiritual received a new premium and, in a vogue word of the day, had become "commodified." Best-selling books, retreat centers, television ministries, charismatic leaders, a New Age movement, Hasidic and mystical Judaism, and recovered mysticisms from the Catholic and Protestant pasts were some of the more visible signs of the new interest. How to account for the shift was more difficult than to point to it. In the eyes of some practitioners of this spirituality, it represented an alternative to old ideologies as these faded. To others, it may have seemed to have risen as a justification for a new worldliness or, conversely, as a compensation when the material world failed its devotees by not delivering prosperity or when the shallowness or poverty of goods without values became evident. For still others, the new spirituality may have seemed a way to reject the sterility of the technical and secular orders. It may also have represented a sense of entitlement in the realm of the soul to match entitlement in respect to bodily needs: God, or Energy, or Connections, in effect, owe me, the spiritual seeker, some satisfactions. However extensive, deep, and lasting the advocacies of mysticism and spirituality turn out to be, they are likely to remain as enhancers rather than supplanters of the practical impulses in American religious energy fields. They are, however, extensions of the affective side of life and thus match what remains a constant, perhaps one that is even being enhanced. The "habitual centre" of cultural energies in religion focus on the affective more than on the intellectual.

THE AFFECTIVE OVER THE INTELLECTUAL

Historian Sidney E. Mead devoted much of his career to showing the effects of Protestant revivalism on the national religious ethos. Other historians have since shown how analogues to revivalism worked similar effects in Catholicism and other complexes. Mead demonstrated, in patterns followed by later historians, that the affective side of religion, symbolized by the revivals, left most Americans posed thus: they could choose to be pious by the standards of piety in their age or to be reasonable by the standards of reason in various moments. Fewer could relate piety to reason, revelation to intellectual life, and the like. Of course, the tensions symbolized by an ancient polarity between Jerusalem and Athens was a constant in Western history. But the era of pietism, revivalism, awakenings, and renewals, in the midst of modernity, accentuate the tensions within it.

For Mead, the religious awakenings "effectively separated the religious from the intellectual life of the society and the two were duly institutionalized in denominations and universities respectively."[10] When scholars use the concept of affectivity this way, they do not necessarily mean hyperemotionalism so much as the whole range of experiential religion. Affection does focus on emotions, sensibilities, and experiences more than on intellectual inquiry and formulation. The trend of devotion to it has increased during the last third of this century. While the enterprises of theology and religious scholarship grow ever more complex, few observers would think of the achievement for the 1970s through the 1990s as being expressive of a generation of creative and influential theological expression. In a conventional inquiry that recalls the name of mid-century giants, people ask, "Where are the Niebuhrs and the Tillichs, the Murrays and Weigels and the Heschels?"

There are few if any peers of these whose names come instantly to mind. The very enterprise of theology itself has become more specialized, less evocative of lay concerns. It is hard to think of any theologian who would be recognized on a *Time* or *Newsweek* cover, the way one can think of religiopolitical, spiritual, and therapeutic celebrities or leaders as candidates for such placement. Yet the fact that the specialization has gone on does not mean that the intellectual enterprise is over; it is being rechanneled. The American Academy of Religion, the Ph.D.-producing university-related schools of religion, and the large journal, monograph, and book industries indicate that energies are also devoted to the intellectual life. But it would not be fair or honest observation to say that, taken together, these represent any challenge or counterpart at all to the affective side of religion.

While women have not specialized in affectivity, or at least while the articulators of religious feminisms

10. Sidney E. Mead, *The Old Religions in the Brave New World* (Berkeley: University of California Press, 1977), p. 89.

would resent being typecast as non-intellectual and only intuitional, the domain of affectivity has increased during a time when another "habitual centre" of cultural life in religion has been visibly expressed: women and women's movements have come into their own.

RECOGNITION OF WOMEN AND WOMEN'S MOVEMENTS

Women probably dominated numerically through all the years of religious expression since Europeans and Africans came five and four hundred years ago to America, and they may have done so in the Native American world before that. However, they were normally excluded from leadership. Most texts were written and interpreted by men, who provided the canons, studied the classics, and held the offices. Women were relegated to auxiliaries, support movements, and the domestic scene.

Perhaps no revolution of this third of the century in American religion will have effects for as long as the one that brought women into leadership, led them to find voice in support of their vision, their gift, and their contribution, and promoted women's consciousness in religion. Accordingly, all the old texts need reinterpretation. Old archives have to be searched, and are being searched, for overlooked women's sources. More and more denominations ordain women, and male leadership in virtually all of these has been challenged to yield hegemony, to complement women, and to learn from them in their enhanced roles. Trends in history writing, for example, as seen in devotion to social history, or history-

from-below, as some call it, particularly result from and produce this women's revolution. Religion gets reworked for its role in care, nurture, generation of life, adolescence, marriage, sexual relations, domestic life, inspiration for women's self-consciousness—at the expense of religious inquiry devoted merely to who had been in power and what they did when men alone were in power.

Men have not fled the ranks. Some have noted, not always without concern, that the clergy may in a generation become predominantly a women's profession. Yet in the healing, practical, and affective lives of religious people, men have remained active, often adaptively and sometimes in resistance. The rise of one realm complicates the life of another but does not do away with it. The same is the case with the "habitual centre" of cultural energies in religion, which flow through channels for particular expressions more than under "the sacred canopy" of civil religion.

PARTICULAR EXPRESSION PREFERRED TO CIVIL RELIGION

Having commented on the decline of denominations, one must still note that most Americans see their religion when institutionalized at all as expressed through specialized institutions and not primarily through the nation, under what Peter Berger has called "the sacred canopy" in which a civil religion thrives. For a quarter of a century, concern has been expressed by those who are devoted to the common good lest Americans in their localisms, particularisms, and denominationalisms or parachurch movements desert all regard for the civil or public religious life, of some coordinating and coalescing sorts. The concern is well placed. Robert Bellah's classic essay on civil religion, expressive of life in the Eisenhower-Kennedy-Johnson presidential eras up to 1965, turned out to be an end-of-the-era statement of observation, not a harbinger of the emergent.[11] Since that time, Americans have been too divided and specialized, in society in general as well as in religion in particular, to follow the scholars in their extensive pursuit of such civil or public religion.

What survived of civil religion in the ensuing period became much more partisan than before, as Bellah himself would note when Richard Nixon occupied the White House and seized the symbols of public religion. Such religion tended to appear in times of militant expression, as was seen briefly during the Persian Gulf war of 1991, but became recessive after the postwar parades had marched down the street. And still, while under the sacred canopy citizens have experienced its leaks, heard the sound of its flapping in the breeze, and seen the arrival of unwelcome newcomers—immigrants—under it,

11. Robert N. Bellah, "Civil Religion in America," *Daedalus*, 96(1):1-21 (Winter 1967).

the canopy does remain and many do transact their concerns with the sacred through American public or civil religion. Political candidates have more recently been trying to seize the symbols of such religion, but they have tended to reduce it to partisan claims and justifications and have failed to match the aspirations of the whole of society. Religion in America is easier to discover, discern, and define than is American religion.

THE TRIAL BALANCE
ON AMERICAN RELIGIOUS
ENERGIES TODAY

American religion involves 200-250 million people in their almost infinite varieties as they face numberless choices in ever shifting modes of life. In other words, citizens display so many energies that it would be unfair to be too exclusive while making an effort to direct attention to where the main outlets and passages are. Like riverbeds, these change from time to time: they broaden or deepen or even find new locations. The energies remain, to the surprise of those who thought secularity would see the dissipation, not the rechanneling, of such vitalities. In William James's terms, for the culture as for the individual, there remain "hot places."

ANNALS, *AAPSS*, **527**, May 1993

Supply-Side Explanations
for Religious Change

By ROGER FINKE and LAURENCE R. IANNACCONE

ABSTRACT: Traditional scholarship approaches religious history from the demand side, attributing developments to the shifting desires, perceptions, and circumstances of religious consumers. This article advocates an alternative, supply-side approach that emphasizes the opportunities and restrictions confronting religious organizations and their leaders. Supply shifts lie at the root of major religious changes in America. Colonial revivalists, Asian cult leaders, and contemporary televangelists all prospered when regulatory changes gave them freer access to America's religious marketplace. The article concludes with a discussion of recent judicial decisions that threaten to restrict the future supply of religious innovation in America.

Roger Finke is associate professor of sociology at Purdue University. He recently completed a book with Rodney Stark, The Churching of America, 1776-1990: Winners and Losers in Our Religious Economy.

Laurence R. Iannaccone is associate professor of economics at Santa Clara University and the author of numerous articles on the economics of religion.

28

THE ANNALS OF THE AMERICAN ACADEMY

FROM upstart sects to controversial cults, new faiths and new approaches to faith permeate America's religious history. Traditional interpretations of these developments have proved curiously one-sided, attributing most innovations to the would-be believer's altered desires, perceptions, or circumstances. Religious historians describe the increased revivalism in the eighteenth and nineteenth centuries as Great Awakenings in which Americans demanded new worldviews more consistent with the existing political and economic environment. Social scientists trace the surge in Asian-style cults in the 1960s to the birth of a "new religious consciousness" among America's youth. Scholars and journalists explain the growth of fundamentalist churches and the rise of televangelist preachers as an escapist "flight from modernity." These and other familiar interpretations of religious events share the unexamined assumption that religious change usually occurs in response to the shifting desires and needs of religious consumers.

This article turns the traditional assumption on its head and asserts that the most significant changes in American religion derive from shifting supply, not shifting demand. Colonial revivalists, Asian cult leaders, and contemporary televangelists all prospered when regulatory changes gave them freer access to America's religious marketplace. These and other important religious developments derive from change in the incentives and opportunities facing religious producers, not some sudden shift in the material or psychological state of the populace. Of course, religious markets respond to the equilibrating forces of both supply and demand, but, as a matter of historical fact, religious demand proves much more stable than religious supply.[1] Hence it is the market's neglected supply side that time and again provides the key to specific religious developments.

Through its emphasis on religious markets, this article implicitly models religion as an object of choice and production. The market model views churches and their clergy as religious producers who choose the characteristics of their product and the means of marketing it. Consumers in turn choose what religion, if any, they will accept and how extensively they will participate in it. In a competitive environment, a particular religious firm will flourish only if it provides a product at least as attractive as its competitors'. As in other markets, government regulation can profoundly affect the producers' incentives, the consumers' options, and the aggregate equilibrium. Together, these assumptions provide a new paradigm in the social-scientific study of religion, which previously we have analyzed in some detail.[2]

1. We suspect that this occurs because the underlying determinants of religious demand —people's tastes, beliefs, socialization, and so forth—are rooted in fundamental human needs, whereas religious supply is strongly affected by governmental policy. For data on the stablility of religious belief, see Andrew M. Greeley, *Religious Change in America* (Cambridge, MA: Harvard University Press, 1989).

2. For further discussion of the market paradigm, see Laurence R. Iannaccone, "Religious Markets and the Economics of Religion," *Social Compass*, 39(1):123-31 (1992); Roger

Here, we apply the paradigm to a series of turning points in American religion that range from the eighteenth century through the present.

SUPPLY-SIDE SHIFTS
IN EARLY AMERICA

Histories of American religion devote much attention to the Great Awakenings that ran from 1730 to 1760 and 1800 to 1830. As the term "awakening" suggests, scholars view these years as periods of surging demand. For example, William McLoughlin describes awakenings as "cultural transformations affecting all Americans," and he claims that they "begin in periods of cultural distortion and grave personal stress, when we lose faith in the legitimacy of our norms, the viability of our institutions, and the authority of our leaders in church and state."[3]

Following Finke and Stark,[4] we contend that the so-called Great Awakenings were nothing more—or less—than successful marketing campaigns of upstart evangelical

---

Finke and Rodney Stark, *The Churching of America, 1776-1990: Winners and Losers in Our Religious Economy* (New Brunswick, NJ: Rutgers University Press, 1992); R. Stephen Warner, "Work in Progress toward a New Paradigm for the Sociological Study of Religion in the United States," *American Journal of Sociology* (Mar. 1993). We owe our use of the terms "supply side" and "demand side" to private conversations with Stephen Warner.

3. William G. McLoughlin, *Revivals, Awakenings, and Reform* (Chicago: University of Chicago Press, 1978), pp. 2, 59. The analogy is that of "breaking out of the dead skin of the past" and seeking something new.

4. Finke and Stark, *Churching of America*. See also Jon Butler, "Enthusiasm Described and Decried: The Great Awakening as Interpretive Fiction," *Journal of American History*, 69:305-25 (1982).

Protestants. These campaigns arose when restrictions on new sects and itinerant preaching diminished. Early American religion flourished in response to religious deregulation.

The character and consequences of colonial deregulation

To appreciate the impact of deregulation, one must recall that the American colonies did not begin as bastions of religious freedom. Rather, the various groups of religious immigrants sought to create enclaves in which their own religion, such as Puritan Congregationalism, enjoyed preeminent status. Most of the colonies had their own established, state churches, and only by virtue of necessity did religious toleration come to the United States. Toleration grew in large part from the need for political compromise among the colonies and the difficulty of maintaining religious uniformity across a diverse immigrant population sparsely settled over vast areas. The transition to a free and competitive religious market began in the late colonial era[5] and accelerated thereafter. The new principles of religious freedom attained their clearest expression in the Constitution and Bill of Rights.[6]

Support for establishment ran deepest and lasted longest in New

---

5. Sidney E. Mead, "From Coercion to Persuasion: Another Look at the Rise of Religious Liberty and the Emergence of Denominationalism," *Church History*, 25:317-37 (1956). See also Roger Finke, "Religious Deregulation: Origins and Consequences," *Journal of Church and State*, 32:609-26 (1990).

6. Article IV of the Constitution stated that "no religious test shall ever be required as qualification to any office or public trust under

England. For nearly two centuries, New England's Congregational churches enjoyed the state's direct and indirect support. They received tax revenue and exercised local authority, while members of other religions paid taxes to subsidize the establishment and risked persecution, including imprisonment, for their support of a dissenting faith. All this changed in the late eighteenth and early nineteenth centuries.[7]

Deprived of its privileged position and financial support, Congregationalism lost market share at a remarkable rate. In 1776, it dominated the New England market with more than two-thirds of all religious adherents; by 1850 its share had plummeted to only 28 percent. In contrast, the dissident upstarts—Baptists and Methodists now freed from regulatory constraint—rocketed from 12 percent of all adherents in 1776 to 41 percent in 1850 (see Table 1 for details).[8]

As the upstart sects successfully fought for followers, they also managed to enlarge the market. Total rates of religious adherence doubled, from a mere 17 percent of the population in 1776 to 34 percent in 1850. One is hard-pressed to attribute these gains to crises or shifts within the American psyche. Increased competition, aggressive marketing, and religious entrepreneurship provide a much more credible explanation. We will examine this process more closely.

The rise of religious entrepreneurs

By all accounts, the Grand Itinerant, George Whitefield, stood at the center of America's First Great Awakening. Yet few scholars seem to appreciate Whitefield's marketing skills and religious entrepreneurship. Whitefield was, in fact, a master of advance publicity who sent a constant stream of press releases, extolling the success of his previous revivals, to cities he intended to visit.[9] His success dramatically illustrates the producer's role in the promotion of faith. Conversely, the New England establishment's response to Whitefield illustrates how regulatory constraints can, and often do, stifle such faith-promoting entrepreneurship.

Whitefield was a minister with credentials, being a graduate from

the United States," and the First Amendment stated that "Congress shall make no law respecting an establishment of religion, or prohibiting the free exercise thereof."

7. The profit from Vermont's Glebe rights or "ministry lands" was redistributed among all clergy (1794); New Hampshire passed toleration acts for Episcopalians (1792), Baptists (1804), and eventually all Christians (1819); Connecticut eased the standards of exemption from religious taxes (1784-91); and Massachusetts's Religious Freedom Act of 1811 eased the constraints on dissenting religions. Religious taxation, the final remnant of establishment, ceased in 1807 in Vermont, 1818 in Connecticut, 1819 in New Hampshire, and 1833 in Massachusetts. William G. McLoughlin, *New England Dissent, 1630-1833* (New York: Cambridge University Press, 1971); John K. Wilson, "Religion under the State Constitutions, 1776-1800," *Journal of Church and State*, 32: 753-74 (1990).

8. Although Catholics eventually became the largest denomination in New England,

Catholic immigration had little to do with the Congregationalists' early decline. By 1850, Roman Catholics constituted only 11 percent of all religious adherents.

9. Frank Lambert, " 'Pedlar in Divinity': George Whitefield and the Great Awakening, 1737-1745," *Journal of American History*, 77: 812-37 (1990).

TABLE 1
PERCENTAGES OF ALL ADHERENTS IN MAJOR DENOMINATIONS, 1776 and 1850

	1776	1850
New England*		
Congregational establishment	67	28
Baptists and Methodists	12	41
Roman Catholics	0	11
Maine		
Congregational establishment	61	19
Baptists and Methodists	8	58
Roman Catholics	0	6
New Hampshire		
Congregational establishment	63	30
Baptists and Methodists	9	46
Roman Catholics	0	3
Vermont		
Congregational establishment	65	29
Baptists and Methodists	10	44
Roman Catholics	0	6
Massachusetts		
Congregational establishment	72	29
Baptists and Methodists	15	33
Roman Catholics	0	17
Connecticut		
Congregational establishment	64	37
Baptists and Methodists	9	39
Roman Catholics	0	11

NOTE: On calculation of rates, see Rodney Stark and Roger Finke, "American Religion in 1776: A Statistical Portrait," *Sociological Analysis*, 49:39-51 (1988); Roger Finke and Rodney Stark, "Turning Pews into People: Estimating Nineteenth-Century Church Membership," *Journal for the Scientific Study of Religion*, 25:180-92 (1986).

*New England totals exclude Rhode Island, which never supported an established church.

Oxford University, and he made no attempt to found his own denomination. Yet his presence provoked heated resistance. The president and faculty of Harvard condemned Whitefield for "going about, in an Itinerant Way."[10] An association of Congregational ministers in Marlborough

County bore "publick and faithfull *Testimony* . . . against Mr. *Whitefield's* appearing as an *Itinerant* Preacher, or *Evangelist*, and traveling from Town to Town." The Congregational ministers of Bristol County complained that "for a Minister to invade another's Province and preach in his Charge without his leave, is disorderly and tends to Confusion, and hurteth the Work of God."[11]

10. *The Testimony of the President, Professors, Tutors and Hebrew Instructor of Harvard College in Cambridge, against the Reverend Mr. George Whitefield and His Conduct* (Boston: T. Fleet, 1744), p. 3.

11. *The Testimony of an Association of Ministers Convened at Marlborough, January 22,*

To appreciate these attacks, one need only see that itinerants were unregulated competitors in the religious marketplace, foreign competition that threatened the privileges and profits of a domestic cartel. In colonial America, the established clergy maintained a system of territorial monopolies, dividing the land into geographical units—often called "parishes"—and granting each minister exclusive authority over the religious activity in his area. Itinerants like Whitefield threatened to undermine this cartel, thereby reducing its power and profits.

New England's clergy moved quickly to defend their interests and squelch the revival. In 1742, following a recommendation of the General Consociation of ministers, the Connecticut legislature prohibited itinerants "from preaching in any parish without the approval of the minister of that parish." Yale students and faculty were required to take an "oath affirming their orthodoxy," and any clergy who protested the law were "called before the legislature, publicly rebuked, and deprived of their offices."[12] Restrictions like these spelled the end of the First Great Awakening.

By the early nineteenth century, however, the erstwhile establishment no longer enjoyed the official support needed to suppress competition. With the power of the parish system in decline, a new generation of religious entrepreneurs sprang up.

Histories usually label this second surge of itinerant evangelism and the concomitant growth of Methodist and Baptist sects as the "Second Great Awakening." In fact, it was the direct result of new religious freedoms.

This time around, the evangelists did not limit themselves to preaching but instead sought to found new churches wherever they went. The famous Methodist itinerant Peter Cartwright emphasized this point when a Presbyterian minister asked him not to start a church "in the bounds of his congregation."

I told him that was not our way of doing business; that we seldom ever preached long at any place without trying to raise a society. He said I must not do it. I told him the people were a free people and lived in a free country, and must be allowed to do as they pleased.[13]

Freed from restrictions, the upstart sects soon overtook the old-line faiths in New England and throughout the nation.

The road not traveled

The story would read quite differently had the religious establishments remained strong and their regulatory power endured. To glimpse history as it might have been, we need only compare the paths of American and English Methodism. Whereas the American Methodists embraced itinerancy and camp meetings, the Methodist hierarchy in England opposed these, viewing both

---

1744, against the Reverend George Whitefield and His Conduct (Boston: T. Fleet, 1745), p. 3; *The Testimony of a Number of Ministers in the County of Bristol against Mr. Whitefield* (Boston: T. Fleet, 1745), p. 8.

12. McLoughlin, *New England Dissent*, 1: 363.

13. Peter Cartwright, *Autobiography of Peter Cartwright, the Backwoods Preacher*, ed. W. P. Strickland (Cincinnati: Cranston & Curts, 1856), p. 123.

activities as a threat to the "fragile nature of religious toleration."[14]

British historian David Hempton notes that "how far Methodism should be allowed to shelter under the umbrella of the Church of England . . . became one of the most controversial legal problems of the period between 1740 and 1820." Initially, the Church of England had tolerated the Methodists' rigorous behavioral standards, exclusive membership, and lay and female itinerancy because Methodists had organized as a society within the Church of England and because John Wesley could guarantee their allegiance to the English church and state. But by the 1790s, Wesley's death and the growth and independence of Methodist societies had pushed Methodists beyond the protective shelter of Anglicanism. The Methodists could no longer call themselves the "Church of England at prayer"; they had become dissenters.[15]

As tensions mounted, Lorenzo Dow, an eccentric American Methodist itinerant, arrived to introduce camp meetings to the British Isles. Fearing reprisals, the Methodist hierarchy quickly moved to block his activities. According to Dow, "They warned the Methodists against me, to starve me out . . . [and] they offered to pay my passage home, if I would quit the country, and promise never to return, which in conscience I could not do."[16] Dow and other itinerants soon found support among the laity, but the Methodist Conference ruled against their frontier-style revivalism, stating that " 'it is our judgment, that even supposing such meetings to be allowable in America, they are highly improper in England, and likely to be productive of considerable mischief: and we disclaim all connections with them.' "[17]

The English Methodists knew whereof they spoke. A few years later, in 1811, Lord Sidmouth sought virtually to abolish itinerancy through a bill that limited preaching certificates to ministers attached to specific congregations. Although the bill failed to win approval, the threat of parliamentary regulation forced the Methodists to further curtail the activities of their itinerants. According to Hempton, the English "Methodists realized that their preaching privileges depended upon continued loyalty and good order."[18]

Thus Methodism in Great Britian faltered while American Methodism soared. As the Methodists in Great Britain struggled to keep pace with population growth, the percentage of Methodists in America continued to climb. From 1776 to 1850, Methodist membership in America rose from less than 3 percent of all church adherents to 34 percent, and the num-

14. Nathan O. Hatch, *The Democratization of American Christianity* (New Haven, CT: Yale University Press, 1989), p. 50.

15. David Hempton, "Methodism and the Law, 1740-1820," in *Sects and New Religious Movements*, ed. A. Dyson and E. Barker, *Bulletin of the John Rylands Library*, 70:94 (1988); see also idem., *Methodism and Politics in British Society, 1750-1850* (Stanford, CA: Stanford University Press, 1984).

16. Lorenzo Dow, *History of Cosmopolite or the Four Volumes of Lorenzo Dow's Journal, Sixth Edition* (Wheeling, VA: Joshua Martin, 1849), p. 256.

17. As quoted in Hatch, *Democratization of American Christianity*, p. 50.

18. Hempton, *Methodism and Politics in British Society*, p. 104.

ber of Methodist congregations sky-rocketed from 65 to more than 13,000.[19] Such meteoric growth could never have occurred under a hierar-chy that restrained its itinerants and opposed camp meetings.

SUPPLY-SIDE SHIFTS IN MODERN AMERICA

Against the backdrop of disestab-lishment, one might suspect that con-temporary changes in religious regu-lation deserve scant attention. But economic reasoning also applies to small shifts and is in some sense most useful at this level, since it draws attention to events that are otherwise ignored or misinterpreted. Any careful observer could have an-ticipated a major response to the total restructuring of the religious market in early America, but the same cannot be said for recent court decisions, new immigration quotas, or an apparently minor change in Federal Communications Commis-sion (FCC) guidelines.

Prime time preachers:
Televangelism
and the FCC

The Communications Act of 1934 authorized the FCC to grant broad-casting licenses, which amounted to monopoly rights over specific fre-quencies in certain areas. In return for these monopoly rights, broadcast-

ers—first radio and then television—have had to submit to FCC regula-tions, including a requirement to de-vote a portion of their air time to the public service. Because FCC guide-lines on public service programming listed religion as one of its suggested categories, broadcasters have always deemed it prudent to devote some air time to religious programs.[20] More-over, because the FCC favored "sus-taining-time," or free, public service programming over commercially sponsored, or paid, programming, most religious broadcast time was provided free of charge.[21]

FCC guidelines thus virtually re-quired broadcasters to supply a scarce commodity—air time—to a certain segment of demanders—preachers—free of charge. Not sur-prisingly, the demand for such time greatly exceeded its supply. Unable to ration through price, the networks fell back on strategies that mini-mized their costs and favored their friends. Most turned their time over to the Federal Council of Churches, a cartel-like association of America's "respectable" Protestant denomina-tions.[22] Of course, the council always denied acting as a cartel. But in the words of one of its own executives, it enabled the member denominations to control "the allocation of time among themselves on radio and tele-

19. Finke and Stark, *Churching of Amer-ica*. For data on Methodist membership in Great Britain, see Robert Currie, Alan Gilbert, and Lee Horsley, *Churches and Churchgoers: Patterns of Church Growth in the British Isles Since 1700* (New York: Oxford University Press, Clarendon Press, 1977), pp. 161-65.

20. Peter G. Horsfield, *Religious Televi-sion: The American Experience* (New York: Longman, 1984), p. 13.

21. See Finke and Stark, *Churching of America*, pp. 218-23.

22. See Jeffrey K. Hadden and Anson Shupe, *Televangelism: Power and Politics on God's Frontier* (New York: Henry Holt, 1988), pp. 46-47.

vision" and thereby avoid "competition among the churches."[23] Above all, the council worked to keep conservative—that is, fundamentalist and evangelical—Protestant denominations off the airwaves. It did so by denying them access to free time and by pressuring national networks and local stations not to provide any additional commercial air time.[24] As television broadcasting grew in the 1950s, the council again successfully pressured the networks to exclude conservative Protestants and again campaigned against paid religious broadcasting.

With little access to commercial network time and no free programming, the conservatives had to fight to survive in the broadcast market. In the 1930s, when they still could buy unrestricted time on Mutual's network, they learned to produce radio programs that covered their costs through listener solicitations. When later forced off the networks, they syndicated these programs, selling them to numerous local stations across the country. They also formed the National Religious Broadcasters to lobby Congress, the FCC, and the National Association of Broadcasters.

The National Religious Broadcasters' lobbying efforts paid off in 1960, when the FCC finally ruled that it would no longer distinguish between free and paid religious programming when evaluating broadcasters' license renewals. Stations and networks could now satisfy their public service obligations with commercial time. Free broadcasts, which accounted for 47 percent of total religious programming in 1959, had dropped to 8 percent by 1977. By the late 1980s, the networks had abandoned free weekly religious programming altogether.

The former beneficiaries of the free broadcasts, the so-called respectable denominations, never recovered. Like the colonial Congregationalists, they proved incapable of any vigorous response. In the wake of the new FCC ruling, they did not even try to compete in the commercial program market and thus quickly faded from the scene. Fundamentalist and Pentecostal preachers—Jerry Falwell, Oral Roberts, Pat Robertson, Jim Bakker, and many others—soon dominated the religious airwaves. They had honed their skills at the fringes of the industry and now aggressively competed for its heartland. In the process, the number of religious broadcasters rose sharply, religious viewership increased, contributions to religious broadcasters grew dramatically, the technical quality and expense associated with religious programming increased, and televangelists became leaders and symbols of the so-called "fundamentalist phenomenon."[25]

The rise of televangelists shocked America's political, academic, and media elites. They proclaimed a massive demand-side outbreak of religious-

23. Roswell P. Barnes, "The Ecumenical Movement," in *Religion in American Society*, ed. Richard D. Lambert, *The Annals* of the American Academy of Political and Social Science, 332:135-45 (1960).

24. Hadden and Shupe, *Televangelism*, p. 47. For examples of the cartel rhetoric used by members of the Federal Council of Churches, see Finke and Stark, *Churching of America*, pp. 221-22.

25. See Hadden and Shupe, *Televangelism*, pp. 155-56, 292.

political conservatism spawned by economic frustration, reactionary sentiments, or postmodern anxiety.[26] In fact, the evangelical-fundamentalists had been present and growing in number throughout the century, but FCC regulations and other cartel-like arrangements had functioned to keep them out of the limelight and off the airwaves.

The new religious consciousness

Throughout the 1970s, no subject within the sociology of religion received as much attention as the rise of America's new religious movements. Scholars rushed to explain the "flowering" of Asian-born and Asian-inspired "cults" and usually pinned the blame on a "new religious consciousness" grown up among America's youth to challenge Western materialism, individualism, and rationalism.[27]

In truth, American demand for Eastern religion dates back more than a century. Gordon Melton has documented how Harvard professors, upper-class Bostonians, the Unitarian Church, and various Spiritualist organizations brought numerous Eastern religious teachings and, above all, Eastern religious teachers to the United States in the late 1800s. This process of cultural importation largely ceased when, in the wake of World War I, Congress passed a series of exclusion acts that dramatically cut Asian immigration and denied potential citizenship to Asians already in America. Thenceforth, Americans interested in exploring Eastern religion had to rely on books, travel abroad, American teachers, or the occasional Eastern visitor on a tourist visa.

In 1965, President Johnson rescinded the Oriental Exclusion Acts. The effects were profound. Indian immigration rose from 467 in 1965 to 2293 the next year and now runs around 25,000 each year. A sudden jump in the supply of Asian teachers released the pent-up demand for Eastern teachings. According to Melton,

The growth of the so-called new religions (primarily the old religions of Asia newly arrived in the West) can be traced to the movement of Eastern teachers to take up residency in the United States beginning in 1965:

1965 Swami Bhaktivedanta (ISKON)
      Sant Keshavadas (Temple of Cosmic Wisdom)
      Thera Bode Vinita (Buddhist Vihara Society)
1968 Yogi Bhajan (Sikh Dharma)
1969 Tarthang Tulku (Tiebetan Nyingmapa)
1970 Swami Rama (Himalayan Institute)
1971 Swami Satchindananda (Integral Yoga Institute)
      Gurudev Chitrabhanu (Meditation International Center)
      Maharaji Ji (Divine Light Mission)
1972 Sun Myung Moon (Unification Church)
      Vesant Paranjpe (Fivefold Path)[28]

26. For an example, see Martin E. Marty, *A Nation of Behavers* (Chicago: University of Chicago Press, 1976), p. 71. For an alternative account of the mainline's decline, see Finke and Stark, *Churching of America*, pp. 245 ff.

27. Charles Y. Glock and Robert N. Bellah, eds., *The New Religious Consciousness* (Berkeley: University of California Press, 1976).

28. J. Gordon Melton, "How New is New? The Flowering of the 'New' Religious Con-

Given the prior existence of a sizable demand for books and periodicals concerning Eastern wisdom and the occult, it should come as no surprise that when gurus finally arrived to market their services in person, they had little trouble finding followers. It was not so much that Eastern faiths had struck a new chord in the American counterculture as that their growth had been artificially thwarted until then.[29]

In failing to perceive the supply shift in Eastern religion, scholars mistakenly invented a demand shift: a "new religious consciousness." This in turn led to appalling exaggerations regarding the entire affair and contributed to the hysteria concerning brainwashing of the late 1970s and early 1980s.[30] Subsequently, more sober studies proved that the vast majority of Asian cults attracted fewer than 1000 followers. Indeed, even the largest and most successful, the Moonies and the Krishnas, never enlisted more than 10,000—though for a time it seemed these all were simultaneously stationed in America's airports.[31] An economic orienta-

tion, emphasizing rational choice, stable preferences, and slightly shifted market equilibrium would have better served both scholars and the public.

Future shocks? Reregulating religion in the 1990s

By all accounts, religious regulation remains an important issue in the 1990s. Though nothing like religious reestablishment looms on the horizon, recent developments suggest a trend toward significant reregulation. American courts are poised to seriously circumscribe the activities of new and nonconventional religious movements.

Attempts to regulate religion have increased sharply in recent years. According to Franklin Littell, "In the last two decades there have been more court cases (all levels of the judiciary) involving religious liberty issues than in the entire history of the United States."[32] More and more, new religious movements find themselves drawn into costly litigation, charged with kidnapping, fraud, tax evasion, brainwashing, and clergy malpractice. Although the vast majority of these cases are dismissed or decided in favor of the religion, they frequently generate damaging publicity, and even one adverse decision has the potential to destroy a new or

sciousness since 1965," in *The Future of New Religious Movements*, ed. David G. Bromley and Phillip E. Hammond (Macon, GA: Mercer University Press, 1987), p. 52.

29. See Finke and Stark, *Churching of America*, pp. 242-44.

30. According to several scholars, the cult scare has led to court and Internal Revenue Service rulings that seriously threaten longstanding freedoms of nonmainstream religions in the United States. See David Bromley and Thomas Robbins, "Government Regulation of Marginal Religious Movements" (Working paper, Virginia Commonwealth University and Santa Barbara Centre for Humanistic Studies, 1992).

31. In 1984, a Toronto magazine estimated that there were 10,000 Krishnas in that city

alone. When Hexham, Currie, and Townsend studied the matter, they found that the correct total was 80! See Irving Hexham, Raymond F. Currie, and Joan B. Townsend, "New Religious Movements," in *The Canadian Encyclopedia* (Edmonton: Hurtig, 1985). See also Melton, "How New Is New?"

32. Franklin Hamlin Littell, "Religious Freedom in Contemporary America," *Journal of Church and State*, 31:222 (1989).

small movement.[33] Increased litigation and regulation affect all religions, but they especially burden the small and politically powerless, the new and nonconventional. Next, we will review a recent court decision that particularly threatens the supply of such religions in America.

Revising free exercise

On 17 April 1990, the Supreme Court ruled that Oregon's Employment Division could deny unemployment benefits to two men, Alfred Smith and Galen Black, who had been fired from their jobs as rehabilitation counselors because they had ingested peyote during a Native American Church ceremony. The court did not dispute peyote's use as an ancient and genuine sacramental practice, but nevertheless it concluded, " 'We cannot afford the luxury of deeming *presumptively invalid . . . every regulation of conduct that does not protect an interest of the highest order.*' " [34] In a single ruling, the Court thus appears to have abandoned the compelling interest test which has shaped its decisions governing the First Amendment's free exercise clause for fifty years.

If government no longer need demonstrate a compelling interest when enforcing laws that inhibit religious practice, then it may pass any number of "formally neutral" and "generally applicable" regulations that seriously constrain the activities of specific religions. Michael McConnell, a University of Chicago law professor, therefore calls the *Smith* decision " 'the biggest free-exercise change in doctrine ever.' "[35] James Wood, editor of the *Journal of Church and State*, claims that "by almost any measure, the *Smith* decision . . . constitutes a substantial abridgment of the free exercise of religion, while providing for far greater state authority and regulation of religious practices and religious institutions."[36] Justice Sandra Day O'Connor issued a similar warning in her dissent to *Smith*: " 'For the Court to deem this [compelling interest] command a "luxury," is to denigrate the very purpose of the Bill of Rights.' "[37]

The Court's new doctrine has already begun to have an impact. For 15 years males of the Sikh religion have been exempt from federal regulations requiring construction workers to wear helmets, because their religion requires them to wear turbans. But in 1990, the exemption was lifted due to the *Smith* ruling.[38] In another case, pending before the Supreme Court, the city of Hialeah, in southern Florida, has passed four ordinances to prevent the killing of animals for religious sacrifice. If the Court evaluates these ordinances as "neutral" and "generally applicable," then the followers of Santeria, an

33. Thomas Robbins and James Beckford, "Religious Movements and Church-State Issues" (Paper delivered at the annual meeting of the Society for the Scientific Study of Religion, Pittsburgh, PA, 1991).

34. As quoted in James E. Wood, Jr., "The Religious Freedom Restoration Act," *Journal of Church and State*, 33:673 (1991).

35. As quoted in ibid.

36. James E. Wood, Jr., "Abridging the Free Exercise Clause," *Journal of Church and State*, 32:749 (1990).

37. Quoted in Wood, "Religious Freedom Restoration Act," pp. 674, 677.

38. Wood, "Religious Freedom Restoration Act."

Afro-Caribbean religion, have lost their right to ritually sacrifice animals (mostly goats and chickens).[39] Could *Smith*, coupled with laws prohibiting the consumption of alcohol, deny Christians the right to celebrate Holy Communion with wine? Probably not. Ironically, the ruling may prove most pernicious precisely because it is unlikely to be applied in this way. *Smith* may eventually constrain all religions, but the smallest and least powerful will bear the brunt of its force. As Justice O'Connor observed in her dissent, " 'The history of our free-exercise doctrine amply demonstrates the harsh impact majoritarian rule has had on unpopular or emerging religious groups.' "[40] It remains to be seen whether majoritarian rule will increasingly stifle the future supply of religious innovation.

CONCLUSION

This article has made a case for supply-side scholarship in religion. It has sought to counteract a bias of traditional scholarship that reduces most every innovation to a psychic shift among religious consumers:

"cultural realignments," "crises of faith," "flights from modernity," and so forth. In a series of examples that run from colonial times to the present, from constitutional amendments to apparently minor regulations, we have shown how market forces govern the incentives and opportunities facing religious producers. Add to these examples a growing body of empirical research that finds few significant trends in the underlying beliefs of the American population,[41] and a reallocation of scholarly resources appears to be in order.

We are struck by the number of religious innovations that occur in response to religious deregulation. The colonial sects began their meteoric rise when the support for established religions faded. Evangelical preachers rushed to the airwaves when a new FCC ruling facilitated their entry. Eastern religions gained a serious following when new rules allowed their teachers to immigrate. In each case, freer access to the religious marketplace expanded and invigorated the supply of religion.

Recent court decisions threaten to reverse this trend, reregulating the religious marketplace and stemming supplies of religious innovation. The immediate casualties of these decisions are new and nonstandard religions. But if history offers any guide, the long-run threat is to the vitality of the entire religious marketplace.

39. See Douglas Laycock, "The Remnants of Religious Freedom," *Supreme Court Review 1990*, pp. 1-68 (1991). The authors thank Derek Davis, associate editor for the *Journal of Church and State*, for updating us on the progress of this case.

40. Quoted in Wood, "Abridging the Free Exercise Clause," p. 747.

41. See, for example, Greeley, *Religious Change in America*.

ANNALS, *AAPSS*, **527**, May 1993

American Religious Exceptionalism: A Reconsideration

By EDWARD A. TIRYAKIAN

ABSTRACT: The first part of this article deals with religion in the United States in the context of American exceptionalism. At least since Tocqueville, observers have noted that a distinctive national characteristic of the United States is its religious vitality. In addition to commonly cited aspects of religious activism, it is also argued here that this exceptional vitality is reflected in the periodical mass or public renewals of the religious life and, stemming from Puritanism, in the diffusion of religious elements to other social contexts. A second theme presented in this article is that the three major religious orientations—Protestantism, Catholicism, and Judaism—not only fill an important niche as providers of social identity but also have found in the United States an exceptional historical setting.

After teaching at both Princeton and Harvard, Edward A. Tiryakian joined the Duke University faculty and has been professor of sociology there since 1967. He is past president of the American Society for the Study of Religion (1981-84) and of the International Association of French-Speaking Sociologists (1988-92). He has published widely in the United States and abroad in the areas of sociological theory, sociology of religion, modernization and modernity, sociocultural change, and nationalism.

NOTE: An earlier version of this article appeared as "L'exceptionelle vitalité religieuse aux Etats-Unis: Une relecture de *Protestant-Catholic-Jew*," *Social Compass*, 38:215-38 (Sept. 1991).

40

A T different historical junctures, or periods of transition, in American history, the question of national identity has become problematic, especially in the past hundred years as the United States became a major world actor. Today, the 1990s are another such unsettled period, a time of far-reaching structural and ideological change at home and abroad wherein we seek to make sense of the direction of a post-Communist era, which is also a post-Reagan era, in a deconstructed world that is no longer bipolar.[1] It is also the last decade of the century, and the last decade of a millennium, both of which, and especially the latter, historically have been stimuli for complex symbolisms, often underlying radical movements seeking a new social order.[2] With these factors in mind, in this article I will consider the question of religion in the 1990s

1. Zaki Laïdi, "Sens et puissance dans le système international," in *L'ordre mondial relâché: Sens et puissance après la guerre froide*, ed. Zaki Laïdi (Paris: Presses de la Foundation Nationale des Sciences Politiques & Berg, 1992).
2. On eschatological ideas of the 1890s, see John Stokes, ed., *Fin de Siècle / Fin du Globe* (New York: St. Martin's Press, 1992). As to the vast literature on millennial movements and utopias, a good introduction is the classic study by Norman Cohn, *The Pursuit of the Millennium* (New York: Harper Torchbook, 1961). The United States has had its share, from the eve of the Revolution to the present; see, for example, Henri Desroche, *The American Shakers, from Neo-Christianity to Presocialism* (Amherst: University of Massachusetts Press, 1971). For a broad overview of utopian and fundamentalist movements as alternate visions of "Axial-Age civilizations" such as ours, see S. N. Eisenstadt, "Fundamentalism, Phenomenology and Comparative Dimensions," in *Fundamentalisms Compared* (Chicago: University of Chicago Press, forthcoming), vol. 5.

by dealing with a complex issue, that of American religious exceptionalism, which highlights the very exceptional period of our contemporary setting.

As an introduction to American religious exceptionalism, it may be well to relate a contemporary East-West encounter at an international airport between two high-technology salesmen, one an American going to Japan for the first time, the other a Japanese coming to the United States for the first time. "How have you prepared for your trip?" the Japanese asked politely. The American opened a large briefcase, revealing dozens of statistical reports, market surveys, sophisticated graphics, and materials from the Commerce Department. "These are the data about Japan that I am taking with me to understand our market potential. What data sets about the United States do you have?" Smiling, the Japanese opened his briefcase and took out its only content: a Bible. "From what I have heard about your country," he said, "this seems to be the essential document to study!"

AMERICAN EXCEPTIONALISM: TOCQUEVILLE, WEBER, SOMBART

Although the story adequately makes the point, social scientists might wish that the briefcase also contained Tocqueville's masterpiece, *Democracy in America*[3] (hereafter *DA*). First published in 1835, it has been of lasting importance as a perceptive and comprehensive analysis

3. Alexis de Tocqueville, *Democracy in America* (1835), ed. J. P. Mayer (Garden City, NY: Doubleday Anchor, 1969).

of American society, its institutions, its belief systems, and its interaction with the environment. Tocqueville and his travel companion to America, Gustave Beaumont, had prepared for their trip to the New World much as the American salesman did, fully arming themselves with factual information. But, once they arrived in the United States in 1832, they encountered a cultural phenomenon that was not part of the then-extant European landscape: a widespread religious vitality.

So struck with this was Tocqueville that in the first chapter of *DA*, where he lays out the essential traits of Anglo-American civilization, he points out how exceptional that civilization was in making "a marvelous combination" of the spirit of religion and the spirit of freedom, two distinct elements that in other societies clashed with each other.[4] Distinctive in having adopted the separation of church and state as a principle of its federal government and distinctive in making religious affiliation a matter of voluntary association, the new country provided religion with a greater and more extensive vitality than was the case in Europe.[5] Tocque-

ville did not reduce American exceptionalism to features of its religious dimension in New England Puritanism, but it is in this cask that I shall later endeavor to pour some new wine.

Before doing so, it is appropriate to note that three-quarters of a century after Tocqueville's visit and observations on the nexus between American democracy and religious vitality, another keen European observer was also struck with the social significance of religion in everyday American life. Max Weber, invited with other distinguished European scholars, including Werner Sombart, to an international congress at the St. Louis World's Fair in 1904, used the occasion for intensive travels, observations, and reflections, including the relation of religion to modernity. Shortly after his return to Germany, he published what became a seminal study in the sociology of religion, *The Protestant Ethic and the Spirit of Capitalism*, which is in some sense a sociological interpretation of Zarathustra's lament, "God is dead and we have killed him!" In this magistral overview of how the confluence of religion and economic development in the West stimulated a distinctive capitalistic civilization, Weber echoed Zarathustra's lament in concluding that the spirit of the religious calling in mundane activities, so pronounced in the early modern period of capitalism, had left the Western scene, leaving us with an "iron cage."[6]

4. Ibid., 1:46-47. Tocqueville may be seen as an early critic of secularization theory, which in the 1960s argued that with the development of modernity and its rational structures, religion would become increasingly vestigial in the public sphere. Based on his observations in America, Tocqueville chided the early formulators of that theory, the Enlightenment "philosophes" who argued that "religious zeal . . . was bound to die down as enlightenment and freedom spread." Ibid., 1:295.

5. "European Christianity has allowed itself to be intimately united with the powers of this world. Now that these powers are falling,

it is as if it were buried under their ruins." Ibid., 1:301.

6. Max Weber, *The Protestant Ethic and the Spirit of Capitalism* (1904-5), trans. Talcott Parsons (New York: Scribners, 1958), p. 181.

If not exceptional in the sense of not being subject to the same laws of historical development as all other modern societies, the United States for Weber was unusual in the enduring strength of Protestantism well after industrialization had taken place. Unlike the European scene, the footprints in a trail leading from an overtly materialistic, capitalist civilization back to its Protestant religious chrysalis were still fresh and clearly visible. "Nobody who visited the United States fifteen or twenty years ago, that is, before the recent Europeanization of the country began, could overlook the very intense church-mindedness which then prevailed in all regions," he wrote.[7] He noted that as recently as 25 years before, only 6 percent of the American population was unchurched (to use a contemporary term), a figure still very low though rising at the time of his visit, that American commoners contributed a significant part of their annual income to maintaining their churches, that there was spirited competition between sects for members, and that it was important for one's social identity to belong to a denomination, though which one to belong to was "rather irrelevant."[8]

As I shall discuss shortly, these traits of American religious life have continued to inform discussions of American religious vitality, as the United States seems to defy Weber's overall pessimistic prognosis of its imminent secularization.[9] However, it might be pertinent to mention first another influential study of American exceptionalism, Werner Sombart's *Why Is There No Socialism in the United States?* which appeared in the same journal and at the same time as Weber was publishing *The Protestant Ethic and the Spirit of Capitalism.*

Sombart's comparative analysis begins by asking at a time when in Europe industrial workers were reacting to advanced capitalism by identifying with new left socialist parties, why did their American counterpart have such an aversion? What made this even more paradoxical, Sombart noted, was that the United States was not a laggard in the development of a capitalist system. It was in fact the quintessential modern society where capitalism reached its zenith, where "the entire life-style of the people adopted a manner suited to capitalism," where there is gigantic capital accumulation and enormous social inequality, in brief, where essential elements of

7. "The Protestant Sects and the Spirit of Capitalism" (1906), in *From Max Weber: Essays in Sociology*, trans. and ed. H. H. Gerth and C. Wright Mills (New York: Oxford Galaxy, 1958), p. 302. The "recent Europeanization" Weber mentions refers, of course, to the influx of non-Northern, non-Protestant Europeans who began coming in great numbers in the 1880s. Their impact on American institutions and ultimately on American democracy led to a great anxiety in Protestant religious circles and became a stimulus of the Social Gospel movement, which Weber does not seem to have observed.

8. Ibid., p. 307.

9. "Closer scrutiny revealed the steady progress of the characteristic process of 'secularization,' to which in modern times all phenomena that originated in religious conceptions succumb." Ibid. One must keep in mind that Weber's fin de siècle Europe, at least the urban industrial centers, had for the most part undergone the transformation aptly discussed in Owen Chadwick, *The Secularization of the European Mind in the Nineteenth Century* (New York: Cambridge University Press, 1975).

the American national character are derived from capitalism and in turn reinforce it.[10] Given similarities in structural conditions, why the difference in political outcomes?

I am not concerned here with the various empirical factors that Sombart adduced to account for the political exceptionalism of American workers in distancing themselves from socialism,[11] but two points might be made. First, Sombart's provocative essay has over the years been very heuristic in comparative political studies by providing one major pole of American exceptionalism: the absence of a social condition that one expects to be attendant of a modern, industrial society.[12] Second, the literature stemming from Sombart has tended to focus on socioeconomic and/or sociopolitical factors but has benignly neglected the possibility of

religion as a major intervening factor in curtailing class cleavages; the latter in continental Europe led to the formation of class parties, including those espousing socialist ideologies of radical economic restructuring.

Following the lead of Elie Halévy's masterful and suggestive interpretation of the British case, in which the great French historian highlighted the role of Nonconformity sects in framing the working classes with a progressive but nonrevolutionary "alternative vision,"[13] let me propose in passing that religious vitality has also been a significant factor in dampening socialism in the American scene. The high levels of religious participation throughout American society—for example, church membership, religious attendance, participation in church-related voluntary associations, traditional religious beliefs such as belief in God or in the afterlife[14]—may be interpreted to point to religious communities as being a more important base for American industrial workers than socialist parties, which in continental Europe did become recreational and inspirational communities for the proletariat.

Space limitation necessitates sidestepping recent controversies in American historiography as to whether in

10. Werner Sombart, *Why Is There No Socialism in the United States?* (1905-6), ed. C. T. Husbands, trans. Patricia M. Hocking and C. T. Husbands (White Plains, NY: International Arts & Sciences Press, 1976), p. 14.

11. For a useful critical discussion, see the introductory essay by C. T. Husbands in *Why Is There No Socialism?* pp. xv-xxxvii. Some of the factors advanced by Sombart, such as the social mobility of American workers and their ability to acquire property, making them feel part of the system, unlike the situation of European workers, had already been advanced by Tocqueville, who is not mentioned by Sombart.

12. See, for example, John H. M. Laslett and Seymour Martin Lipset, eds., *Failure of a Dream? Essays in the History of American Socialism* (New York: Anchor Press, 1974); Seymour Martin Lipset, "Why No Socialism in the United States?" in *Sources of Contemporary Radicalism*, ed. Seweryn Bialer and Sophia Sluzar (Boulder, CO: Westview, 1977); Gary W. Marks, *Union in Politics: Britain, Germany and the United States in the Nineteenth and Early Twentieth Centuries* (Princeton, NJ: Princeton University Press, 1989), chap. 6.

13. Elie Halévy, *A History of the English People in 1815* (London: Ernest Benn, n.d.), esp. pp. 365-74, although the entire chapter "Religion and Culture" in vol. 3 merits attention. See also his follow-up study, *Imperalism and the Rise of Labour*, rev. ed. (London: Ernest Benn, 1951).

14. This has been repeatedly documented. See, for example, Kenneth D. Wald, *Religion and Politics in the United States* (New York: St. Martin's Press, 1987), pp. 6-15.

our new global age it makes sense to talk about American exceptionalism at all.[15] Nonetheless, in support of the exceptionalist perspective, let me propose a complementary aspect of American exceptionalism: the absence of a political factor present in other modern societies and the presence of a complex factor of religious vitality that is absent in other industrial Western societies. The two deserve to be treated as opposite sides of the same American coin.

FEATURES OF AMERICAN RELIGIOUS VITALITY

I will not linger on the well-trodden trail of religious factors in which the United States is an enduring outlier among modern industrial nations,[16] nor will I dwell on the various explanations and controversies surrounding the American case.[17] In re-

cent years, economic models, ultimately inspired by Adam Smith, seem to be gaining currency in viewing religious vitality to be a function of deregulated markets that stimulate healthy competition. The United States would appear to be par excellence a market religious economy, characterized by "consumers' preferences," including opportunities to "switch brands."[18] To be sure, there are still espousers of the centrality of political factors, revolving around the separation—or lack thereof—of church and state, this centrality being a primary point in Tocqueville. Regardless of the particular interpretation, there is a consensus that religion is usually better off, in terms of its social vitality, in societies where it is not a state-regulated monopoly.

At this macro or national level, there are two other features of the American scene that are very distinctive and that, taken with the usually cited factors, strengthen the case for American exceptionalism in its religious dimension. The first is the periodic recurrence of religious revivals on the American scene, or what may

15. For an internationalist refutation, see Ian Tyrrell, "American Exceptionalism in an Age of International History," *American Historical Review*, 96:1031-55 (Oct. 1991); and its rejoinder by Michael McGerr, "The Price of the 'New Transnational History,'" ibid., pp. 1056-67. For a lucid overview of the case for American exceptionalism by a leading comparative scholar, see Seymour Martin Lipset, "American Exceptionalism Reaffirmed," in *Is America Different?* ed. Byron E. Shafer (New York: Oxford University Press, 1991), pp. 1-45.

16. Theodore Caplow, "Contrasting Trends in European and American Religion," *Sociological Analysis*, 46:101-8 (Summer 1985); Wald, *Religion and Politics in the United States*; Andrew M. Greeley, "American Exceptionalism: The Religious Phenomenon," in *Is America Different?* ed. Shafer, pp. 94-115.

17. See, for example, Caplow, "Contrasting Trends"; Roy Wallis, "The Caplow-de Tocqueville Account of Contrasts in European and American Religion: Confounding Considerations," *Sociological Analysis*, 47:50-52 (Spring 1986); Laurence R. Iannaccone, "The Conse-

quences of Religious Market Structure: Adam Smith and the Economics of Religion," *Rationality and Society*, 3:156-77 (1991); Rodney Stark, "Do Catholic Societies Really Exist?" ibid., 4:261-71 (July 1992); Mark Chaves and David E. Cann, "Regulation, Pluralism, and Religious Market Structure: Explaining Religion's Vitality," ibid., pp. 272-90; Raymond Boudon, "The Understanding of Religious Vitality Needs Additional Factors," ibid., 4:467-76 (Oct. 1992).

18. For quantitative and qualitative aspects of denominational switching, which is particularly noteworthy among Protestants, see Wade Clark Roof and William McKinney, *American Mainline Religion: Its Changing Shape and Future* (New Brunswick, NJ: Rutgers University Press, 1987), pp. 162-77.

be termed the periodic revitalization of American religious vitality. There is no need to belabor the point that the colonization of New England was essentially a religious undertaking to establish a "City on the Hill," a "new Jerusalem." This sense of mission has clung to the American scene in different guises down to the present.[19] Other societies have felt a sense of being chosen, but what is remarkable about the American case is the periodic rekindling of the sense of mission, of collective purpose, via the phenomenon of a string of major revivals. The leading historian of revivals, William McLoughlin, has categorized American history in terms of four major cycles of "awakenings," from the first, which began in the 1730s, to the current one, which he sees as starting in the 1960s.[20] In his words, "Our history has been essentially the history of one long millenarian movement. Americans, in their cultural mythology, are God's chosen, leading the world to perfection. Every awakening has revived, revitalized, and redefined that culture core."[21]

The social significance of the revivals has been considerable, in part because the regenerated evangelical impulse has spilled over to or stimulated various social undertakings, frequently in the nature of social reform movements, new voluntary associations, and renewal of political cohesion.[22] Moreover, an important aspect of the American case, at least since the religious awakening of 1858, is that the large-scale revivals have taken place in urban centers and have utilized modern technology to reach their constituents. Unlike so much of the European urban scene, the espousal of modern technology and certain adaptations to modern popular culture—for example, in music—have prevented urban America from becoming a religious wasteland. In this connection, it should be recalled that the beginnings of American sociology and related social sciences owe much to the Social Gospel movement that was part of the turn-of-the-century religious revival.[23] A large number of the first generation of academic social scientists were either ministers or sons of ministers involved in the Social Gospel movement. They sought to understand the ways of new arrivals from Europe who were culturally vastly different from native-born Americans, to improve the social conditions of these immigrants by scientific knowledge, and ultimately to help keep the faith in American democratic institutions

19. Edward A. Tiryakian, "Puritan America in the Modern World: Mission Impossible?" *Sociological Analysis*, 43(4):351-67 (1982).

20. William G. McLoughlin, *Revivals, Awakenings, and Reform* (Chicago: University of Chicago Press, 1978). For the controversy regarding the reality of cyclical awakenings, see the various pieces in *Sociological Analysis*, vol. 44 (Summer 1983).

21. McLoughlin, *Revivals, Awakenings, and Reform*, p. 19.

22. A masterful discussion of this in terms of the United States in the first half of the nineteenth century is Perry Miller, *The Life of the Mind in America* (New York: Harcourt, Brace & World, 1965), bk. 1.

23. Leon Bramson, *The Political Context of Sociology* (Princeton, NJ: Princeton University Press, 1961); Dorothy Ross, *The Origins of American Social Science* (New York: Cambridge University Press, 1991); Arthur J. Vidich and Stanford Lyman, *American Sociology: Worldly Rejections of Religion and Their Directions* (New Haven, CT: Yale University Press, 1985).

and their underlying voluntarism. Ipso facto, nascent American social science was a secular extension of the religious reform movement of evangelism.

There is a subtle feature of religious vitality in the United States that needs to be mentioned, however all too briefly, given its general import. It is what I see as a tacit trade-off, an unwritten covenant, so to speak, that in return for the separation of church and state, the Puritan spirit of creating a "Holy City"—de facto a modern theocracy, which briefly occurred in Calvin's Geneva—could roam free anywhere in the wider society and attach itself to any part of the human condition, thereby transforming it into a moral aspect. The initial Pilgrim's "errand into the wilderness"[24] has become a near-permanent feature of modern American society. The religious impulse to find evil—or a fall from grace—in empirical conditions calling for a mass mobilization—in earlier periods known as a crusade—to redeem a flawed world underlies the propensity for an exceptional American moralism that can be directed at any mundane target either at home or abroad. Domestic targets in recent decades have included poverty, civil rights, smoking, dieting, and physical fitness, while overseas targets, more personalized, have ranged from "the evil empire" to Saddam Hussein. The energy, attention, and resources given to eradicating the conditions involved might appear incommensurate from a strictly secular perspective, yet once the

moral mobilization appears on the scene, there is no checking the impulse, no cost accounting of the national effort. It is in this phenomenon of moralization that the United States shows a this-worldly activism that both perplexes and stimulates the rest of the world.

Since American moralism has been a well-observed aspect of the American scene, I will not pursue the theme further than having mentioned its nexus to American religious exceptionalism. Still, it may be appropriate in closing this section to point out an interesting paradox of the American situation: on the one hand, an increasing, if any, separation of religion from the public sphere—except at times of political conventions—and, on the other, a continuing high level of moralization of all social spheres, including those that in other societies are treated as morally indifferent, such as the sexual comportment of public officials.

PROTESTANT-CATHOLIC-JEW
REVISITED

In the postwar era of the late 1940s and 1950s, the economic boom in America's postwar recovery, an unexpected God-sent prosperity took place side by side with a political crisis over so-called un-American activities. The problematics of national identity, and of trust and distrust in public servants and intellectuals, were some of the aspects that loomed large as the United States defined its mission to the world as the containment of Communist aggression abroad. This led some patriotic zealots to see as a corollary the strong curbing of Communist subversion at

24. Perry Miller, *Errand into the Wilderness* (Cambridge, MA: Harvard University Press, Belknap Press, 1956).

home. Besides this, other aspects of the postwar American scene germane here were problematics of personal identity in a changing and more depersonalized world, reflected in the popularity of existential philosophy and in sociological works such as David Riesman's *Lonely Crowd* and William Whyte's *Organization Man*.

It is in this general setting that a new cycle of religious activity began. Quantitatively, church membership and affiliation increased, and, qualitatively, a new generation of religious figures in all three major faiths—such as Norman Vincent Peale, Billy Graham, J. Fulton Sheen, and Joshua Loth Liebman—became well-known inspirational leaders, reaching national audiences via best-sellers, syndicated columns, radio, and eventually television.

It was as part of the times that the first popular work in the sociology of religion, Will Herberg's *Protestant-Catholic-Jew*, appeared.[25] As an updated version of the social-identity-of-religion perspective that one can find in Tocqueville and Weber, Herberg's analysis argued that social identity is conferred for second- and third-generation Americans by membership in one of the three main faith communities. These stand on a par with each other as "equi-legitimate subdivisions of the American people."[26] The communities are ethno-religious or religioethnic ones: they are basic props of the American way of life and are instrumental in social-

izing new arrivals into the mainstream of American institutions. To come back to our starting point, it is thus as agencies of socialization that Protestantism, Catholicism, and Judaism exemplify American religious exceptionalism.

There are both merits and pitfalls in Herberg's analysis that deserve ampler discussion than can be given here.[27] What I would like to do in this section is to reconsider the Herberg thesis in proposing that the American historical and environmental experience has been a singular, or exceptional, one for all three major religious communities.[28]

Protestant

The religious matrix of the United States in Calvinism and the social

25. Will Herberg, *Protestant-Catholic-Jew: An Essay in American Religious Sociology* (1955; new rev. ed., Garden City, NY: Anchor, 1960).

26. Ibid., p. 211.

27. On the debit side, see the criticisms of John Wilson, *Religion in American Society: The Effective Presence* (Englewood Cliffs, NJ: Prentice-Hall, 1978), pp. 310-12. In addition, Herberg made no discussion of Islam in America, but in recent years it has become problematic as to whether in the United States—or in Europe, for that matter—the Islamic community can attain parity as an "equi-legitimate subdivision" of society. Can one, for example, see Islamic holidays publicly recognized or imams asked to give the invocation at commencement ceremonies of Ivy League schools? On the plus side, Herberg's study would suggest as a research topic that various immigrant groups have higher levels of socioreligious participation in the United States than that of their immediate kin in the country of origin. If this were empirically validated, it would cast further doubt on the assumption that modernization and secularization are collinear.

28. For a more detailed discussion of the distinctive condition of each major religious community in the United States, see E. A. Tiryakian, "L'exceptionnelle vitalité religieuse aux Etats-Unis: Une Relecture de Protestant-Catholic-Jew," *Social Compass*, 38:224-34 (Sept. 1991).

reflection of this cultural floor in the (formerly) hegemonic white Anglo-Saxon Protestant (WASP) sector of the population are universally recognized and require no discussion. What needs to be underscored, however, is that Protestantism was, from the first, the religion of the land, the religion of the very first group of latecomers (since the Indians were, after all, the original settlers).[29] Unlike the European setting where they began as dissidents, as protesters against an established church and hierarchical social order, Protestants in America were from the beginning the arbiters and formulators of the norms of social life. They did not have to fight against an establishment; they established their own social order.

Essentially, the American setting gave rise to the first large-scale Puritan civilization, one that, freed from the worries of a repressive social environment, turned its missionary impetus into a gigantic enterprise of harnessing an equally gigantic physical environment that was viewed as wilderness. Max Weber and one of his leading interpreters, Talcott Parsons, have keenly observed that in reorienting the quest for salvation to "this-worldly asceticism," Protestantism introduced a powerful "cognitive breakthrough," a "lever for social change."[30] In seeing themselves not primarily as benefactors but as

stewards or trustees of God's purpose in placing them in front of wilderness, the Puritans and their descendants, even unto today, helped to create and then re-create not just what Lipset aptly termed "the first new nation"[31] but what in fact was equally the first Protestant nation.

As I have discussed in the previous section, the ethical code of Protestants, oriented to the rational mastery of the world as God's fiduciary agents, has suffused in principle all social spheres. This is a unique feature of the American situation, which I trace to the Americanization of Protestantism—and to the Protestantization of America. It has led, among other things, to a unique emphasis on service as a component of American capitalism, namely, that capitalist enterprises have to be sanctified or justified by the service they provide, to customers and to the larger community; in the latter case, the Puritan commitment to education is reflected in America in the substantial giving to higher education from the private sector, a feature mostly absent in European capitalism until well into the present century.

Catholic

A paradox of Catholics in America is that overtly and covertly they have been subject to harassment, suspicion, and vilification from the Puritans down to Paul Blanshard and Jimmy Swaggart, yet they have flourished in the United States more than in any other modern society. Viewed as potential subversives because of

29. For the purpose of the argument, I include the Anglican Church and its later Episcopalian derivative as part of the Protestant orientation in America.

30. Talcott Parsons, "Introduction," in *The Sociology of Religion*, by Max Weber (Boston: Beacon Press, 1963).

31. Seymour Martin Lipset, *The First New Nation* (New York: Basic, 1963).

loyalty to a foreign power, the papacy, Catholics have been in fact among the staunchest supporters of American nationalism and its civil religion of the American way of life, even to the extent of supporting the American episcopacy and laity leading the fight for modernism against Vatican traditionalism.[32] Catholic laypersons, whether as union leaders, such as George Meany, or in high rungs of government, such as J. Edgar Hoover and Alexander Haig, have been the bitterest foes of alien ideologies, particularly Marxist socialism. Part of the reason why there is no socialism in America probably lies with the Catholics. While they form the largest religious denomination in the United States, Catholics have not organized their own political party, such as Christian Democratic parties on the European continent. Instead, one might venture to say that, outside the South, the Democratic Party for most of the twentieth century—from the 1920s through the 1960s—has been a sort of secularized Catholic Church, with Catholic laity prominent among the party's curia.

The distinctive historical feature of Catholics in the United States is that from the start of the American colonization—with the brief exception of Maryland—they were a minority within a Protestant host majority. In spite of vigorous demographic increases in the nineteenth and twentieth centuries, stemming just as much from immigration as from natural increase, and in spite of rapid economic and educational progress, Catholics seem to have a tacit image of self as a minority group, as a sort of grateful guest worker in a host Protestant society who has to watch his or her manners and not act as a unified bloc to bring about legislation or policy, domestic or foreign, that might be branded as mixing religion with politics. As noted by Tocqueville long ago, Catholicism in America is as committed to the ideals of republican democracy as any other constituent part of American society, yet it is this socioreligious grouping that has the hardest time being accepted as fully American. Ironically, moreover, it is the least politically organized.

Although Catholics constitute more than one-fifth of the American population and make up the single largest denominational grouping in seven of ten regions of the United States,[33] their rise to the top of the political and professional ladder of higher administration outside of Catholic institutions has been checkered, as observed by a noted priest-sociologist-novelist.[34] Only two Catholics have run for the American presidency, with equally dire results. Alfred E. Smith, the first Catholic descendant of immigrant stock to present himself for the presidency, was initially blocked at the 1924 Democratic convention as "Rum and Romanism" became the issue. A popular governor of New York State, he

32. See, for example, Lester R. Kurtz, *The Politics of Heresy: The Modernist Crisis in Roman Catholicism* (Berkeley: University of California Press, 1986).

33. Bernard Quinn et al., *Churches and Church Membership in the United States, 1980* (Atlanta, GA: Glenmary Research Center, 1982), pp. 1-9; *Mission and Context* (Glenmary Research Center), 3:2-3 (Summer 1992).

34. Andrew M. Greeley, *The American Catholic* (New York: Basic Books, 1977).

carried the nomination in 1928, but, despite his vow to maintain strictly the separation of church and state, the 1928 campaign against him utilized the most sensational sort of anti-Catholic propaganda, complete with the circulation of a spurious Knights of Columbus oath that made this Catholic voluntary association seem treasonable and subversive of the social order.[35]

The election of John F. Kennedy, representing another new generation of American voters, has been hailed as a demonstration that Catholics have finally divested themselves of a political pariah status at the highest level of office. But the rejoicing may be premature, for Kennedy was assassinated in office, and so was his brother Robert, who was in 1968 on his way to the Democratic nomination. Thirty years later, there is still grave doubt as to whether the official accounts of the day have told the full story. Moreover, symbolically, Catholic candidates have been taken out of contention: in 1972, when the Democratic vice presidential candidate was replaced after the reporting of his medical history, and in 1984, when another Catholic vice presidential candidate was politically neutralized because of her husband's alleged economic wrongdoings in New York. All in all, then, at the political level, the jury is still out as to when Catholics may aspire to a normal seeking and filling of presidential office.

Yet, a final aspect of the paradoxical condition of Catholics in America is that they have become an integral part of American culture, particularly in the area of leisure and entertainment. Evidence includes the national following of the Fighting Irish football team, the number of Catholic athletic coaches in non-Catholic schools and in professional sports, and the frequent use of Catholic priests, nuns, and churches in movies and television shows wishing to portray traditional religious figures.

Jew

At the heart of American exceptionalism concerning Jews in America is that, while, for Jews, the United States is not and cannot be ontologically and existentially "the land" the way Israel is, it has been more of a rewarding and accepting home than any other setting outside Israel itself.[36] To be sure, interspersed with some calamities, Jews have flourished as a distinctive group in diverse historicopolitical settings, from absolute kingdoms and authoritarian regimes, as in ancient Egypt and the Ottoman empire, to modern constitutional monarchies and democratic republics. What makes the American case different from the others?

35. Donn C. Neal, *The World beyond the Hudson: Alfred E. Smith and National Politics 1918-1928* (New York: Garland, 1983); Karl Schriftgiesser, *This Was Normalcy: An Account of Party Politics during Twelve Republican Years, 1920-1932* (Boston: Little, Brown, 1948).

36. For an insightful discussion of territoriality and Israel, see W. D. Davies, *The Territorial Dimension of Judaism* (Berkeley: University of California Press, 1982). For a general discussion of Jews and America in the present context, see Seymour Martin Lipset, "A Unique People in an Exceptional Country," in *American Pluralism and the Jewish Community*, ed. Seymour Martin Lipset (New Brunswick, NJ: Transaction, 1990).

I would propose that Jews in America have not been marginalized as "wholly other" by virtue of their religion; there has been no historical ghetto experience, no pogroms. In fact, because of a deep-structure affinity of Calvinist Puritanism for Judaism, it is in America that Jews have increasingly found full societal and cultural participation and acceptance, symbolized by widespread acceptance in recent years of the term "Judeo-Christian."

This statement may initially be challenged by the question of anti-Semitism in America, if not now then in an earlier part of the century. Undoubtedly, Jews faced restriction in an earlier period in gaining admission to certain highly prestigious schools and social clubs. But for the most part, these restrictions may have been applied as a function of class and ethnicity, rather than of religion, not only to Jews but also to other non-WASP first- and second-generation ethnics. These restrictions have also to be measured against the more virulent racism shown toward Asians—for example, the Chinese and the Japanese—and toward blacks. In addition, unlike Catholics, whose loyalty to America has been questioned because of alleged loyalty to a foreign power, Jews have not felt their commitment to Israel subject to public scrutiny.

In brief, I would argue that being Jewish in America, far from carrying culturally disadvantageous baggage, has on the contrary had some very distinctive cultural advantages, rendering the American experience exceptionally felicitous. What are these advantages? At the surface level, general aspects of the American situation such as the absence of a feudal past with ascriptive social structures, the separation of church and state, the commitment to higher education, and a strong work ethic that rewards actors as individuals in terms of performance are conditions in which Jews readily found opportunities for social advancement. But since these are characteristic of the modern sector of society anyway, one has to go to a deeper cultural level to find something exceptional. The clue is presented in a passage by Weber: "Puritanism always felt its inner similarity to Judaism, but also felt the limits of this similarity. . . . The Jews who were actually welcomed by Puritan nations, especially the Americans . . . were at first welcomed without any ado whatsoever and are even now welcomed readily."[37]

Weber did not go further in the matter of the "elective affinity" of Puritanism and the Jews, but had he looked closely at the American situation he would have found a sociocultural environment uniquely favorable and receptive to Jews.

First and foremost, the Puritans had a deep identification with Israel. The Bible, particularly the Hebrew Scriptures, was a constant referent for everyday action and legitimation, stemming from the Puritan identification of themselves as fleeing from Egypt—corrupt civilization—into the land of Canaan, hence the name of the town New Canaan, Connecticut. Shedding civilization and creat-

37. Max Weber, *Economy and Society*, ed. Guenther Roth and Claus Wittich (Berkeley: University of California Press, 1978), 1:622-23.

ing a "City on the Hill" meant a repudiation of the false gods and graven images of that civilization. The Puritans de-emphasized Christian names and Christian holidays associated with Rome, paganism, or idleness. Thus Christmas was not celebrated, but Thanksgiving, derived from the Jewish harvest festival of Succoth, became the major holiday; similarly, the Puritans extensively used first names taken from the Old Testament in preference to Christian first names.

Second, the esoteric dimension of American civil religion is one in which Freemasonry has played a leading role from the very beginnings of the Republic, to which it has contributed some of the very basic symbols of the American polity, such as the Great Seal of the United States. Many of the leading figures of the independence movement were Masons, and the Declaration of Independence itself—as was the case for the French counterpart, the Declaration of Human Rights—is a manifestation of Masonic principles, including universalism, the equality and brotherhood of all men, and the freedom of conscience. Central to Freemasonry are symbols, rituals, and mythologies that are linked to the kabbalistic tradition; so, for example, speculative Masonry relates itself to the ancient craft of architecture whose master architect was Solomon, the builder of the Temple, and Freemasonry utilizes the Hebraic rather than the Christian calendar.

In brief, the Masonic dimension of American culture—a particularly strong but covert presence in American life, especially in the formative period of the country—provided Jews with important cultural support and legitimation.[38] As Dumenil has remarked, "Jews . . . could also find in Masonry a religious spirit congenial with their traditions and could have the satisfaction of knowing that much of Masonry was drawn from the Old Testament."[39]

In the past two decades, American foreign policy has evolved or accentuated a "special relationship" with Israel, a diffuse commitment that it has with no other nation, save perhaps with Great Britain. I do not think this can be adequately accounted for in instrumental, rational terms of strategic benefits accruing to the United States or in terms of effective domestic political mobilization by political action committees. While both are operative, there is also a strong core of emotional, cultural support that provides readiness and legitimation for massive American support. That support comes from not only the Masonic-secular tradition mentioned earlier but also from the contemporary fundamentalist sector of American religion, which treats Israel with great reverence, not only for its biblical setting but also for its eschatological significance.

38. Indicative is a Masonic statement of 1823 that declares, " 'To the Jewish nation we are indebted for all that is ancient, judicious and distinct in Masonry. From them under the great I AM, we derive all we know of the history of man and the will of Heaven.' " Cited in Dorothy Anne Lipson, *Freemasonry in Federalist Connecticut* (Princeton, NJ: Princeton University Press, 1977), p. 183.

39. Lynn Dumenil, *Freemasonry and American Culture 1880-1930* (Princeton, NJ: Princeton University Press, 1984), pp. 69-70.

CONCLUSION

To conclude what must perforce be only an introduction to a vast field of analysis, several caveats must be entered. First, I have not brought into the discussion of American religious exceptionalism its nexus to the international scene, that is, the overseas missionary activities and their bearing on American foreign policy, both in support of or against the latter, at different periods.[40]

Second, the presentation of religious exceptionalism should not mean that everything is rosy, that the religious scene is exempt from factionalism, dissent, and conflict. There have been and will continue to be conflicts within and between major religious orientations regarding, for example, homosexuality, female ordination, and the like. And there will continue to be acute conflict regarding the interpretation of the separation of church and state. Thus, as champion of secularism, the American Civil Liberties Union has taken and will continue to take legal actions seeking to nullify religious vitality in the public sphere. And the more that Christian symbols are driven from the public sphere, the more this is likely to generate counterreactions that may feed into the politically disaffected.

Finally, in this transition period marked by oscillations between affirmations of national pride regarding political and military triumphs over external foes and increasing self-doubts about how many Americans can today realize the American dream, American exceptionalism is beginning to appear in a new, more somber color. In his introduction to a recent issue of *Daedalus*, Steven Graubard admonishes that our country's "drug problem" is linked "to any number of conditions that make the United States truly 'exceptional,' though in ways few care to reflect on."[41] The uniqueness of the United States, he continues, is no longer its prosperity relative to other advanced modern societies but its problematic race and interethnic relations, its inadequate medical care system, its run-down and dangerous inner cities, its archaic criminal justice system, and its public education system.[42]

It is hard to anticipate what lies ahead in the remaining years of this millennium for American religion and American society, particularly in light of how much unexpected historical change has taken place in less than a generation. To echo Weber's conclusion in *The Protestant Ethic and the Spirit of Capitalism*, perhaps a truly secular age will emerge, characterized by the total absence of the religious factor from the public sphere and the petrification of religion in social consciousness. Or perhaps, in the face of domestic crises, confrontations, and questions of national identity, religious vitality will undergo a new cycle of this-worldly activism, as it did one hundred years ago.

40. See, for example, William R. Hutchinson, *Errand to the World: American Protestant Thought and Foreign Missions* (Chicago: University of Chicago Press, 1987).

41. Stephen R. Graubard, "Preface," *Political Pharmacology: Thinking about Drugs*, vol. 121, *Daedalus*, p. vi. (Summer 1992).

42. Ibid.

ANNALS, *AAPSS*, **527**, May 1993

Religion and Ethnicity in Late-Twentieth-Century America

By PHILLIP E. HAMMOND and KEE WARNER

ABSTRACT: A tie to the old-country religion remains one of the ways by which ethnic group identity is expressed and maintained in America. Recent survey results suggest, however, that this relationship between religion and ethnicity is not as strong as it once may have been. Moreover, the degree of ethnic and religious identification, as well as the strength of their corelationship, varies from one ethnic group to another. After a presentation of these facts, we then discuss what they mean for ethnic assimilation and religious development in these waning years of the twentieth century.

Phillip E. Hammond is professor of religious studies and sociology, University of California, Santa Barbara. He is the author or editor of a number of books, the latest being Religion and Personal Autonomy *and* The Protestant Presence in Twentieth Century America.

Kee Warner is assistant professor of sociology, University of Colorado, Colorado Springs. His recent work focuses on the politics of local environmental reforms and urban development.

AFTER three decades of heightened ethnic consciousness by African Americans, Mexican Americans, Asian Americans, and Native Americans, asserting that assimilation in America remains the greater trend in ethnic relations may seem absurd. Indeed, controversies over "multiculturalism" in the college curriculum, the "rise" of "unmeltable" white ethnics, and the persistence of vibrant ethnic organizations, newspapers, and fund appeals would suggest that ethnicity remains a powerful force in American society. And so it does.

Nonetheless, such persistence defies the larger and more prevalent trend toward assimilation. Unlike the long-standing situation in Belgium or Northern Ireland, for example—or the situation recently exposed in Yugoslavia—U.S. society was not formed by territorially combining already existing ethnic populations. Rather, the vast majority of American citizens are immigrants, or the children of immigrants, who, upon arriving on this continent, found an ongoing culture to which some kind of accommodation was, and is, required. As Stephen Steinberg puts it, such transplanted minorities, "ripped from their cultural moorings and lacking a territorial base," could hardly survive here with their culture intact. "American society provided only a weak structural basis for ethnic preservation. The very circumstances under which ethnic groups entered American society virtually predestined them to a gradual but inexorable decline."[1]

Inexorable decline need not be uniform, however. Common sense alone would suggest that various groups differentially diminish their differences with the host culture, by accommodating to it and/or having it accommodate in return. Moreover, events can occur that in some sense reverse the assimilation process. Seen vividly in the case of Jews during and since the Holocaust, such episodes of ethnic renewal may be long- or short-term, widespread or narrowly experienced, but they may also temporarily halt or redirect the inexorable decline. Thus, for example, the percentage of American Jews marrying non-Jews went down from 6.7 percent in 1941-50 to 5.9 percent in 1956-60, but it then returned to an escalating rate: 17.4 percent in 1961-65, 31.7 percent in 1966-71,[2] and is even higher now.

ASSIMILATION AND SECULARIZATION

A parallel exists between ethnic assimilation and religious secularization. While there are many meanings of secularization, we mean by the term simply the decline of religion's social significance. Thus both ethnicity and religion, we are saying, are vulnerable to forces that diminish their social importance. Individuals may, of course, choose to assign great importance to their ethnicity and/or their religion, but the processes of assimilation and secularization minimize the likelihood that such personal importance trans-

1. Stephen Steinberg, *The Ethnic Myth* (Boston: Beacon Press, 1981), p. 43.

2. Egon Mayer, *Love and Tradition: Marriage between Jews and Christians* (New York: Plenum Press, 1985), p. 48.

lates into generalized social significance. Indeed, it may be precisely the
freedom to choose that renders the
choices—whatever they are—less salient in social relationships.

This increasing freedom to choose
reveals yet another feature common
to ethnicity and religion: their declining inheritability. The notion that
ethnicity may not be inherited is not
as readily apparent as the declining
inheritability of religion, which is
widely understood and well documented in the United States.[3] In fact,
the belief that ethnicity is inherited—passed on through generations—is one of its defining features.[4]
In the United States, most people
claiming an ethnic identity believe
that the ethnicity they inherit is
traceable to some geographic territory and that their myth of origin is
tied to that territory. Such beliefs
need not be taken literally, of course,
especially in the case of such diaspora
peoples as Jews and Armenians or in
the case of a new ethnic group such
as Mormons, where territory is real
enough in the myth, though disputed
as geographical reality. In other
words, what matters is the belief, not
the actuality.

Thus, while the process of choosing whether to remain loyal to one's
parents' religion is fairly obvious, the
analogous process in the case of
ethnicity, though similar, is not so

obvious, probably because of the belief that ethnicity is inherited. There
are, for example, those cases where
the precise nature of the ancestry has
simply been forgotten, thus allowing
persons to select from a variety of
ethnic progenitors or to select no
foreign ancestry at all. Not surprisingly, in the United States this
last option—of declaring oneself simply American—is more often found in
those border southern (Appalachian)
states with sizable Scots-Irish, German, and English immigration in the
eighteenth century but relatively little in-migration since.[5] After all, one
need back up only four generations to
find 16 different ancestors, and it is
a rare American who knows much
about even a minority of those 16.
Genes may be inherited, but the social meaning of those genes will, in
some sense, be voluntarily selected in
a way that parallels the decision of
whether and how to remain loyal to
one's inherited religion.

A third feature common to ethnicity and religion is the role played by
intermarriage in the processes of assimilation and secularization. Just
as marriage across ethnic boundaries
need not weaken the ethnic identity
of either partner but often does, so
may marriage occur across religious
lines without weakening religious
identity. But religious intermarriage
is often discouraged for fear of just
such loss because that loss, like lost
ethnic identity, frequently occurs.

And how could it be otherwise?
One or both partners in an intermar-

3. Phillip E. Hammond, "The Extravasa-
tion of the Sacred and the Crisis in Liberal
Protestantism," in *Liberal Protestantism: Realities and Possibilities*, ed. R. S. Michaelsen
and W. C. Roof (New York: Pilgrim Press,
1986), pp. 51-64.
4. The other defining characteristic is the
existence of a myth of origin, a story accounting
for the peoplehood of those sharing an identity.

5. U.S., Department of Commerce, Bureau
of Census, *Ancestry of the Population by State:
1980*, Supplementary Report P.C. 80-S1-10,
1983.

riage are likely to give up a religious connection and a territorial tie. One or both may relinquish a friendship network and possibly a language. Secular ethnic organizations might be abandoned as well, just as might friendships with persons still attached to the inherited ethnicity.

Individual assimilation, like secularization, occurs in a number of interrelated ways: by diminished social interaction, residential propinquity, language use, newspaper or journal reading, organizational memberships, worship, kinship relationships, and so forth. Among empirical investigations, Reitz makes this point very clear in the case of ethnicity in Canada, as do Stark and Glock in the case of religion in the United States.[6] This suggests that, if both ethnic and religious identities weaken, so may the relationship between ethnicity and religion.

ETHNICITY AND RELIGION

Just as some observers deny that secularization occurs in America, others deny the reality of assimilation. Not surprisingly, therefore, so also have some observers doubted the decline in the relationship between ethnicity and religion. For example, historian J. S. Olson states, "The relationship between ethnicity and religion in the United States is as powerful today as it has been throughout American history."[7] Of course, as our first paragraph acknowledges, ethnicity does remain a powerful force in the United States. Likewise, who can doubt the continued vitality of religion in this society? But persons who argue for no change—by denying assimilation and secularization and/or their co-increase—rely too much on mere descriptive statistics, as Olson relies on reports showing that, for example, French, Irish, Italian, and Polish Catholics are significantly different in their practice of Catholicism.

Of course! But such reports show only that ethnicity remains influential. The church or synagogue was not just an insulating device by which assimilation was resisted; in many instances, it was also a vehicle by which assimilation or acculturation could be facilitated. Thus, for most immigrant Americans, religion has been a major way of exercising one's ethnic identification. The questions addressed here are (1) Is this still the case? and if so, (2) For whom is it stronger, and for whom is it weaker?

PATTERNS OF RELATIONSHIP BETWEEN RELIGION AND ETHNICITY

While it might be assumed that virtually everywhere ethnicity and religion are related, it must be acknowledged that this relationship takes several forms, at least in mixed immigrant societies such as the United States. Following Abramson,[8] we can distinguish at least three patterns:

6. Jeffrey G. Reitz, *The Survival of Ethnic Groups* (Toronto: McGraw Hill Ryerson, 1980); Rodney Stark and C. Y. Glock, *American Piety* (Berkeley: University of California Press, 1968).

7. J. S. Olson, *The Ethnic Dimension in American History* (New York: St. Martin's Press, 1979), p. 436.

8. Harold J. Abramson, "Religion," in *Harvard Encyclopedia of American Ethnic Groups*, ed. S. Thernstrom, A. Orlov, and O. Handlin (Cambridge, MA: Harvard University Press, 1980).

1. Religion is the major foundation of ethnicity; examples include the Amish, Hutterites, Jews, and Mormons. Ethnicity in this pattern, so to speak, equals religion, and if the religious identity is denied, so is the ethnic identity.[9] Let us call this pattern "ethnic fusion."

2. Religion may be one of several foundations of ethnicity, the others commonly being language and territorial origin; examples are the Greek or Russian Orthodox and the Dutch Reformed. Ethnicity in this pattern extends beyond religion in the sense that ethnic identification can be claimed without claiming the religious identification, but the reverse is rare. Let us call this pattern "ethnic religion."

3. An ethnic group may be linked to a religious tradition, but other ethnic groups will be linked to it, too. Examples include Irish, Italian, and Polish Catholics; Danish, Norwegian, and Swedish Lutherans. Religion in this pattern extends beyond ethnicity, reversing the previous pattern, and religious identification can be claimed without claiming the ethnic identification. Let us call this pattern "religious ethnicity."

As a first generalization, we suggest that the first of these patterns, ethnic fusion, is the most firmly institutionalized—that is, religion and ethnicity remain most strongly related and provide the greatest identity—and the third pattern, religious ethnicity, is least firmly institution-alized. Ethnographic evidence testifies to the strength of religion and ethnicity in the first pattern, but that very strength may keep such groups small and insulated and thus obscured in large-scale quantitative studies. In any event, we examine here only examples of ethnic religion and religious ethnicity, though, as will become apparent, in the United States this still leaves room for considerable variation.

A second generalization can also be suggested: If in the first pattern, religion and ethnicity are more or less fused, in the case of ethnic religion it is more likely that ethnicity helps to uphold religion, while in the case of religious ethnicity it is more likely that religion helps to uphold ethnicity. With ethnic religion, in other words, everyone in a church probably shares an ethnicity as well as a religion, but there are fellow ethnics not found in church; with religious ethnicity, everyone in a church probably shares only a religion, though ethnic parishes were a well-known but now declining phenomenon.

Religion and ethnicity differ culturally in one respect, however, which warrants inquiring into the relative stability versus changeability of the two identities. We have discussed the belief in the inheritability of ethnicity. This belief alone no doubt serves to help maintain ethnicity; at most, one may play down its importance to the point where one even loses track of what was inherited ethnically, but only rarely would a person exchange one ethnicity for another.

For religion, the situation is quite otherwise. National polls report overwhelming agreement with the notion

9. In actuality, of course, there can be exceptions, as the labels "jack Mormon," "banned Amish," or "cultural Jew" suggest.

that "an individual should arrive at his or her own religious beliefs independent of any church or synagogue." In the survey we introduce shortly, 77 percent agreed with this statement, a figure that helps to interpret the next finding. When asked, "Do you see the church as something passed on from generation to generation, or as something that needs to be freely chosen by each person?" two-thirds—65 percent—answered "freely chosen," and only 23 percent answered "passed on from generation to generation." The Protestant principle of individual religious responsibility permeates American culture, in other words, even for those persons with strong ethnic ties. Consequently, all else being equal, religious loyalty will likely weaken before ethnic loyalty weakens. Thus Greek Orthodox Americans become Roman Catholic, Armenian Americans become Episcopalian, Japanese Americans become Methodist, or Jewish Americans become secular, often as a result of intermarriage, without necessarily giving up Greek, Armenian, Japanese, or Jewish identity.

Seldom is all else equal, however, so the opposing pattern is also found, especially in America among ethnic Catholics, who of course represent the pattern of religious ethnicity. Thus, for example, Alba reports an intermarriage rate as high as 70 percent among Italian Americans who are third generation in this country and under 30 years of age, noting that "intermarrying Italians married freely with other Catholic groups,"[10]

which is to say that religious loyalty could be said to have been stronger than ethnic loyalty in these instances.

THE STRENGTH OF THE ETHNICITY-RELIGION RELATIONSHIP

If it is a truism that ethnic or religious identity may each range along a weak-to-strong continuum, it is also the case that little is known empirically about the relationship of the two identities. Of course, as with many major challenges in the social sciences, this one would be best addressed with time-series data, especially across two or more generations. Ideally, researchers would have measures of the strength of both ethnic and religious identities at several chronological points in order to observe which changed first and with what effect. But studies of this sort are rare in the annals of social research, and surrogate studies must often take their place.

AN EMPIRICAL INQUIRY

Although the data about to be reported were collected (in 1988 and 1989) for another purpose,[11] they permit at least a provisional investigation of the issues raised earlier in this article. The sample comes from four states—California, Massachusetts, North Carolina, and Ohio—via randomly dialed telephone interviews with about 650 adults between the ages of 25 and 63 in each state. From the resulting 2600 interviews, 1691

10. Richard D. Alba, *Italian Americans* (Englewood Cliffs, NJ: Prentice-Hall, 1985), p. 89.

11. Phillip E. Hammond, *Religion and Personal Autonomy* (Columbia: University of South Carolina Press, 1992).

cases can be classified on measures of
ethnic identity and religious loyalty.

*Ethnic identity
    measure*

Three pieces of information were
used to classify people as high in ethnic identification. One question
asked, "From what countries or part
of the world did your ancestors
come?"[12] We noted whether persons
claimed single or multiple foreign ancestry or, in 17 percent of the cases,
only U.S. ancestry or no answer. Another question asked about the ethnic ancestry of one's spouse. We noted
whether respondents married within
their ethnic group. The third question asked, "Would you say, in general, that you feel pretty close to
other people from the same national
background, or that you don't feel
much closer to them than to other
people?" We noted whether respondents reported feeling closer or not.

Persons judged to be high in ethnic
identification included those who reported feeling closer to fellow ethnics
and those who claimed a single foreign ancestry and/or were in-mar-
ried. This way, unmarried persons
could be classified as high in ethnic
identity provided they regarded
themselves as having a single ethnic
ancestry and felt closer to fellow ethnics. Similarly, persons could also
score as high despite mixed ethnic
ancestry provided they were married
to someone sharing one of those ethnic heritages and felt closer to people
of that heritage.

12. This question followed one that determined whether the respondent was native- or
foreign-born.

By this rather stringent measure,
only 16 percent of our 1691 cases
score as high, though this percentage
ranges from 36 percent, in the case of
Mexican Americans, to 3 percent, in
the case of Swedish Americans. This
is a much lower rate of strong ethnic
identity than common sense would
suggest. For example, the rate for
blacks, 35 percent, seems unexpect-
edly low. The explanation—for blacks,
anyway—probably does not lie in low
levels of in-marriage or feeling closer
to fellow ethnics but lies instead in
the question about foreign origin. For
persons whose ancestors emigrated
from Sweden or Japan or Italy, little
ambiguity exists. But for blacks in
America, the situation can be quite un-
clear. African Americans, of course,
came from somewhere other than these
shores, but Africa is not a "country,"
nor were the "parts of the world" from
which they came identifiable as na-
tion-states at the time. Add the history of slavery, forced marriage, separation, transciency, and inadequate
record keeping, and it is understand-
able that many blacks in America do
not readily name Africa as the source
of their ethnic identity. Only if they
did name Africa in this survey as
their country of origin, however, could
they then affirm the same identity for
their spouses, report feeling closer to
persons like themselves in this respect, and thus score high on our
measure. Even though this measure
is thus too blunt to detect nuanced
ethnic sentiments, it nevertheless is
relatively accurate; persons scoring
high are, in fact, likely to be higher
in ethnic identity than others.[13]

13. A similar complication forced us to exclude Jews from this analysis. Jews answered

Religious identity
   measure

Our measure of religious identity is not as indirect as the ethnic identity measure. As with the ethnic measure, however, the upshot is a conservative device that, to the degree that it works, doubtlessly underestimates the phenomenon it purports to measure. Conceptually, at least, it is straightforward.

Many countries from which Americans emigrated had, and may still have, established churches. Other countries were fundamentally homogeneous in religion even if they gave no formal recognition to a single religion. To varying degrees, therefore, immigrants to the United States often had a religion by which and through which they could carry on old-country culture. The current linkage between religion and ethnicity in America is, of course, the topic of this article, but the historical fact of such linkages provides us with our measure. We consider simply whether people remain attached to the religious tradition historically associated with the countries of their ancestral origins.

This operation was simplified by our decision to use from our sample only those ethnic groups with 25 or more respondents. After Jews were excluded, for the reasons given previously, only 12 groups qualified, which could be religiously characterized as follows: Lutheran, from Norway, Sweden, or part of Germany;

the question of national origin with "Germany," "Russia," and so on, requiring us to use religious identification to determine their ethnicity. That, in turn, meant we could not investigate their ethnicity and religion separately.

Roman Catholic, from France, Ireland, Italy, Mexico, Poland, or part of Germany; Anglican, or Episcopalian, from England; Presbyterian, from Scotland; and black Protestant, from Africa.

Of course, not everyone with roots in a given country is part of that country's religion—for example, this is true of Irish American Protestants—but if persons seek to express their ethnicity religiously, these 12 groups have fairly clear-cut guidelines. Germany, with historically strong Lutheran and Catholic churches, may appear an exception, but by first asking German Americans in our sample if they were raised as Lutheran or Catholic, we can classify them as adults as still loyal to their religious tradition or religiously something else. In the case of persons with African roots, we follow the considerable literature testifying to the central role played by black Protestant churches in the lives of black Americans. Our assumption, in other words, is not that all African Americans are affiliated with a black Protestant denomination—nor are all Norwegian Americans Lutheran; rather, we are assuming that remaining with or returning to the religion culturally and historically associated with one's ethnic origins, rather than departing to another religion or to no religion at all, may to some degree express one's ethnicity.

To the extent that these two indices fall short of measuring exactly what we seek—the strength with which people identify themselves with an ethnic group on the one hand, and with the religion historically linked to that ethnic group on the

TABLE 1

**STRENGTH OF IDENTITY AND RELIGIOUS AFFILIATION,
AND THEIR RELATIONSHIP, IN TWELVE ETHNIC GROUPS**

Ethnic Group Origin	(1) Number of Cases	(2) Percentage High in Ethnic Identity	(3) Percentage Affiliated with Historical Religion	(4) Relationship between (2) and (3)
Mexico	42	36	67	.33
Africa	77	35	68	.18
Italy	115	23	61	.10
Poland	63	19	56	.18
Ireland	309	15	54	.13
Norway	29	14	31	.39
England	373	11	0	.04
Scotland	125	10	15	.14
Germany (Lutheran)	332	10	12	−.01
Germany (Catholic)	110	8	87	.08
France	83	8	30	.18
Sweden	33	3	18	.21
Total	1691	16	33	.15

other hand—we underestimate the true strength of both types of identity as well as the true strength of the relationship between the two types. Our goal per se is not to estimate these things with exactness, however, but to discover for various ethnic groups their relative strengths and the reasons for differences in these strengths. Better measures might do this job more effectively, but it is doubtful that they would discover a different ordering of well-documented differences.

WHAT THE DATA SHOW

Table 1 supplies the data necessary for the ensuing analysis. For each of 12 ethnic groups, it provides the number of respondents in the group; the percentage who score high in ethnic identity, the measurement of which was described earlier; the

percentage who are affiliated with the historical religion of that ethnic group; and the correlation (Pearson's r) between ethnic identity and religious affiliation.

Visual inspection of Table 1 suggests that religious identity tends to be strongly related to ethnic identity at the group level (Pearson's $r = .70$) In other words, groups with high rates of ethnic identity tend also to have high rates of religious identity. At the individual level, by contrast, the average for the total sample (bottom row of Table 1) is a much lower .15, ranging from .39, for Norway, to effectively zero, for German Lutherans. Since, however, some groups are fairly small, making their scores unreliable when treated alone, we aggregated groups by category for more reliable analysis.

The first category includes the first two populations in Table 1, persons tracing their ancestry to Mexico or Africa. They exhibit not only the highest rates of ethnic identity but also the highest rates of historical religious affiliation. It can also be noted that, of the 12 ethnic groups listed in Table 1, these two are most likely to be regarded, by themselves and by others, as racial groups and most subject to political, economic, and social discrimination in American society at large. They are thus more likely than other groups listed to live in ethnic neighborhoods, have friends who are fellow ethnics, and so on. Combined, the two groups' correlation score between ethnic and religious identity is a significant .23; that is, persons in these groups who are most strongly identified ethnically are also more likely to be affiliated with their ethnic group's religion.

The characteristics of this first category suggest an antithetical second grouping made up of those ethnic groups that, unlike the first category, have low rates of both ethnic and religious identity. England, Scotland, Germany (Lutherans), and Sweden all seem to fit here without squeezing. Norway, too, qualifies except for a moderately high rate, 31 percent, of religious attachment to Lutheranism, though with only 29 respondents, this percentage is unreliable. These five groups also share, of course, a history of early entry into the United States, white skin, and cultural similarity to the amalgam culture dominant in America. Consequently, these groups show the highest rates of assimilation found among the 12 groups of Table 1.

Three of the five remaining groups (Italy, Poland, and Ireland) are in the middle of the table with respect to both ethnic and religious identity. Catholic Germany is anomalous because of its uncharacteristically low ethnic identity rate and high—the highest—religious identity rate. Some of the explanation may lie in the fact that German Catholics in this sample come disproportionately from Ohio, where Cincinnati remains a traditional center of old German American Catholic culture.[14] France is also anomalous, with measures closer to Norway than Italy, Poland, and Ireland but still higher on religious identity than all others in the second grouping. As rough conjecture, one might say that German Catholics in America are highly assimilated—by intermarriage, for example—but highly distinctive by religious heritage. Correlatively, French Americans are also highly assimilated by intermarriage but relatively low when it comes to identity with their historical religion.

ANALYSIS

What is the historical religion of French Americans? It is, of course, Roman Catholicism—the same as the historical religion of Italian, Polish, and Irish Americans, plus those German Americans raised as Catholic. The contrast with the second grouping is all the more striking, therefore, because all five populations in that grouping are Protestant.

14. This is not the entire explanation, however, as is seen from a parallel study to be discussed later in this article. There, with a sample that is national and 50 percent larger, the same characteristics are found among German American Catholics.

TABLE 2

STRENGTH OF IDENTITY AND RELIGIOUS AFFILIATION, AND THEIR RELATIONSHIP, IN THREE CATEGORIES OF ETHNIC GROUPS

Category	(1) Number of Cases	(2) Percentage High in Ethnic Identity	(3) Percentage Affiliated with Historical Religion	(4) Relationship between (2) and (3)
Minority (Mexico, Africa)	119	35	67	.23
Catholic (Italy, Poland, Ireland, Catholic Germany, France)	680	15	57	.13
Protestant (Norway, England, Scotland, Lutheran Germany, Sweden)	892	10	8	.05

If we thus combine all five Catholic ethnic groups, not including Mexican Americans, and all five Protestant ethnic groups, not including African Americans, we can observe that, while the ethnic identity rate of the Catholics is only modestly higher than that of the Protestants—15 percent versus 10 percent—the religious identity rate is significantly higher: 57 percent versus 8 percent (see Table 2).[15] The inference is strong, therefore, that—to use the terminology of earlier pages—Catholic Americans have assimilated at nearly the rate of Protestant Americans, but they have secularized at a lesser rate. Religious identity, if this inference is correct, thus helps to maintain ethnic identity more than nonreligious ethnic identity helps to maintain religious identity, at least in the case of

15. The procedure of combining ethnic groups this way gives greater weight to groups having more members. If, instead, the several group scores are averaged, the results are nearly identical.

Catholic Americans. For them, the religious identity lingers longer than the nonreligious ethnic identity. We are perhaps too late to observe this pattern among the greatly assimilated and greatly secularized Protestants. Correlatively, the very low rates of assimilation and secularization of Mexican and African Americans mean that it is too soon to tell, should that point come, whether ethnic or religious identity will erode first.

A REPLICATION

The analysis just presented was replicated using data from the General Social Surveys, 1983-90, of the National Opinion Research Center at the University of Chicago. Not only was this sample three times the size of the four-state sample—5235 compared to 1691—but it also allowed the inclusion of Puerto Ricans in the minority category, the inclusion of Spain and French Canada in the

Catholic category, and the inclusion of Denmark in the Protestant category. Measures of ethnic identity and affiliation with historical religion were nearly identical in the two analyses. Remarkably similar percentages and correlations appeared, especially in the case of our Table 2.

On the basis of these two studies, therefore, it would seem plausible to argue that religion and ethnicity maintain a significant relationship in late-twentieth-century America, but it is just as plausible to note that this relationship systematically varies from one kind of ethnic group to another. Three generalizations seem warranted. First, ethnic identification and loyalty to the religion of one's ethnic group have tended to diminish together in the American context. That is, assimilation and secularization are correlated. Second, the processes of assimilation and secularization occur at a slower pace in ethnic groups regarded as minorities and thus discriminated against. Finally, decline of ethnic identity appears to precede decline of ethnic religious loyalty, though—given the nature of the two samples of data used here—we cannot establish whether this sequence is true only of Catholics in America or is a general process already undergone by Protestant ethnics. This is just one more thing we have yet to learn about the complex relationship of religion and ethnicity in America. Historical data might provide an answer.

THE FUTURE

Neither religion nor ethnicity will disappear in the near future, of course, but the linkage between the two is almost certain to decline. That is to say, as religion becomes more and more a matter of individual choice, and persons become increasingly selective in making that choice, ethnicity, along with other background characteristics, will have a declining effect in determining religious identity. This process will be most obvious in suburban, nondenominational churches and in amorphous spiritual groups, but the inroads made by Pentecostal Protestantism into Hispanic Catholicism and by Black Muslims into African American Protestantism also signal further weakening of the link between religion and ethnicity.

As mention of Black Muslims reminds us, however, such a weakening linkage does not mean that religion necessarily fades in importance as a vehicle for expressing ethnic concerns. Indeed, just as black Americans have long used their Protestant churches as organizing devices on a range of issues, so may we expect the growing populations of Arabs and Asians in America to use their religions for such purposes. Moreover, it does not necessarily follow that, just because religion is a matter of choice, its importance declines; it may actually take on greater psychological significance even as its social and ethnic importance diminishes.

The overall trend is predictable, however. The decreasing importance of ascribed characteristics, and the correlative increase in individuals' autonomy, diminishes the inheritability of both religion and ethnicity, and that means the decline in their relationship.

ANNALS, *AAPSS*, **527**, May 1993

The Churches and Social Change in Twentieth-Century America

By CHARLES Y. GLOCK

ABSTRACT: The twentieth century has witnessed a number of major social changes that have affected America's churches by virtue of the changes challenging traditional interpretations of scripture. Among these changes have been declines in anti-Semitism and racial prejudice and discrimination, and transformations in the role and status of women and in sexual practices and attitudes. In the past, scripture has been used to justify anti-Semitism, discrimination against Afro-Americans, women's being subordinate to men, and opposition to divorce, premarital sex, adultery, and homosexuality. Churches have responded to the social changes, sometimes by modifying scriptural interpretations to accommodate them, sometimes by standing fast against them. The differences in response prove to be highly associated with differences in church performance. They also have sharply varying implications for the churches' future, especially their ability to exercise moral authority.

Charles Y. Glock is professor emeritus of sociology, University of California, Berkeley. He has taught at New York University, Columbia University, and the University of California, Berkeley. While at Columbia, he directed the Bureau of Applied Social Research. At Berkeley, he was director of the Survey Research Center. He is coeditor of The New Religious Consciousness *and coauthor of* The Anatomy of Racial Attitudes.

A major abiding problem facing church bodies is how to respond when common understandings about how the world works or should work are challenged. The problem is aggravated when the challenge raises questions about the validity of prevailing interpretations of scripture. Should the challenge be resisted and fought? Should it be accepted and modifications made to accommodate it? Or is ignoring the challenge the wisest course? However answered, the response has consequences, sometimes profound, for the viability of both religion and its institutions.

Throughout their history, Christian churches have faced and survived many such challenges. Based on their past record, they are likely to survive new ones. Still, as in the past, the intriguing question lingers, As new challenges arise and have to be addressed, what will the results be?

Twentieth-century America has witnessed its share of challenges to conventional wisdom. Some have involved profound changes in social arrangements whose justification has been grounded, in smaller or larger part, in scripture. As a result, churches have been obliged to respond. The nature of the social changes, the churches' responses to them, the apparent consequences for the churches, and the implications for the churches' future are the subjects of this article.

SOCIAL CHANGES

The social changes to be focused on bear on the behavior and attitudes of Christian Americans toward Jewish Americans, the civil rights of Afro-Americans, the status of women in the society, and forms of sexual expression including homosexuality.

Anti-Semitism

Anti-Semitism still exists in America. Relatively speaking, however, there has been a sharp decline in the amount of both anti-Semitic prejudice and discrimination. Jews are no longer parodied in the media as they were in the first quarter of the century. Songs with anti-Semitic lyrics and humor depicting Jews in an unfavorable light, which were popular then, have virtually disappeared.[1] Most dramatic, perhaps, has been the effective elimination of discrimination against Jews in employment, in housing, and in higher education. In the first half of the century, it was commonplace for Jews to be refused employment, to be banned from hotels, social clubs, and summer resorts, and to experience quotas limiting college and university admission and fraternity membership if not total disbarment from these institutions.[2] Such forms of discrimination are extremely rare today and, when practiced, highly likely to be abandoned if and when they are publicized.

1. Michael Selzer, ed., *"Kike!" A Documentary History of Anti-Semitism in America* (New York: World, 1972), esp. pp. 114-67; Oscar Handlin, "American Views of Jews at the Opening of the Twentieth Century," in *Antisemitism in the United States*, ed. Leonard Dinerstein (New York: Holt Rinehart Winston, 1971), pp. 48-57.

2. Marcia Graham Synott, "Anti-Semitism and American Universities: Did Quotas Follow the Jews?" in *Anti-Semitism in American History*, ed. David A. Gerber (Urbana: University of Illinois Press, 1986), pp. 233-74.

Public opinion polls also attest to a decline in anti-Semitism. In 1938, 58 percent of a sample of the national population named one or more "objectionable qualities which Jews generally have to an extent greater than other people." In an equivalent 1962 survey, 22 percent named an objectionable quality, a decline of 36 percentage points.[3] Since the 1960s, there have been further declines in the proportion holding negative stereotypes of Jews.[4] In a 1989 national poll in which respondents were asked to say how warm or cool they feel toward Jews, Catholics, and Protestants on a temperature scale ranging from zero to 100, the mean scores for Protestants was 75.3; for Catholics, 73.9; and for Jews, 69.8.[5] Recognizing that Protestants predominated in the sample and that Jews were a very small minority, the differences are negligible and attest to the high regard in which Jews have come to be viewed.

Once again, it is important to emphasize that the change is relative, not absolute. Still, it cannot be gainsaid that, since the early part of the century, a significant change in consciousness has occurred with respect to how Jewish Americans are viewed

and accepted by their non-Jewish counterparts.

Race relations

It is less clear that relations between blacks and whites in America have improved over the course of the century. The spate of recent racial riots argues to the contrary as does the persistence of white discrimination and black ghettoization. There is an abundance of other evidence, however, to demonstrate that improvements have occurred.

The most striking evidence relates to civil rights. Well into the 1940s and 1950s, it was commonplace for Afro-Americans to be denied the right to vote, to work, to housing, to attend the same schools as whites, to intermarry, to obtain accommodations in white-operated motels, hotels, boarding houses, and summer resorts, to eat in restaurants, to attend churches, to travel, and to enter public and private bathing beaches, swimming pools, golf courses, playgrounds, and parks. The list goes on and on.[6] Discrimination in many of these respects remains but in no way as pervasively as before and now without the general acquiescence of public opinion and the law.[7]

Beliefs about and attitudes toward Afro-Americans have also changed substantially over the course of the

3. Results of polls conducted in 1938 and 1962 by the Office of Public Opinion Research, reported in Charles H. Stember et al., *Jews in the Mind of America* (New York: Basic Books, 1966), pp. 54, 65.

4. Gregory Martire and Ruth Clark, *Anti-Semitism in the United States* (New York: Praeger, 1982), pp. 15-30.

5. From the General Social Survey for 1989, an annual poll of the national population conducted by the National Opinion Research Center, reported in *An American Profile: Opinions and Behavior, 1972-1989*, ed. Floris W. Wood (Detroit: Gale Research, 1990).

6. Stetson Kennedy, *Jim Crow Guide: The Way It Was* (Boca Raton: Florida Atlantic University Press, 1990); Jonathan H. Turner, Royce Singleton, Jr., and David Musick, *Oppression: A Socio-History of Black-White Relations in America* (Chicago: Nelson-Hall, 1984).

7. Reynolds Farley and Walter R. Allen, *The Color Line and the Quality of Life in America* (New York: Russell Sage Foundation, 1987).

century, although, as some observers have noted, the frequent failure of the new beliefs and attitudes to be acted upon may undermine their significance as indicators of change. Still, it is highly unlikely that the reduction of discriminatory practices could have occurred had beliefs and attitudes remained fixed.

A belief long associated with past treatment of Afro-Americans is that they are less intelligent than whites. In a national poll conducted in 1942, 42 percent of white Americans denied holding this belief. In 1963, when the question was posed in the same way in an equivalently designed and executed poll, 76 percent denied the belief.[8] In 1963, when asked, "Should there be laws against interracial marriages?" 59 percent of whites in a national population sample replied yes. By 1975, the proportion saying yes had declined to 38 percent, and in 1988, it was 25 percent.[9]

The status of women

The women's movement in America predates the twentieth century. The status of women in society in the early 1900s, consequently, can hardly be said to represent what went on before in American history. It seems fair to say, however, that the changes brought about in the twentieth century were substantially greater than those wrought previously. This is especially evident with respect to the

domestic obligations thought appropriate for women and to their role in the workplace. Before 1900, and indeed, well into the 1900s, the virtually unquestioned view was that women were primarily responsible for the upbringing of children and the care of the home. There was a grudging growing acceptance of women's participation in the workplace.[10] It was not until the 1950s and later, however, that the idea that equality between women and men should prevail in work situations began to gain ascendancy.

In a national Gallup poll taken in 1938, 78 percent disapproved of "a married woman earning money in business or industry if she has a husband capable of supporting her."[11] In 1977, when asked their degree of agreement with the statement, "It is much better for everyone involved if the man is the achiever outside the home and the woman takes care of the home and family," 66 percent agreed, 18 percent strongly and 48 percent moderately.[12] In 1990, the same question produced 41 percent agreement, 10 percent strongly and 31 percent moderately.[13] In a 1937 Gallup poll, when asked, "Would you vote for a woman for President if she qualified in every other respect?"

8. Reported in Rita James Simon, *Public Opinion in America: 1936-1970* (Chicago: Markham, 1974), p. 57.

9. Richard G. Niems, John Mueller, and Tom W. Smith, *Trends in Public Opinion: A Compendium of Survey Data* (Westport, CT: Greenwood Press, 1989), p. 170.

10. Beth Millstein and Jeanne Bodin, *We, the American Women: A Documentary History* ([Englewood, NJ]: Jerome S. Ozer, 1977), pp. 199-226.

11. George H. Gallup, *The Gallup Poll: Public Opinion, 1935-1971* (New York: Random House, 1972), p. 131.

12. Wood, ed., *An American Profile*, p. 531.

13. Based on a privately arranged tabulation of the 1990 General Social Survey, conducted by the National Opinion Research Center.

34 percent said they would.[14] In 1989, 86 percent said yes when asked, "If the party whose candidate you most often support nominated a woman for president of the U.S., would you vote for her if she seemed qualified for the job?"[15]

There is still no woman President, women continue to have more domestic obligations than do men, and women in the workplace have still to achieve status and compensation equal to those of men. Still, it is conceivable now, where it was not early in the century, that a woman will become President. There are more men taking care of children and doing domestic chores than in the past. In the workplace, the gap between men and women is no longer as large as it once was. A complete transformation in beliefs and attitudes about the role of women in society has not occurred; however, the transformation is in process and very much beyond where it was but a few decades ago.

Sexual expression

A further obvious addition to any catalogue of social changes in twentieth-century America would appear to be the growing acceptance of sexual practices previously judged taboo. On examination, however, it turns out that this is true only for some sexual practices, not all of them. The century has certainly witnessed a stark increase in the practice of divorce. The number of divorces per 1000 population in 1910 was 0.9; in 1950, it

was 2.6; and in 1988, it was 4.8.[16] Premarital sex is also more frequent and more acceptable. In 1971, for example, 31.7 percent of U.S. teenage women reported having had premarital sexual intercourse. For 1976, the figure was 39.0 percent and for 1982, 45.2 percent.[17] In a national poll conducted in 1972, 27 percent responded "not wrong at all" when asked, "If a man and woman have sexual relations before marriage, do you think it is always wrong, almost always wrong, wrong only sometimes, or not wrong at all?"[18] Twenty-four percent said "wrong only sometimes." In 1989, to the same question in an equivalent national poll, 41 percent said "not wrong at all" and 23 percent, "wrong only sometimes."[19]

There are no reliable longitudinal statistics on the practice of extramarital sex in America. The attitude data, however, indicate that, unlike premarital sex, it is presently proscribed by the vast majority of the population. Moreover, if anything, the disapproval is increasing, not decreasing. In 1990, only 2 percent of the national population responded "not wrong at all" when asked, "If a married person has sexual relations with someone other than the marriage partner, do you think this is always wrong, almost always wrong, wrong only sometimes, or not wrong

16. U.S., Department of Commerce, Bureau of the Census, *Statistical Abstract of the United States, 1991*, 111th ed., 1991, p. 86.

17. Sandra L. Hoffreth, Joan R. Kahn, and Wendy Baldwin, "Premarital Sexual Activity among U.S. Teenage Women over the Last Three Decades," *Family Planning Perspective* 19(2):48 (Mar.-Apr. 1987).

18. Wood, ed., *An American Profile*, p. 599.

19. Ibid.

14. Gallup, *Gallup Poll*, p. 67.

15. Wood, ed., *An American Profile*, p. 541.

at all?" Another 7 percent responded "wrong only sometimes."[20] In 1972, the same question produced a 4 percent "never wrong" response and 12 percent answered "wrong only sometimes."[21]

There are also no reliable longitudinal statistics on the number of homosexuals in the society. By virtue of homosexuals' coming out of the proverbial closet, however, visible signs of their presence have substantially increased. As to the acceptability of homosexuality, the signals are mixed. Since 1973, there has been no substantial change in the public's acceptance of "sexual relations between two adults of the same sex." In 1973, 73 percent of the national population viewed it as "always wrong." In 1980, the figure was also 73 percent, and in 1990, the same. While no more accepting of homosexuality, the population appears less willing now than in the past to condone discrimination against homosexuals. In 1973, 49 percent of the national population thought that a "man who admits he is a homosexual should be allowed to teach in a college or university." In 1980, the figure was 57 percent, and in 1990, 73 percent.[22]

As with respect to the other social changes being considered, no claim is warranted that old attitudes have been supplanted by new ones. Indeed, as the evidence presented indicates, a substantial part of the popu-

lation, and a majority with respect to adultery and homosexuality, continues to cling to old sexual taboos. Still, these are not as sacrosanct as they once were, and, while some continue to hold sway, others, such as prohibitions against divorce, either have been or are in the process of being transcended. It may be difficult to imagine a time when homosexuality will be commonly accepted as a wholly legitimate sexual preference. It is harder still, however, to conceive a return to the closet.

THE RESPONSE OF THE CHURCHES

By and large, America's churches have not remained aloof from these social changes. All of them involve a challenge to the way scripture has been interpreted and taught. Scripture has been used to justify anti-Semitism, discrimination against Afro-Americans, women's being subordinate to men, and opposition to divorce, premarital sex, adultery, and homosexuality.

The scriptural threat has been experienced by all churches, not just those that subscribe to a literal interpretation of the Bible. In part, this is because there are literalists in all churches. It is also because church members favoring the changes of consciousness have had to cope with reconciling them to their faith.

The responses of churches and of church people have not been the same for all of the changes being considered. Consequently, the responses are considered separately for each change, rather than collectively for all of them.

20. Privately arranged tabulation from the 1990 General Social Survey.
21. Wood, ed., *An American Profile*, p. 603.
22. In this paragraph, 1973 and 1980 figures are from ibid., p. 583; 1990 figures are based on a privately arranged tabulation of the General Social Survey.

Anti-Semitism

Scripture has been used to justify anti-Jewish sentiments throughout Christian history and this was certainly true in America in the first half of the century. Indeed, it remains true today, although to a lesser extent. In the early part of the century, the use of scripture to this end manifested itself more in church people than in the churches as institutions. Overt and explicit anti-Semitism was not, for the most part, an official component of church policy. Nevertheless, the way scripture was interpreted, written about in church publications and educational material, and taught had the effect of fostering and warranting anti-Semitism. The Jews were portrayed as Christ killers and having called on themselves a curse from God for their actions. The doctrines that "salvation is only possible through Christ" and that those who reject Christ are subject to eternal damnation had the effect of the Jews' being portrayed as pariahs.[23] Missions to the Jews, devoted to converting them to Christianity, a highly visible part of the Christian landscape throughout the first half of the century, also contributed to Judaism's being depicted as an inferior religion. In the early part of the century, there was little or no effort to challenge these practices.

The founding and growth in the first half of the century of Jewish defense agencies,[24] the Holocaust, the dramatic increase in the number of college-educated Americans that occurred between 1950 and 1970, and the research done on anti-Semitism by social scientists[25] all combined to raise public consciousness about anti-Semitism. The result, as reported earlier, has been a substantial decline in the incidence of anti-Semitism in America in the last half of the century.

The churches, in the face of this onslaught against anti-Jewish prejudice, did not get on the bandwagon early on or wholeheartedly. Vatican Council II adopted a statement on the Jews that, in part, was intended to combat anti-Semitism; and since then there has been a sharp increase in Christian-Jewish dialogue.[26] For the most part, however, the movement to combat anti-Semitism stemmed from the Jewish, not the Christian, community.

The churches did respond, however, by muting the emphasis on offensive scriptural passages. Increasingly, all mankind has been recognized as being party to Christ's death, not just Jews. The themes that "salvation is to be found only through Christ" and that "all who reject Christ are eternally damned," espe-

23. Bernhard E. Olson, *Faith and Prejudice: Intergroup Problems in Protestant Curricula* (New Haven, CT: Yale University Press, 1963), esp. pp. 32-43, 223-49; Charlotte Klein, *Anti-Judaism in Christian Theology* (Philadelphia: Fortress, 1975), pp. 92-126.

24. See, for example, *Not the Work of a Day: The Story of the Anti-Defamation League of B'nai B'rith* (New York: Anti-Defamation League of B'nai B'rith, 1965).
25. Notably the series of studies conducted under the auspices of the American Jewish Committee by the Institute of Social Research, University of Frankfurt, Germany.
26. Helga Croner, comp., *Stepping Stones to Further Jewish-Christian Relations: An Unabridged Collection of Christian Documents* (New York: Stimulus Books, 1977).

cially as they apply to Jews, have been de-emphasized. There has also been a sharp decline in missions directed toward Jews. Proselytizing Jews to become Christian comes now not from the churches but from Jews for Jesus. More fundamentalist Christians, seeing in the travails of the Middle East and of present-day Israel the fulfillment of biblical prophecy, have come to a new rapprochement with Judaism and with the Jewish people. There are some who view this development suspiciously, but, taken at face value, it represents another indicator that the churches have backed off from scripture that has been shown to nourish and sustain anti-Semitism.[27]

Race relations

Scripture was cited frequently from southern U.S. pulpits as affording support for slavery. Biblical passages, from both the Old and the New Testaments, were interpreted as demonstrating that slavery was enjoined by God and, indirectly, by Jesus as well through his failure to condemn slavery specifically and to include it explicitly among the sins he enumerated. Prominent among the scriptures ascribing slavery as God's intention was Genesis 7:21-27. It was interpreted as God's prophetic determination, through Noah's curse on Ham's son, Canaan, that blacks were to be eternally in a servant state. With the abolition of slavery, such scriptural citation lost some of its currency, but not entirely. Inside

and outside the South, it continued to be used, especially the Genesis reference, to affirm the inferior status of persons of color in God's eyes.[28]

Just how many churches and church people were party to such beliefs by the turn of and into the twentieth century is impossible to say. Certainly, the conception that blacks were of an inferior race was widespread, and it is likely that alleged scriptural support to this effect continues to be expressed. Indeed, as late as 1977, 35 percent of a population sample of the San Francisco Bay Area agreed—21 percent strongly and 14 percent somewhat—that "for reasons we cannot now know, God made the races different as part of his divine plan."[29]

Interpreting scripture to justify discriminatory treatment of Afro-Americans was not formally sanctioned by the churches. There were no official pronouncements affirming the validity of the interpretations. At the same time, however, there were no official pronouncements denying their validity. Institutionally, the churches were relatively silent on the issue. The condemnation of the interpretations, which was considerable, came from individuals, clergy and lay, not from the church bodies themselves.

Before 1929, actually, very few church pronouncements on race relations were made. One study counted six pronouncements by the 17 member denominations of the then Fed-

27. Charles Y. Glock and Rodney Stark, *Christian Beliefs and Anti-Semitism* (New York: Harper & Row, 1965).

28. Forrest G. Wood, *The Arrogance of Faith: Christianity and Race from the Colonial Era to the Twentieth Century* (New York: Knopf, 1990), esp. pp. 84-115.

29. Richard A. Apostle et al., *The Anatomy of Racial Attitudes* (Berkeley: University of California Press, 1983), pp. 38-43.

eral Council of Churches during the period 1908-28. None of these dealt with scripture explicitly or with refuting charges of Afro-American inferiority.[30]

In the 1930s, race relations began to come into its own as a subject for church pronouncements. Twenty-seven statements were endorsed by one or more member denominations associated with the Federal Council of Churches.[31] After 1940, the flood-gates opened, and at most annual meetings of church bodies, one or more pronouncements on race relations became commonplace.[32] Missing still, however, is any reference to past scriptural affirmations of racial discrimination.

Today, based on surface appearances, scripture would seem no longer used to provide a rationale for racism. To be sure, on the fringes of the church, there are extremists who express the old shibboleths. Mainstream Christianity, however, seems above board. Still, a nagging problem remains. Many past observers of black churches have noted a proclivity on their part to be other-worldly. The deprivations of this life, it was taught, will be set right for believers in the next.[33] In research done as late

as the 1960s, this message, it was found, was still being proclaimed.[34] It is, in all likelihood, still being taught, albeit not to the extent that it was in the past. The message, while scarcely a defense of racism, remains, subtly, a means to sustain it.

The subordination of women

Challenges in twentieth-century America to scriptural interpretations of the role of women in society have focused principally on those passages of the Bible that traditionally have been cited (1) to deny women access to ecclesiastical power, (2) to justify women's being in a subordinate status to men, (3) to warrant the assignment of domestic obligations to women, and (4) to certify to the maleness of divinity. These challenges are not new to the century. They have been raised before. It was not until the twentieth century, however, that the challenges were effective in generating more than a token church response and this came, in large part, after the rise of the women's liberation and feminist movements of the 1950s and 1960s.

Churches have responded variously to these challenges. The variety is most pronounced and clear-cut with respect to women's being granted greater access to ecclesiastical power. Some churches, most notably the Roman Catholic and Orthodox churches, continue to refuse to ordain women and essentially on the same biblical grounds as have been

30. Franks S. Loescher, *The Protestant Church and the Negro: A Pattern of Segregation* (New York: Association Press, 1948), pp. 28-30.

31. Ibid., pp. 30-33.

32. Ibid., pp. 34-50.

33. For example, Gunnar Myrdal et al., *An American Dilemma* (New York: Harper & Row, 1944), pp. 861-63; Hortense Powdermaker, *After Freedom* (New York: Viking Press, 1939), p. 285; St. Clair Drake and Horace Cayton, *Black Metropolis* (New York: Harper & Row, 1958), pp. 582-87.

34. Jack Bloom, "The Negro Church and the Movement for Equality" (M.A. thesis, University of California, Berkeley, 1966).

invoked traditionally.[35] In contrast, between the 1940s and the 1980s, most Protestant churches, the Lutheran Church-Missouri Synod and the Seventh-Day Adventists being notable exceptions, authorized the ordination of women where they had not done so before.[36] In every case, some reinterpretation of scripture was part of the grounds for authorizing the change.[37]

The scriptural passages quoted to oppose the ordination of women were also used in the early part of the century to restrict women's participation in church assemblies, boards, councils, and so on. Such restrictions have now all but disappeared. Indeed, in some churches, for example, the United Methodist Church and the Evangelical Lutheran Church in America, quotas have been adopted to ensure women's representation.

Most churches in recent years have tended to downplay traditional interpretations of scripture to the effect that women are to be subordinate to men and responsible for domestic obligations. They have also given more attention to passages that testify to the equality of men and women and that testify to women's signifi-

cant role in scripture. There has also been a sympathetic church response to the charge of sexism in the language of the Bible. By and large, the churches have not found a way to respond effectively to the maleness of God language. They have, however, with varying degrees of success, sought to eliminate sexist language in liturgy and in teaching materials. Churches subscribing to a literal interpretation of scripture have been less accommodating in these respects than churches that do not. No church, however, has been a stalwart defender of past practices and beliefs.

In sum, the churches' response to feminist challenges to scripture have been, at the one extreme, to bend with some if not all of them and, at the other, to embrace them wholeheartedly. Conservative Protestant churches, and the Roman Catholic and Orthodox churches with respect to women's ordination, have been the most resistant to change. Mainline Protestant denominations have been the most open to it.

Human sexuality

Divorce, sexual intercourse before marriage, adultery, and homosexuality were all proscribed by the churches in the early part of the century. By and large, the proscriptions continue to prevail today. Churches still uphold the sanctity of marriage and the desirability of avoiding sexual intercourse outside of marriage. For the most part, heterosexuality continues to be affirmed as the desirable sexual orientation.

Over the course of the century, however, there has been an accom-

35. The Roman Catholic Church's practice on the ordination of women to Holy Orders is contained in the Code of Canon Law, canon 968, 1: *Sacram ordinationem valide recipit solus vir baptizatus* ("only a baptized man receives ordination validly").

36. Michael P. Hamilton and Nancy S. Montgomery, eds. *The Ordination of Women: Pro and Con* (New York: Morehouse-Barlow, n.d.), pp. 82-99.

37. John H. Reumann, *Ministries Examined: Laity, Clergy, Women, and Bishops in a Time of Change* (Minneapolis: Augsburg, 1987), pp. 78-99.

modation to those who do not abide by the proscriptions. The accommodation is most evident with respect to divorce. While virtually all Protestant churches now afford council against divorce, they impose, at most, limited requirements on allowing divorced persons to marry.[38] In the early part of the century, church marriages for divorced persons, except the innocent party in an adulterous relationship, were enjoined.[39] Officially, the Roman Catholic Church has not changed its posture toward divorce. Church marriages are forbidden for divorced persons. In practice, however, the strictures are either avoided through now more liberalized annulment procedures or muted through priests' turning a blind eye to divorced persons' receiving the sacraments.[40] The explicitness of the biblical injunctions against divorce, especially those attributable to Christ, makes their reinterpretation difficult, if not impossible. The growing incidence of divorce has been accommodated scripturally through explaining away passages that forbid divorce as

38. For example, Methodists are now instructed concerning divorce, "Where marriage partners, even after thoughtful consideration and counsel, are estranged beyond reconciliation, we recognize divorce as regrettable but recognize the right of divorced persons to marry." *The Book of Discipline of the United Methodist Church: 1988* (Nashville: United Methodist Publishing House, 1988), p. 94.

39. For example, in 1920, Methodist instruction concerning divorce was, "No divorce, except for adultery, shall be regarded by the Church as lawful." *Doctrines and Discipline of the Methodist Episcopal Church* (New York: Methodist Book Concern, 1920).

40. Andrew M. Greeley, *The Catholic Myth: The Behavior and Beliefs of American Catholics* (New York: Scribner's, 1990), p. 117.

reflecting cultural conditions that existed at the time they were written.

The growing incidence of premarital sex, or at least knowledge of it, came later in the century than the growth in divorce rates. The churches, consequently, have only recently come to grips with the problem, and some are still in the midst of deciding what exactly their response should be. Conservative Protestant churches have opted more or less to stand firm with the past: premarital sexual intercourse remains forbidden. The Roman Catholic Church has chosen this option as well. Mainline Protestant churches have not come to a conclusion. For the most part, they are in the process of studying the matter. Study documents appear to be maintaining avoidance as the most desirable practice, but they are also struggling to establish scripturally justifiable conditions for premarital sex.[41] The struggle is not unlike the one to justify divorce. Sooner or, more likely, later, the outcome is likely to be the same. Like divorce, some churches, and perhaps eventually all of them, will find a way, grudgingly, to accommodate premarital sex.

The churches' response to the increasing visibility of homosexuality has been similar to their response to the growing incidence of premarital sex. Conservative Protestant, Roman

41. See, for example, "Keeping Body and Soul Together: Sexuality, Spirituality, and Social Justice" (Document prepared for the 203rd General Assembly [1991], General Assembly Committee on Human Sexuality, Presbyterian Church [U.S.A.], 1991); *Human Sexuality and the Christian Faith: A Study for the Church's Reflection and Deliberation* (Minneapolis: Augsburg Fortress, 1991).

Catholic, and Orthodox churches continue to consider homosexual behavior a sin. Mainline Protestant churches, on the other hand, are virtually all engaged in study and reflection to decide what their response should be. Judging from the available study documents, there will be no return to scripturally based condemnations of homosexuality.[42] Just how far these churches will go in accepting homosexuality, and on what grounds, is still too early to tell. Much will depend on whether or not homosexuals are accepted for the ministry. Albeit in isolated instances, tradition in this respect has already been broken. It seems unlikely that in mainline Protestant churches, the instances will remain isolated in the future.

Adultery, it was noted earlier, is as unacceptable to most Americans as it was earlier in the century. Consequently, even though the incidence of extramarital sex has increased, the churches have not been under pressure to change their traditional views on the subject and, uniformly, they have not. Just as it was earlier in the century, adultery continues to be judged a sin. Insofar as the increasing incidence of adultery has affected any change, it has been mostly in the direction of condemnation being balanced with overtures of forgiveness, healing, and reconciliation.

THE APPARENT
CONSEQUENCES

At first glance, America's religious denominations do not appear to have

42. See, for example, "Keeping Body and Soul Together," pp. 93-107; *Human Sexuality and the Christian Faith*, pp. 12-27, 41-46.

been affected by these social changes and their responses to them. The proportion of the population who say they were in church last Sunday was around 40 percent in the 1940s. There was a spurt to 59 percent in the 1950s and a decline in the 1960s to 42 percent. Since then, attendance has been pretty steady at 40 percent. It was 43 percent in 1989. The proportion of the population who profess a belief in God has remained at around 95 percent ever since the question was first asked in 1944. Since 1952, the proportion of the population expressing a belief in Jesus Christ as God or Son of God has ranged from 75 to 84 percent. The figure for 1988 was 84 percent. Also holding relatively steady has been the proportion reporting church membership. In 1973, it was 73 percent; in 1989, 69 percent.[43]

These overall figures, however, mask sharp differences in the performance of individual denominations. The differences, it turns out, are highly associated with the openness of denominations to reinterpret scripture to accommodate change.[44]

43. The statistics reported on in this sentence and in the balance of the paragraph are based on Gallup polls of the national population conducted in the indicated years. George H. Gallup, Jr., and Jim Castelli, *The People's Religion: American Faith in the 90s* (New York: Macmillan, 1989), pp. 3-45.

44. Caution should be exercised in interpreting this association. All it tells is that a church's performance and its response to social change covary together. The association is not a demonstration that the one causes the other. It is not possible with existing data to determine the extent to which church performance is a result of church response to social change. It appears self-evident, however, that a church's performance potential is enhanced

Virtually all of the accommodating churches, meaning essentially the mainline Protestant churches, suffered a loss in membership as the process of accommodation unfolded. Earlier on, these same churches had all experienced gains in membership. From 1936 to 1960, for example, the Presbyterians, Episcopalians, Methodists, Disciples, United Church of Christ, American Baptists, and Lutherans (American Lutheran Church and Lutheran Church in America) all gained membership, the first four at rates higher than general population growth. From 1960 to 1988, a period of continuing general population growth, all of these denominations, save the American Baptists, had membership losses, and the Baptists grew by only 1 percent.[45] As might be expected, membership loss was accompanied by loss in net income. Significantly, however, per capita income did not decline.[46]

Like their mainline counterparts, conservative Protestant churches also enjoyed substantial growth prior to 1960. For them, however, the growth has continued since. The Southern Baptist Convention, the Lutheran Church-Missouri Synod, the Assemblies of God, the Nazarene Church, the Church of Jesus Christ of the Latter Day Saints, the Seventh

Day Adventists, and the Jehovah's Witnesses all grew between 1960 and 1988.[47] Comparatively, the Lutheran Church-Missouri Synod and the Southern Baptist Convention grew considerably less than the other churches. This was a result, perhaps, of these churches' experiencing more internal conflict than other conservative churches did about how to respond to the challenge of social change. Growth in income goes along with growth in membership, and the association holds for all of these conservative churches.

A substantial proportion of America's Roman Catholics do not agree with their Church's uncompromising positions on the ordination of women, divorce, premarital sex, and, incidentally, birth control and abortion. A small minority are raising questions about the Church's posture on homosexuality. In a 1987 poll of American Catholics, 46 percent said that Catholic laity should have the right to participate in deciding whether priests should be allowed to marry. Twenty-five percent said that the Church's policy of not ordaining women weakened their faith.[48] In the same poll, 57 percent said that "you can be a good Catholic without obeying the Church's teaching on divorce/remarriage," 66 percent said the same about the Church's teaching on birth control, and 39 percent on abortion.[49] In response to a 1990 poll, 46 percent of American Catholics thought divorce

where its moral authority is accepted, threatened where it is not. The noted association between church performance and response to social change bears this out.

45. J. Gordon Melton and Phillip C. Lucas, *Secularization and Resacralization: Reflections on a Religious Census of the United States* (Santa Barbara, CA: Institute for the Study of American Religion, 1991).

46. Andrew M. Greeley, *Religious Change in America* (Cambridge, MA: Harvard University Press, 1989), pp. 67-75.

47. Melton and Lucas, *Secularization and Resacralization*.

48. William D'Antonio et al., *American Catholic Laity in a Changing Church* (Kansas City, MO: Sheed & Ward, 1989), pp. 95, 139.

49. Ibid., p. 64.

laws should remain the same or be made easier, and 40 percent expressed the view that premarital sex is never wrong. Nineteen percent felt it was never wrong or only sometimes wrong for two adults of the same sex to have sexual relations.[50]

Despite these reservations about the Church's posture, Roman Catholics are not, as would appear to be the case with mainline Protestants, voicing their displeasure by abandoning the Church. Since 1960, the growth in the size of the Catholic population has been increasing and at a rate only slightly below the rate in the general population.[51] Catholics are attending mass less regularly, however. In 1958, 75 percent of Catholics were attending mass regularly; in 1987, the figure was roughly 52 percent.[52] Contributions have also declined dramatically. In 1963, Catholics, on the average, were contributing 2.2 percent of their incomes to the Church; in 1984, the figure was 1.2 percent.[53]

IMPLICATIONS FOR
THE FUTURE

Regarding the immediate and more distant future, it can be predicted with confidence that there will be more social changes, more shifts in consciousness, and more resulting challenges to which the churches will

50. Based on a privately arranged special tabulation of Catholic responses to the General Social Survey for 1990.
51. Melton and Lucas, Secularization and Resacralization.
52. D'Antonio et al., American Catholic Laity, p. 44.
53. Greeley, Catholic Myth, p. 130.

be obliged to respond. The increase in the incidence of abortion has already had an impact on the churches. On the immediate horizon are the issues of euthanasia and the proper use of new knowledge concerning genetic engineering. As is the case with abortion, these issues will be divisive and, by virtue of their raising questions about God's intentions for humankind, the churches inevitably will be engaged.

In the more distant future, presuming that social and economic conditions allow the sciences, especially the social sciences, to blossom, still new knowledge about how the world works will be forthcoming. It, too, can be expected to affect the churches, especially as it touches on such fundamental questions as the existence of free will, the character of human nature, and the contributions of nature and nurture to personality development and the fabric of social and cultural life.

That the Protestant churches that have been least compromising in their response to the social changes of the twentieth century have thrived is no guarantee of their continued viability. While they have not experienced as much dissent from church positions among their constituents as have the Catholic and mainline Protestant churches from theirs, some dissent does exist and, on some issues, it appears to be growing. There is also the danger that these churches will be left behind because change proves inexorable and there will be no one or only a remnant left to subscribe to what these churches advocate.

Favoring a more positive scenario for these churches is, to begin with, their ability to abandon a cause when it is lost. These churches' devotion to particular scriptural interpretations is not inviolate. They are, to be sure, much less prone to compromise than mainline Protestant churches; however, compromise is not wholly alien to them. When changes do prove inexorable, these churches are able and willing to abandon or to radically deemphasize scriptural interpretations previously held dear. Witness, for example, the virtual disappearance from their rhetoric of the "curse of Canaan," of Jews' being blamed, even cursed, for the crucifixion of Christ, and of women's being divinely ordained to be subordinate to men.

Also supporting a prognostication of continuing vitality for these churches is that new challenges make old ones less salient and, in some instances, cause them to be forgotten entirely. Consequently, even where these churches are losing out in their advocacy of an old challenge, they have a chance to recoup on the new one. For example, once blue laws passed into oblivion in America, continuing to support them was obviously a lost cause for conservative churches. Since then, however, new issues such as abortion and homosexuality have arisen on which conservative churches have also taken a partisan stand. Losses sustained because these churches lost out in their advocacy of blue laws have been more than made up for in the new supporters gained from their opposition to abortion and homosexuality. In effect, these churches' prospects for re-

newal can be as never ending as their ability to accommodate eventually to old changes in consciousness and to initially oppose new ones.

Finally, among other strengths, these churches have the advantages of strong financial support and high membership consensus in religious belief and practice. Some pundits, including this one, anticipated that with the spectacular rise in the 1950s and 1960s in the number of college graduates in the United States, the commitment to orthodox religious beliefs would decline.[54] This has not happened. It seems unlikely to happen in the present era, when the nation's commitment to and ability to support higher education is in decline.

The prospects for the mainline Protestant churches are more difficult to judge because it is not clear whether or not and, indeed, how they can solve the problems they face. Especially troublesome is that their constituencies are divided not only about how the church should respond to social change but about fundamental articles of faith, including how scripture is to be read and understood. Moreover, among their members, the strongest opponents of the churches' efforts to accommodate to social change and to compromise on traditional interpretations of scripture also tend to be the doctrinally most orthodox, the most regular church attenders, and the largest financial contributors.[55]

54. Rodney Stark and Charles Y. Glock, *American Piety: The Nature of Religious Commitment* (Berkeley: University of California Press, 1968), pp. 204-24.

55. Robert Wuthnow, *The Restructuring of American Religion: Society and Faith since*

Despite the divisions, there exists a loyalty to these churches that can be counted on to ensure their survival. Because of the divisions, however, it is hard to conceive a way for these churches to contain, much less reverse, the declines in membership they have been experiencing.

There are some who see a solution in developing a way to read and interpret scripture, based on modern biblical scholarship, that would afford a clear alternative to its being read and interpreted literally, in effect, as one spokesman for this view has put it, "rescuing the Bible from fundamentalism."[56] The difficulties to be overcome, especially the need to raise the level of biblical literacy from its currently low state, are formidable. Moreover, even were it possible to develop the alternative envisioned, it is unlikely that it would be acceptable to the more traditionally oriented folk who continue to attend the mainline churches. The alternative course of trying to turn things around by letting the traditionalists call the tune seems even more untenable.

Another prospect is for these churches to break up and to form new churches of like-minded believers. Haphazardly, this is already happening to a limited extent, mostly through more conservative congregations' severing their denominational ties and through more avant garde congregations' being ousted from their denominations. The chances that division will occur more exten-

sively and in a more systematic fashion are remote if only because of the difficulties attending the division of church properties and resources. Still, the possibility of the mainline churches' being reconstituted cannot be ruled out entirely. The future course of their histories may dictate it. Indeed, the best hope for the revitalization of mainline churches may be in their becoming, through division, smaller and more ideologically homogeneous.

The future of the Roman Catholic Church in America is also enigmatic. Survival almost certainly will not be at issue. Otherwise, a lot will depend on the positions that the Vatican adopts on new issues and on whether or not it remains unbending on old ones. Being conservative on new issues, as it has been already on abortion and euthanasia, will continue to be divisive and alienating. Based on the record of this century, mass defections of members from the Church are not in the cards. The Church does face, however, the prospect of still lesser financial support. Also likely is the continuing erosion of the Church's moral authority as Catholics, more and more, simply act in ways contrary to Church teachings. The option, which conservative Protestant churches have adopted, of abandoning or becoming silent about church positions when the social changes they oppose prove unstoppable is not as available to the Catholic Church because of its worldwide constituency. A social change may reach the point of being inexorable in the United States without the same thing happening elsewhere. Still, it is conceivable that some of the Church's

---

World War II (Princeton, NJ: Princeton University Press, 1988), esp. pp. 35-70.

56. John Shelby Spong, *Rescuing the Bible from Fundamentalism* (San Francisco: Harper San Francisco, 1991).

strictures, such as those on birth control, may be so universally disobeyed as to cause the Vatican to yield. There is also the possibility that survival needs will dictate a change. The shortage of priests and nuns, for example, may become so intolerable at some point as to decree a retreat from celibacy and perhaps, but less likely, the nonordination of women.

A temporary effect of any retreat will be to reduce Catholics' feelings of alienation from their Church. The reduction is not likely to be maintained, however, when positions are adopted on new issues with which a substantial number of Church members are in disagreement. In this regard, the Roman Catholic Church suffers in comparison with conservative Protestant denominations, which, by virtue of their more highly consensual memberships, can resist change with greater impunity.

ANNALS, *AAPSS*, **527**, May 1993

Critical Junctures:
Theological Education Confronts Its Futures

By BARBARA G. WHEELER

ABSTRACT: During the 1980s, an extensive literature critical of North American theological education appeared. It challenged basic and widely accepted premises of theological study: its orientation toward clerical tasks, its conceptions of theory and practice, and the way studies were structured in a fourfold pattern of Bible, theology, history, and practice. Deploring the fragmentation that clericalism, theory-practice dualism, and disciplinary dispersion had produced, many of the authors called for a unifying theological emphasis, by which they meant that theological study should form habits of intellect and character that enable a person to make theological judgments. In the same period, however, social trends and developments pushed theological schools to diversify, offering new specialized programs for ministers and laypersons as well as new program formats for older, less mobile students. The call for unity and coherence and the countervailing trend toward diversification and diffusion will force theological schools to make choices in the 1990s that will influence the shape of religious life and leadership in the century to come.

Barbara G. Wheeler is president of Auburn Theological Seminary and director of its Center for the Study of Theological Education. She has conducted a series of studies of theological education and has edited and contributed introductions and chapters to several books, including Beyond Clericalism: The Congregation as a Focus for Theological Education, *coedited with Joseph C. Hough, Jr., and* Shifting Boundaries: Contextual Approaches to the Structure of Theological Education, *coedited with Edward Farley.*

THEOLOGICAL education in North America finds itself at a crossroads, facing choices that will determine its character in the next century. Powerful and conflicting social, religious, and cultural forces make these choices unavoidable. Indeed, the cumulative pressures on theological schools and the programs they conduct are so great that it can fairly be said that everything about theological education—the nature of the institutions that house it, its constituencies, its practices of teaching and scholarship, and even its purposes—is now up for grabs or will be during the present decade.

The extent of the contest over the nature and future of theological education is illustrated by the fact that the very term is controversial. Adopted by old-line Protestant denominations to describe the work of the postbaccalaureate schools in which most of their clergy and many theological scholars were educated, "theological education" had come by the middle of the twentieth century to refer to graduate-level training of clergy in any religious tradition.

Increasingly, however, the adequacy of the term has been challenged. Roman Catholics and Jews have shown a preference for terms of their own, "priestly formation" and "rabbinical training," respectively. Black and white evangelicals who represent groups that do not require their leaders to have graduate degrees argue that theological education occurs in many settings, including colleges, correspondence courses, and clergy conferences and institutes. Even the descendants of the term's inventors are uncomfortable with its usual definition as graduate-level clerical training. Some mainline Protestant writers argue that theological education is appropriate, indeed necessary, for all Christians, not just ordained leaders. Others, Protestant and Roman Catholic, have pointed out that study of and education in theology is preparation for advanced teaching and scholarship as well as pastoral leadership.[1]

These semantic differences within and between religious groups are not trivial. They are signs of major developments—increased religious and cultural pluralism, realignment of social and educational classes, and significant intellectual shifts—that are reshaping American life. The next sections of this article will explore two sets of these developments: one presses theological education toward greater unity and coherence; the other pulls it in the opposite direction, toward greater multiplicity and dispersion. The article will conclude with reflections about how different ways of resolving this tension might affect religion and society more broadly.

CALLS FOR CLARITY AND COHERENCE

Arguably, the most remarkable development in theological education during the past decade has been the appearance of a literature about its nature and purposes, a stream of

1. See Edward Farley, *Fragility of Knowledge: Theological Education in the Church and the University* (Philadelphia: Fortress Press, 1988), pp. 85-92; Thomas F. O'Meara, "Doctoral Programs in Theology at U.S. Catholic Universities," *America*, 3 Feb. 1990, pp. 79-103.

books and articles by respected theological scholars that examine theological education's history, criticize its current state, and propose alternatives. Complaints about seminaries and calls for their improvement are not, of course, a novelty. Throughout the history of theological schools, critics—most often church leaders—have accused them of unsound teaching and laxity in admissions and have suggested how these failures might be corrected. The charges have been answered and sometimes anticipated by seminary presidents, who from time to time have set forth reform proposals of their own. As in other branches of higher education, however, it is rare for senior faculty in central academic disciplines to write serious, scholarly works about the educational enterprise itself. The publication of a whole shelf of such works in a brief period, after nearly a quarter century in which very little had been published about theological education,[2] suggests that dissatisfaction runs deep among those who have the most power to determine what the directions and content of theological education should be.

The first publication in the new theological education literature, a book by Edward Farley, a Protestant theologian teaching at the Divinity School at Vanderbilt University, did indeed deliver an unsettling message. Farley's work, *Theologia: The Fragmentation and Unity of Theolog-ical Education*, alleged that the standard patterns of theological education that dominate Protestant theological schools, have heavily influenced Roman Catholic theologates, and are beginning to affect rabbinical schools make very little sense. These widely accepted patterns are a mishmash, a pastiche of educational pieces that have accumulated by accident rather than by design. Theological educators, Farley charged, do not know what they are doing and why.

Sources of confusion

In *Theologia* and subsequent monographs and essays, Farley shows how this situation developed.[3] In the late Middle Ages and early Reformation period, theology was unified and coherent. It was understood to be something that occurs within the person who undertakes theological learning. Originally, theology was neither propositions nor methods but deep personal wisdom, a disposition, a habit of turning to God. A series of developments undermined both theology's personal character and its unity.

First, the pietists injected a practical note. For them, theology as wisdom was inadequate. It needed a goal beyond itself, namely, the holy life.

2. The last major work on theological education before the early 1980s was the comprehensive study by H. Richard Niebuhr, Daniel Day Williams, and James M. Gustafson, *The Advancement of Theological Education* (New York: Harper & Brothers, 1957).

3. Farley's historical and critical argument as recounted in this article is set forth in *Theologia: The Fragmentation and Unity of Theological Education* (Philadelphia: Fortress Press, 1983); idem, "Theology and Practice outside the Clerical Paradigm," in *Practical Theology*, ed. Don S. Browning (San Francisco: Harper & Row, 1983), pp. 21-41. Farley's constructive proposals for theological education are found in his *Fragility of Knowledge*, pp. 103-91.

Thus theology subtly evolved from a personal wisdom into a set of studies leading to holiness. These studies, like the theological literatures of an earlier period, reflected contemporary ideas about religious knowledge: Scripture was the first authority, theological exposition of Scripture came next, and practice last, as a goal or result.

The Enlightenment preserved these divisions but made other significant changes. Each division of study became a separate, formal academic discipline; and in the nineteenth century the goal of the whole process was redefined as clerical practice.[4] North American theological education inherited the results of all these developments and added its own: it divided the practice of ministry into a number of functional specialties, each of which had a body of specialized studies to go with it.

The outcome of these developments is the jumble Farley identified: ancient field divisions onto which had been laid much later ideas about religious knowledge and theory's relation to practice, plus modern criteria for academic disciplines, and all of this finally had been harnessed to functional ministerial specialties, what Farley called "the clerical paradigm," that are defined as the goal of the whole enterprise.

Results of the confusion

Farley and some of the several dozen writers whose essays and monographs on theological education

have appeared since 1983[5] have reviewed the perennial complaints about theological education and show how they are rooted in this history and its messy results:

1. The theory taught in theological schools does not seem relevant for the practice of ministry. That, say the writers, is because the theory-practice distinction that has come down to us through the past several centuries, in which practice was understood as the point of application for theological theory, is outworn. Most contemporary views either portray the reciprocal relationship of theory and practice or reject the distinction altogether.

2. The content elements of the fourfold pattern of studies—Bible, theology, history, and practice—are not readily integrated. The reason, according to the writers, is that these elements have for so long been autonomous academic disciplines, each developing on its own without reference to the others. The problem of fragmentation is compounded by the fact that what once held the disciplines together was a view of religious authority—Scripture first, practice last—that has been widely challenged.

3. The graduates of theological schools are unprepared for the complex demands and stresses of ministry practice. This serious problem, the widely reported—and often self-reported—judgment that ministers are not adequately prepared for their roles, can, in the view of the writers,

---

4. In Farley's account, this change is marked by the publication of Frederich Schleiermacher's *Brief Outline of Theological Study*. Farley, *Theologia*, pp. 84-88.

5. For a bibliography of these works, see W. Clark Gilpin, "Basic Issues in Theological Education: A Selected Bibliography, 1980-88," *Theological Education*, 25(2):115-21 (Spring 1989).

be traced to the shift to a view of theology as a body of studies to be mastered. Lost in this shift was the goal of forming the whole person, of imparting a comprehensive set of capacities that dispose the theological student both to understand God's will and to respond to it.

Toward theological coherence

Farley and other authors propose alternatives to the present practices of theological education. To clear the way for change, most agree, the conventional description of theological education as theory-applied-in-practice must be abandoned, and the four-fold pattern of studies must be recognized for what it is, an aggregate that has no rationale and that may or may not include the requisites of an adequate theological education. Then comes the critical step: to decide what the purpose of a theological education should be and to put in place a principle of coherence that accords with its purpose and helps to determine the elements and order of the educational process.

On the question of purpose, there is near consensus among the writers of the last decade: the purpose of a theological education is theological, not in the modern academic sense but along the lines of earlier views of theology as the capacities required "to understand God truly"[6] and to do what that understanding requires. There is no reason why a theological

6. The phrase was introduced by David H. Kelsey, *To Understand God Truly: What's Theological about a Theological School* (Louisville, KY: Westminster/John Knox Press, 1992).

education, construed this way, should be restricted to those preparing to be clergy, but even if a school intends all of its graduates to become religious professionals, the writers insist, an education oriented toward theology is preferable to one shaped by the clerical paradigm. True competence in ministry is more likely to be achieved indirectly, through the theological formation of a person's judgment, aptitudes, and habits, than it is directly, by technical training.

The writers who produced the recent literature on theological education hold various theological views, and thus their proposals for what should give shape to theological formation vary considerably: critical interpretation of faith, the world situation, and vocation (Farley); reflection on experiences of oppression and liberation (the feminist collective Mud Flower); and reflection on the practices (as opposed to the functions) of leadership (Joseph Hough and John Cobb) or on the practices of congregations (James Hopewell).[7] But they agree on the central point: theological education must be more than a "clutch of courses"[8] in academic and practical

7. Farley, *Fragility of Knowledge*, pp. 133-70; Mud Flower Collective, *God's Fierce Whimsy: Christian Feminism and Theological Education* (New York: Pilgrim Press, 1988); Joseph C. Hough and John B. Cobb, *Christian Identity and Theological Education* (Chico, CA: Scholars Press, 1985); James F. Hopewell, "A Congregational Paradigm for Theological Education," *Theological Education*, 21(1):60-70 (Autumn 1984).

8. David H. Kelsey, "A Theological Curriculum about and against the Church," in *Beyond Clericalism*, ed. Joseph C. Hough, Jr. and Barbara G. Wheeler (Atlanta, GA: Scholars Press, 1988), p. 37.

subjects. It must be an intense, focused process whose goal is theological capacity and understanding.

Though the authors and their proposals are diverse, most of the authors are mainline Protestants. One early reaction from theological educators of other traditions was to identify the judgment threaded through the publications—that theological education is both ineffective and confused—as a symptom of the larger crisis in old-line Protestantism. Some mainline Protestants further suggested that the literature's preoccupation with matters of rationale and purpose narrowed its relevance even further, to the nondenominational, often university-related institutions in which many of the writers had studied and taught. Church-sponsored seminaries, they argued, are at least clear about whom they are serving.

More recently, however, other groups have begun to ask similar questions about the nature and purpose of theological education, and their explorations have moved in directions that suggest that many of the most troubling problems cross the lines of religious traditions. Roman Catholics, for instance, have found themselves in general agreement with the criticisms advanced by the Protestant writers, especially their attacks on the professional paradigm and the autonomous academic disciplines. As the price of accreditation by the Protestant-dominated Association of Theological Schools,[9] Roman Catholic seminaries had

stepped up their emphasis on professional training and academic training, sometimes at the expense of the formation programs that were the core of their own educational model. Some Roman Catholics deplored this loss; for this group, the Protestant calls for attention to education as the formation of capacities and habits were welcome indeed, though the theological bases for formation that the Protestants proposed were usually not congenial.[10]

As the numbers of men seeking to enter the priesthood plummeted, with diastrous effects on seminary enrollments, Catholics also found themselves asking questions about the constituency of theological education akin to those raised by the mainline Protestants. For whom is a theological education intended? Absent sufficient numbers of candidates for the priesthood, can and should the "programs of priestly formation" that seminaries now offer serve as theological preparation for lay Christian life and leadership?

Evangelicals, too, have begun asking themselves pointed questions about theological education.[11] Though less clerical in their orientation and more comfortable than their

9. Roman Catholics joined this organization—then the American Association of Theological Schools—in large numbers in the years

1968-73; most received their accreditation between 1970 and 1977.

10. George P. Schner, "Evaluation" (Manuscript, Auburn Theological Seminary, 1990).

11. See Richard A. Muller, *The Study of Theology: From Biblical Interpretation to Contemporary Formulation* (Grand Rapids, MI: Zondervan, 1991); Robert W. Ferris, *Renewal in Theological Education: Strategies for Change* (Wheaton, IL: Billy Graham Center, 1990). A small group of scholars from seminaries serving several branches of evangelicalism has begun to meet at Fuller Seminary and plans further publications.

mainline colleagues with the priority that the fourfold pattern gives Scripture, evangelical theological educators struggle with their own version of the theory-practice problem. Evangelical schools have been far more open than others to the human sciences and technology. Now, as they watch some of the huge conservative churches develop training programs that are much more technocratic than their own, they have begun to ask themselves what unwelcome cultural values they may have imported along with social science theory and techniques and what the impact has been on both orthodoxy and piety. Inevitably, this has stirred conversations about theological learning and formation akin to those going on elsewhere.

Finally, rabbinical schools face many of the same issues. The academic dimension of rabbinic training has dominated it for many centuries; in this country, a professional dimension has been added, writes Neil Gillman, as "American rabbis assumed the pastoral, clerical and administrative functions of Christian clergy."[12] The story Gillman tells is closely parallel to the one Farley recounts: under the influence of modernity, the Torah, the central focus of the curriculum, ceased to be "viewed as a single, internally coherent, and consistent body of discourse";[13] it was secularized, leaving no locus for the personal "religious

quest" of the rabbinical student. Gillman reports that his institution, the Jewish Theological Seminary of America, views the issue of the religious education of future rabbis—which Gillman rephrases as the problem of "religious authenticity in Judaism"—as *the* Seminary issue."[14] Gillman, like Farley and the other writers, proposes a reconception: rabbinic education should equip the student with capacities to conduct the "subtle, complex, messy, anxiety-filled" process of ferreting out meaning and truth[15] and to lead Jewish communities that seek to do the same.

It would be inaccurate to suggest that self-examination and radical reconception are popular activities among theological educators. The writers cited here have received only spotty attention, and the conventional formulas with which theological education has long been explained and criticized ("the need to integrate theory and practice") are still in wide use, despite their rough treatment in the recent literature.

The number and scholarly quality of the critiques of the present and the accompanying calls for change suggest, however, that, among thoughtful leaders across the range of Judeo-Christian traditions, a critical and constructive movement is building. From important scholars and teachers in widely separated religious corners come the same charges: inherited patterns of theological study are deficient—fragmented, impersonal, mechanistic, and ineffective. These

12. Neil Gillman, "On the Religious Education of American Rabbis," in *Caring for the Commonweal: Education for Religious and Public Life*, ed. Parker J. Palmer (Macon, GA: Mercer University Press, 1990), p. 112.

13. Ibid., p. 115.

14. Ibid., pp. 120, 123.

15. Ibid., p. 129.

influential figures seem also to be building a consensus, at least on a general level, about the direction that educational change must take: theological education must reclaim the kind of formative power it had in earlier times, refitting its procedures, of course, to contemporary circumstances and intellectual constructs but aiming as before to instill dispositions, virtues, understanding—a wisdom that shapes the whole person who seeks to understand and respond to God.

PRESSURES FOR DISPERSION

The sort of education that theological education's internal critics are calling for, the formative kind that they insist is required to address what amounts to crises of coherence in theology and of competence in the ministry, cannot be achieved by curriculum change alone. Historian Glenn Miller points out in his review of the recent literature that education as formation has institutional requisites far broader than the rearrangement of course lists:

We need to stop thinking about education in the modern system of courses, disciplines and the like. The type of learning that promotes leadership occurs in the dialectical relationship between a student and an educational environment. The study of Tacitus in the privacy of a student's home did not contribute to the development of a leader. However, the reading of Tacitus in an English liberal arts college or academy did have that effect. If we wish to develop the kind of leaders who can transform the contemporary church, we must find the theological equivalent of the liberal arts college. To redefine theological education is first to

reconceive the institutions that teach theology.[16]

Though Miller and the other writers do not provide full-scale designs of these reconceived theological institutions, the kind of school their proposals would require can be derived from the proposals themselves. It would indeed resemble the excellent liberal arts college: a school that is small enough for the faculty to know the students' minds and characters and to take a direct interest in their development; a school whose location and pattern of life permit the kind of intense involvement in a community of reading, writing, talking, and practicing that is likely to form deep habits and capacities.

There are few indications that community, intensity of focus, and the kinds of institutions that would support these emphases will be easy to achieve. In the decade when calls for coherence have been mounting, existing theological schools have been pressed in the opposite direction: to diversify their programs, to spread them out geographically, and to accommodate part-time and individualized patterns of study. These pressures are rooted in economic, social, and cultural conditions that affect all of American higher education but that are bearing down on seminaries and divinity and rabbinical schools with special force.

Economic pressures

During the last year, a new financial crisis in American higher educa-

16. Glenn T. Miller, "The Virtuous Leader: Teaching Leadership in Theological Schools," *Faith and Mission*, 9:31-2 (Fall 1991).

tion has been widely remarked, if not fully analyzed. As the 1990s began, a handful of major universities announced the reappearance of large and intractable deficits. Several interconnected developments—the continuing recession; low yields on invested funds; fast-rising costs, especially for medical insurance; and deep cuts in state and federal support for higher education—soon swelled the numbers of institutions in or on the verge of serious finanical trouble.

Most theological schools are especially vulnerable to these adverse financial developments. They must shoulder all the responsibilities of advanced education, but with fewer resources than almost any other kind of school. They do not enjoy the economies of scale available to larger institutions.[17] Tuitions are strikingly low; except in university-based schools, they rarely exceed $7000 and are often less than half that amount.[18] Earnings of and, correspondingly, contributions from graduates are also low. Most public funds that support higher education are not available to theological schools, and

the denominational support on which they have relied instead is generally declining, as American religious bodies face financial crises of their own.

These factors create a constant state of financial anxiety in theological schools. In periods like the present, as uncertainty shades into genuine difficulty in some institutions, most are actively seeking ways to cut expenses and to increase revenues for both the short and long terms. The devices available are generally at odds with the requirements of a focused, pedagogically intensive educational community.

One strategy, for instance, has been to attract new enrollment and tuition revenue by creating new programs. In the last twenty years, U.S. theological schools have invented a professional doctoral degree and a wide variety of master's programs for both general and specialized professional audiences. These programs have drawn students. Without rapid growth first in the new doctoral program and later in master's programs, seminary enrollments would have declined substantially during the period.[19]

Some of the new programs offer general studies for nonprofessionals and thus seem to coincide with themes in the recent literature that oppose clericalism. At the same time, however, the new programs, with

---

17. Warren Deem, a financial consultant who studied seminaries, has pointed out that the average theological school, with its full-time equivalent student enrollment of fewer than 200, is "more analogous [in its pattern of organization and level of resources] to a neighborhood primary school than to a modern graduate professional institution." Warren Deem et al., *Theological Education in the 1970s: Redeployment of Resources, Theological Education,* 4(4):779 (Summer 1968). The enrollment figure is from Gail Buchwalter King, *Fact Book on Theological Education for the Academic Year 1990-91* (Pittsburgh: Association of Theological Schools, n.d.), p. 29.

18. Figures are for a year of full-time professional study. King, *Fact Book,* pp. 78-82.

19. Doctor of ministry enrollments have increased from a handful twenty years ago to over 7000 (headcount), or 13 percent of total enrollment in 1990. In the short interval between 1989 and 1990, enrollment in nonprofessional master's programs increased by about 6 percent while enrollment in the core professional program, the three-year master of divinity, decreased 8 percent. King, *Fact Book,* p. 31.

their diverse purposes and multiple foci (many of them in specialized areas of clerical practice), have added to the overspecialization and the confusion about goals that have been the target of so much criticism. The resulting program sprawl, it is charged, has taken its toll especially on faculty members, whose newly diversified teaching responsibilities divert them from giving careful attention to individual students and from the kinds of theological scholarship that the reconception and reformation of theological education demand.[20]

*Social and
cultural pressures*

The fragmenting effects of financial pressures have been intensified by several closely linked social and cultural trends. These trends are sharply evident in the changed profile of contemporary seminarians. Seminary students are markedly older than seminarians twenty years ago: the mean age in 1972 was about 26 years; in 1988, 31.[21] Many more of the students are women: the percentage has tripled in the last two decades, reaching about 30 percent in 1990. The two developments are related: female theological students were, in 1988, significantly older than male students.[22] It can be in-

ferred from other data that both these changes are linked to program diversification as well: women and older students are more likely to enroll in programs other than the master of divinity.

These interrelated changes have had salutary effects. They have, for instance, bolstered enrollments that would probably have remained stagnant otherwise,[23] and they have brought much needed social and intellectual diversity. They have also, however, created serious institutional strains and pressures. Older students generally have heavier financial obligations than do younger students and, unless they are married, fewer sources of outside support. As a result, they are more likely to enroll part-time and to press for schedule arrangements that give them as much time as possible to work for pay.[24] Many younger students also have high earning needs and have seconded such requests. Almost all theological schools have had to provide the option of part-time study; the exceptions have been the few that can provide adequate financial aid for all who need it.

Even part-time programs are not enough to attract some older and financially pressed students who are not willing to leave jobs or social net-

20. For an especially vehement account of the overcommitment of theological schools and its consequences, see James M. Gustafson, "Priorities in Theological Education," *Theological Education*, 23 (supplement):69-87 (1987).

21. Ellis L. Larsen and James M. Shopshire, "A Profile of Contemporary Seminarians," *Theological Education*, 24(2):22 (Spring 1988).

22. Ibid., p. 27.

23. Two phenomena, the establishment of the doctor of ministry degree and the advent of women in substantial numbers in theological schools, seem to account for virtually all the increase in total enrollment in the last 25 years.

24. Between 1978 and the present, full-time equivalent enrollment as a percentage of total enrollment has dropped from 78 percent to 69 percent. See Larsen and Shopshire, "Profile," p. 54; King, *Fact Book*, p. 37.

works in order to move to a distant seminary campus. To serve these immobile students, an increasing number of theological schools have created satellite centers and extension programs at which students can complete at least part of a degree program, usually on a part-time basis. Such programs have become sufficiently common that the professional accrediting organization, the Association of Theological Schools, adopted new and less restrictive standards for nonresidential programs at its 1992 meeting.[25] Some supporters of these new educational formats argue that they pave the way for new kinds of educational service, to racial and ethnic minorities and to other groups in areas that do not have theological schools nearby. Others point out that theological school enrollments are no longer growing; the survival of particular institutions and the enterprise as a whole, they insist, depends on finding new sources of students and public support. Against these arguments, a few seminary leaders have expressed hesitation about the adequacy of part-time and extension study as educational formation, but their concerns have not, so far, had much of a braking effect.

CHOICES AND
THEIR CONSEQUENCES

Theological schools face some critical choices. It might be protested that they have been posed here too sharply; educational focus and quality, on the one hand, and flexible for-

25. A copy of this document can be obtained from the Association of Theological Schools, 10 Summit Park Drive, Pittsburgh, PA 15275-1103.

mats and schedules, on the other, are not necessarily an antinomy. It is certainly the case that campus-based programs that provide regular contact between students and between students and teachers do not guarantee the formation of mind and character. Indeed, the functionalist, disjointed pattern of studies that recent writers have criticized so harshly became entrenched in a period when traditional residential programs were the norm. Nor do unconventional locations and arrangements rule out effective education. The history of educational innovation shows that program experiments, especially in their early stages, can have powerful formative effects.

Nonetheless, the ideas and forces prevailing on North American theological education buffet it from different sides and push it in different directions. Respected scholars inside the schools, joined by some religious and university leaders, advocate singleness and clarity of purpose, educational intensity, and institutional discipline—doing a few things much, much better than they have been done in the past. Meanwhile, large segments of the schools' constituencies as well as many of their leaders assert that their future depends on more varied forms of educational programs that are more accessible to more people in more places. As noted earlier, the sides are remarkably balanced with respect to religious tradition—Roman Catholics, Jews, evangelicals, and mainline Protestants are all found in each camp. They are ideologically balanced as well: some feminists, progressives, conservatives, and so on favor focus, others a broader reach. How, then, shall theological schools set a course? Which set of goals and ideals should they adopt?

There are good reasons to choose a pragmatic, entrepreneurial approach, to devise plans for the future that work with rather than against social, cultural, and economic trends. As Glenn Miller has pointed out, seminaries, which were an American invention, took shape by adapting to their environment, often turning stubborn difficulties and even nasty surprises into opportunities. Theological schools, he says, became "masters of the *ad hoc*"; clear and convincing rationales for their actions were frequently devised after the fact.[26]

Especially now, amid the multiple restructurings of American religion, one could argue that these capacities for self-invention and adaptation ought to be used. The dependable old sources of protection and support are in trouble: mainline Protestant denominations are greatly weakened, evangelical organizations and churches are fighting among themselves, Roman Catholics and Jews find their resources for education diminished or needed elsewhere. What better time for theological schools to reach out to local communities and constituencies, to create, reshape, and export programs as a way of building new, more durable networks of support for the future?

The arguments for focus and coherence may, however, be even more compelling. The well-being of theological schools in the longer term may

depend less on building a new clientele for their services than on the contribution they can make to the renewal of leadership for American religious communities.

There are many signs that religious leadership needs such attention. The interest of the ablest college graduates in religious professions has plummeted.[27] Public confidence in the leadership of religious institutions is moderate rather than high.[28] Some observers maintain that the ministry has been "deprofessionalized" to a remarkable degree, stripped, that is, of its authority and basis in expertise.[29] Whether or not this is the case, there is certainly evidence that the status of clergy, especially Protestant clergy, is slipping. The changes in educational patterns described in this article support such a view. Education for high-status roles in American life is selective, de-

26. Conversation with Glenn Miller, 1992.

27. A survey of Phi Beta Kappa members shows that in the years 1945-49, equal numbers chose medicine/dentistry and the ministry/priesthood/rabbinate—about 4 percent in each case; in 1975-79, 19 percent chose medical professions and less than 1 percent, religious professions. Howard R. Bowen and Jack H. Schuster, *American Professors: A National Resource Imperiled* (New York: Oxford University Press, 1986), p. 227.

28. In the General Social Survey from 1972 to 1988, about one-third of respondents indicated that they had "a great deal" of confidence in the leaders of religious institutions. Scientifically based professions ranked higher; education was about the same; legally based professions, government, and the press ranked lower. *General Social Surveys 1972-89: Cumulative Code Book* (Chicago: National Opinion Research Center, 1989), pp. 185-89.

29. This thesis is advanced in Sherryl Kleinman, *Equals before God: Seminarians as Humanistic Professionals* (Chicago: University of Chicago Press, 1984), pp. 1-23 and passim.

manding, rigorous, and usually expensive. Education designed to be convenient, widely accessible, and affordable—qualities that have been the hallmarks of new seminary programs in recent years—confers much less authority and social power.

Status does matter; the esteem in which religious leaders are held is a fair indication of a society's openness to religious groups and perspectives in its common cultural life. Status considerations alone, though, should not determine the future of theological education. To opt for theological education that is selective, demanding, campus based, and full-time only because it confers more prestige on its graduates would be to deal in appearances.

The brief for focused, formative theological education answers a deeper need as well. The continued viability of religious institutions and traditions depends on their ability to offer models of thought and action that make a real difference to both their own adherents and to those who honor their values but do not share their systems of belief. Such widely observed trends as diminished worship attendance, the increasing circulation of members among denominations and faith traditions, and the marginalization of religious thought in American intellectual life strongly suggest that many religious groups are failing the test. Theological schools and programs that take seriously the formation of mind and character not only produce leaders who can teach and demonstrate religious thinking and behavior. Such institutions also become centers to which religious communities can bring their deepest questions and best ideas about what their models of faith and action in contemporary circumstances should be. Contending with these questions is, of course, theological activity. The recent writers may be right: the reform of theological education as theological formation may be in everyone's best interest.

ANNALS, *AAPSS*, **527**, May 1993

Another Look at New Religions

By J. GORDON MELTON

ABSTRACT: Two decades of intensive study of nonconventional religion in North America has provided a large data base to examine some of the basic ideas about the new religious movements that have become so prominent in the last generation. Common ideas about the ephemeral nature, lack of historical context, and the role of charismatic leaders, derived from studies of rather small samples of new religions, are challenged in this article by a study of 836 new religions that have operated in North America this century. They are best viewed not as marginal cultural phenomena, that is, as cults, but as products of the massive diffusion of the world's religions globally. The number of new and nonconventional religions has grown steadily since the passing of new immigration laws in 1965 and will continue to grow in the light of even higher quotas for Asian and Middle Eastern immigrants passed in 1990.

J. Gordon Melton is the director of the Institute for the Study of American Religion in Santa Barbara, California, and a research specialist with the Department of Religious Studies at the University of California—Santa Barbara. He is the author of a number of reference books on American religion, most notably the Encyclopedia of American Religions *(4th ed., 1992).*

A generation ago we thought we understood the phenomenon of marginal religions. On the edge of the religious community there was a handful of different kinds of religions, some exotic, some exploitive, and a few troublesome. They were a problem only to a few sociologists who were trying to place several difficult leftovers into their typology of religious groups and Evangelical Christians disturbed by their unorthodox teachings. Through the first seven decades of the twentieth century, the term "cult" had come to be applied to these marginal religions. Yinger summarized what was known about the cults in his oft-quoted statement of the mid-1950s:

The term cult is used in many different ways, usually with the connotations of small size, search for a mystical experience, lack of an organizational structure, and presence of a charismatic leader. Some of these criteria (mysticism, for example) emphasize cultural characteristics that are inappropriate in our classification scheme; yet there seems to be the need for a term that will describe groups that are similar to sects, but represent a sharper break, in religious terms, from the dominant religious tradition of a society. By a cult, therefore, we will mean a group that is at the farthest extreme from the "universal church" with which we started. It is small, short-lived, often local, frequently built around a dominant leader (as compared with the greater tendency toward widespread lay participation in the sect). Both because its beliefs and rites deviate quite widely from those that are traditional in a society (there is less of a tendency to appeal to "primitive Christianity," for example) and because the problems of succession following the death of a charismatic leader are often difficult, the cult tends to be small, to break up easily, and is relatively unlikely to develop into an established sect or denomination. The cult is concerned almost wholly with the problems of the individual, with little regard for questions of social order; the implications for anarchy are even stronger than in the case of the sect, which is led by its interest in "right behavior" (whether the avoidance of individual sin or the establishment of social justice) back to the problem of social integration. The cults are religious "mutants," extreme variations on the dominant themes by means of which men try to solve their problems. Pure type cults are not common in Western society; most groups that might be called cults are fairly close to the sect type. Perhaps examples are the various Spiritualist groups and some of the "Moslem" groups among American Negroes.[1]

As social scientists were absorbing this understanding of cults as small, ephemeral marginal groups, the culture was also grasping a shift in the nature of America's religious establishment. Herberg suggested that the Protestant establishment of the previous generation had been replaced by a new establishment of Protestants, Catholics, and Jews.[2] We seemed to have comprehended the basic structures of the religious community, at least in the United States.

As we were accepting this more plausible religious universe, however, forces somewhat outside of our vision were already at work to render it obsolete. Along with its destruction, World War II also spurred such an improvement in transportation

1. J. Milton Yinger, *Religion, Society and the Individual* (New York: Macmillan, 1957), pp. 154-55.
2. Will Herberg, *Protestant-Catholic-Jew* (Garden City, NY: Doubleday, 1955).

and communication as significantly to shrink the world and launch new waves of international shifts in populations and religious ideas. For the West, the most important shift was the arrival of Eastern ideas. Certainly, since the 1890s, some Eastern thought had slipped through the significant legal barriers that had been erected to keep it out. However, immediately after the war, European countries began to invite outsiders into Europe to rebuild the labor market. With no thought to the religious ideas they would bring with them, Western Europe welcomed Chinese Buddhists, Turkish Muslims, and Indian Hindus. And with a new consciousness of the world, Westerners began to travel to the East not just as explorers of their geography but as seekers in the spiritual terrain. Upon making a great discovery, these new explorers returned to open Japanese-style zendos, Sufi enclaves, and incense-filled ashrams.

Then in 1965, the major barrier to the entry of Eastern and Middle Eastern ideas into the American religious mix fell. Diplomats pursuing global political maneuvers in southern Asia had encountered a minor problem; Asians were insulted by American immigration policies. New friends in Asia demanded changes if America expected cooperation in the Southeast Asia Treaty Organization. With the immigration bill that was produced in 1965, barriers to Asian immigration were dropped. Asians and Middle Easterners, Asian and Middle Eastern religious teachers, and Asian and Middle Eastern religious ideas started a flow that to this

day shows no sign of slowing and every sign of increasing.

The impact of change brought by the dropping of the immigration barrier was somewhat hidden by a diverting sideshow. The postwar baby-boom generation was reaching adulthood in a culture that was not prepared to absorb it. With insufficient openings in the culture, the baby-boomers came to create a counterculture that looked for alternatives everywhere—art, politics, economics, living arrangements, and religion. Among the alienated of the counterculture were the first converts to the new Asian religions.

Such ferment as the 1960s witnessed had parallels in American history, but now a new factor had been added. For the first time, a variety of Asian teachers, not just books, placed the full spectrum of Asian belief-practice systems before a public seemingly hungry for new wisdom. A set of new ideas from the East, from the Sikhism of a Yogi Bhajan to the interesting variation on Christian themes by Korean evangelist Sun Myung Moon, presented themselves, accompanied by teachers ready and eager to instruct a generation of seekers of alternative religious truths.

The coincidence of the beginning of the wave of Asian teachers with the counterculture's reaching its climactic stage had several dramatic and, I would suggest, distorting effects on our perception of what was happening. First, the scholars who initially called our attention to the burst of new religious activity, especially on the West Coast, were also individuals enthused with the counterculture, and they erroneously tended to see the new religious impulse as a product of that counterculture. Thus as the counterculture died, they stopped tracking the continual influx of new religions, which has persisted unabated to the present.

Second, the movement of the first new religions among participants in the counterculture produced an intense reaction that took form as the anti-cult movement. While there is every reason to believe that some reaction to the growth of new religions would have developed, among Evangelical Christians, for example, the virulent form it took was directly related to the peculiarities of the counterculture. During the summers of the late 1960s and early 1970s, numerous college-age youths dropped out of school to spend time in California among the street people. Many, at the end of a summer in the counterculture, simply never returned to their old ways. Some of these people were recruited by one of the new religions and when seen again, in the glowing enthusiasm of their new faith, appeared to parents, family, and former friends as religious fanatics. What could explain such a change? It had to be some illegitimate influence that had entered the lives of their sons and daughters. By the time the counterculture had died, and the new religions had moved on to more visible and recognizable recruitment techniques, a philosophy of destructive cults, brainwashing, and deceitful recruiting had entered the popular mind.

The combination of the continuing emergence of new religions for the last thirty years and intense controversy caused by the reaction of the anti-cult movement to their presence has had among its results a flowering of scholarship. Where, in 1960, one could hardly find a specialist in nonconventional religions, today several hundred can be found in the United States alone. As might be guessed, this flowering of scholarship has allowed a reexamination of all of our assumptions concerning the so-called cults. The rest of this article will attempt to bring together the major insights concerning what has been learned about the new religions and propose a new perspective as to how they may be viewed in the future.

TOWARD A NEW BASE
FOR THE STUDY OF
NONCONVENTIONAL RELIGION

Through the 1980s, the Institute for the Study of American Religion conducted a broad survey of American religious groups in preparing the text for the third edition of the *Encyclopedia of American Religions* (*EAR3*), published in December 1988, a 1991 supplement and, more recently, the fourth edition of *EAR*.[3] The *EAR* first appeared in 1979 as the focus of a continuing project to gather data on every primary religious body—denomination—that now operates or has ever operated in North America, and it is the only single source containing such data. As part of the survey, besides assembling basic descriptive material of a

3. J. Gordon Melton, *Encyclopedia of American Religions*, 3d ed. (Detroit: Gale Research, 1989); ibid., Supplement (1991); ibid., 4th ed. (1992).

historical and theological nature, the institute made an attempt to gather information that could at a later date be quantified.

The survey has centered upon the 1586 different religious groups that appear in *EAR3*, including over 700 nonconventional religious groups. For the purposes of this article, the groups in the original sample of 1586 identified as either mainline Christian churches or sectarian Christian churches—all the groups in chapters 1-10—were deleted. From the remaining chapters, those religious bodies serving primarily an ethnic and/or immigrant membership—Jewish groups, the Buddhist Churches of America, Arab Muslim associations, and so on—were deleted while at the same time recognizing the important role that the ethnic-immigrant groups play in the development of nonconventional religions. The deletions left 755 groups to be included in the survey. Supplementing the sample of 755 groups from *EAR3* were an additional 81 nonconventional groups about which research has been completed and that either appeared in the *EAR3* supplement or are slated to appear in *EAR4*. Also among the 755 groups were 50 groups whose date of origin could not be determined within a decade, though most had been formed since 1940.

Table 1 presents a breakdown of the total of 836 nonconventional religions, considered in 15 groupings and showing how many individual new nonconventional religious groups of each type were formed decade by decade since 1940. As the table shows, prior to World War II 169 cults had

been formed. Thirty-five additional nonconventional religious groups were formed in the late 1940s, 88 in the 1950s, 175 in the 1960s, 216 in the 1970s, and 103 thus far have been located that formed during the 1980s. The Adventist churches, while more properly considered sects rather than cults, have nevertheless been included in the survey, since a number of prominent Adventist groups have frequently been labeled as cults—the Seventh-Day Adventists, the Jehovah's Witnesses, the Worldwide Church of God, and the Identity churches. The overall conclusions of the survey are not changed by their inclusion.

The large sample of new religious groups allows us to move beyond some of the earlier studies of new religions, which based their generalizations about new religions on exceedingly small samples. Popular texts by Beckford,[4] Bromley and Hammond,[5] Bromley and Shupe,[6] Levine,[7] Tipton,[8] and Wallis[9] based their theoretical conclusion upon direct reference to the same small sample of 10 to 15 contemporary cults with only passing and perfunctory

4. James A. Beckford, *Cult Controversies* (London: Tavistock, 1985).

5. David G. Bromley and Phillip E. Hammond, eds., *The Future of New Religious Movements* (Macon, GA: Mercer University Press, 1987).

6. David G. Bromley and Anson D. Shupe, *Strange Gods* (Boston: Beacon Press, 1981).

7. Saul Levine, *Radical Departures* (San Diego: Harcourt, Brace, Jovanovich, 1984).

8. Steven M. Tipton, *Getting Saved from the Sixties* (Berkeley: University of California Press, 1982).

9. Roy Wallis, *The Elementary Forms of the New Religious Life* (London: Routledge & Kegan Paul, 1984).

TABLE 1
NONCONVENTIONAL NEW RELIGIONS INCLUDED IN THIS SURVEY

	Date of Formation					
	Before 1940	1940s	1950s	1960s	1970s	1980s*
Adventists	24	6	8	8	20	9
Atheism	5	2	1	6	6	1
Mail Order			1	5	4	1
Mormon	17	3	6	1	10	3
Communal	11	2	4	9	4	1
Metaphysical	20	1	5	8	6	2
Psychic	36	10	25	48	23	18
Ancient Wisdom	29	3	14	14	16	8
Magick	2	2	2	24	45	29
Islamic	3	1	3	4	14	4
Other Middle East	4		1	2	1	
Hindu	10	1	6	24	33	10
Other Indian	1	1		4	6	2
Buddhist-Taoist	5	3	11	16	255	10
Miscellaneous	2		1	2	4	5
Total	169	35	88	175	216	103

Date of origin unknown: 50
Number of groups: 836

SOURCE: J. Gordon Melton, *Encyclopedia of American Religions*, 3d ed. (Detroit: Gale Research, 1989).

NOTE: In the case of groups that have migrated to North America from other countries, the date of establishment in North America has been used as the date of origin.

*Data for the 1980s are for only the first half of the decade.

acknowledgment that hundreds of others also existed.

THE EPHEMERAL NATURE OF NONCONVENTIONAL RELIGIONS

In the 1950s, Yinger characterized cults as short-lived groups, generally taken to be one generation in duration. Yinger, with no attempt to pose in scholarly neutrality, pictured nonconventional religions as small unstable groups at the opposite extreme from the ideal ecclesia. They were, to use his term, "mutants." He cited the Spiritualists and the Black Muslims as examples. This ephemerality of new religions was among the first elements of the common understanding of nonconventional religions to be challenged.

In the 1960s, Geoffrey K. Nelson attacked the issue in his important study, *Spiritualism and Society*.[10] It should be noted that Nelson used an entire movement as the subject of his research. Spiritualism (in contrast to, for example, a single Spiritualist group such as the National Spiritualist Association of Churches or the Church of the White Eagle Lodge) is analogous to the New Thought Metaphysical Movement (in contrast to

10. Geoffrey K. Nelson, *Spiritualism and Society* (New York: Schocken Books, 1969).

TABLE 2

NONCONVENTIONAL NEW RELIGIONS REPORTED AS DEFUNCT AS OF 1990

Date Formed	Number Formed	Number Defunct
Before 1940	169	38
1940s	35	7
1950s	88	8
1960s	175	29
1970s	216	30
1980s*	103	2
Unknown	50	11
Total	836	125

Number of nonconventional religions in survey: 836

SOURCE: Melton, *Encyclopedia of American Religions*, 3d ed. (1989).
*Data for the 1980s are for only the first half of the decade.

any particular group such as the United Church of Religious Science or the Unity School of Christianity). Nelson's argument, however, did not distinguish between Spiritualism as a movement and any one of its prominent components. Spiritualist organizations have survived for over a century, and the more prominent ones show no sign of demise. The two major Black Muslim organizations, cited by Yinger, have survived since 1926 and 1929, respectively, and both seem destined to survive for many decades to come.

In like measure, the survey of currently existing nonconventional religions shows a decade-by-decade growth in the number of additional religious groups and no rapid decline of groups after their allotted generation. Of the 836 groups surveyed, only 125 are now defunct. Of the 125 defunct groups, only 38 are among those groups formed prior to 1940. (See Table 2.) Thus approximately 200 nonconventional religious groups— that is, those formed prior to 1950— are in at least their third generation.

Many, such as Jehovah's Witnesses, Theosophy, and Christian Science, have a firmly established place in America's religious landscape and have become the seedbed from which a number of variations have sprouted. While a few nonconventional religions do in fact come and go quickly— 30 of the 216 groups formed in the 1970s have already ceased to exist— and while most pass through unstable phases, especially in their first generation, the great majority of those that survive the first decade continue to become stable organizations with a lasting place in the religious ecology of their communities.

Thus the data currently available suggest, contrary to the understanding of nonconventional religions as ephemeral phenomena, that they are permanent religious phenomena that will tend to grow and evolve through the same normal stages of development as seen in the culturally mainline religions as they move from more informal organizations to a bureaucratic structure. Given the large number of individuals who are either religiously unattached—still representing millions, even though a relatively small percentage of the population—or loosely attached—an even larger group available for entirely new religious affiliation—new religions are never lacking for potential recruits.

This observation concerning the longevity as opposed to the transitory nature of nonconventional religion makes a direct comment upon the failure of the secular anti-cult movement to reach one of its stated goals. It has worked on the tacit assumption that the nonconventional religions were less than genuine religions and that with a combination of social pressure and legal force they could be destroyed. They were considered unstable cancer cells that could be surgically treated with some due attention. The opposite seems to be the case, however. The anti-cult movement, while bringing much pain to individuals and causing some groups to divert resources to defend themselves, has had no measurable effect on the development of the nonconventional religions, which, in the decade since Jonestown, have continued to grow, consolidate gains, and expand.

THE AHISTORICITY OF NONCONVENTIONAL RELIGIONS

If new religions are ephemeral, it can be—and frequently is—assumed, though rarely stated, that they can be treated apart from their history. Thus individual nonconventional religions are rarely considered with reference to like groups (do they exist?) or to predecessor groups (do these exist, since the current groups were developed by the singular religious visions of the founder?). Thus the Hare Krishna movement is considered apart from any reference to the centuries-old Vaishnava tradition of Bengal and the Gaudiya Math out of which it developed, not to mention the growing Indian American community, which now supplies it with much of its support. The Divine Light Mission is treated quite apart from the Sant Mat tradition and the role of the guru in that tradition. The Church Universal and Triumphant is treated as the product of its founders without reference to the Theosophical tradition, from which it derived most of its traditions, and the "I AM" Religious Activity, which served as an immediate predecessor. Unidentified flying object contactee groups can be treated without reference to the Theosophical and Spiritualist groups, upon which they have modeled their life.

The truncated perspective of a nonconventional religion apart from the larger religious context within which it operates significantly distorts not only our understanding of it but our assessment of its impact as part of a larger integrated religious movement. While the Hare Krishna movement, in and of itself, may have little overall impact on middle America, as part of the larger Hindu and Asian religious incursion into America, it is participating in the reorientation of American religious life away from an exclusively Western Jewish-Christian format. Thus much of the distortion of our estimate of the significance and future of nonconventional religions derives from the disregard of the tradition that grounds and supports individual groups and supplies them with multiple avenues of influence.

In examining the various nonconventional religions currently operating in the United States, it was found that almost every group was related to a number of quite similar groups from which it had derived and/or with which it shared common roots. As William Sims Bainbridge put it, "In modern society, cults are born out of older cults, and most of them are known to cluster in family lineages."[11] That is, "nonconventional" ideas and behavior patterns originated either in a culture—Japan, India, Turkey—in which they were normative or, in the case of homegrown religions, in a subgroup—the metaphysical occult community—where they were supported by a larger grouping of sympathetic people. Such diverse ideas can then be tested and refined over a period of decades, if not centuries, through the interaction of a cluster of groups that can be seen to constitute a movement.

Thus the concept of prosperity consciousness as currently espoused by, for example, the United Church and Science of Living Institute originated in the nineteenth-century metaphysical community. The ideas and practices associated with prosperity consciousness were then processed by the numerous metaphysical churches and practitioners only to be passed to the United Church's flamboyant pastor, Rev. Ike, in the 1960s. Rev. Ike's message is shared by over twenty

11. William Sims Bainbridge, "Cultural Genetics," in *Religious Movements: Genesis, Exodus, and Numbers*, ed. Rodney Stark (New York: Paragon, 1985), p. 159.

metaphysical church groups that existed before he came on the scene and was discussed in over 200 books by different metaphysical authors. His contribution has not been in the generation of new ideas but in his forceful presentation of these ideas to the African American community.

Thus, contrary to the popular understanding of cults as new innovative religious impulses, current data suggest that nonconventional religions fall within a relatively small number of long-standing religious families and traditions. Not only do the particular groups grow and develop, but the family of similar groups evolves much as the more conventional religions do. The Methodists are now divided into over thirty denominations and the Baptists into over sixty. What in the West are considered nonconventional religious alternatives—the Hare Krishna movement, Zen Buddhism, the Sufi orders—are primarily denominations of the mainline dominant religion of another country. Like the great majority of Christian bodies, these individual groups exist as schisms and variations within their long-standing particular religious tradition.

The problem of succession in nonconventional religions

It is generally assumed that nonconventional religions, as ephemeral ahistorical groups, have a problem of succession on the death of their founder-leader. Drawing upon the discussion of charismatic leaders that originated with Max Weber, Yinger proposed what has become another truism about nonconventional religions, namely, that the death of the founder or charismatic leader of the group is experienced as a traumatic near-fatal event, "because the problems of succession following the death of a charismatic leader are often difficult, the cult tends to the small, to break up easily, and is relatively unlikely to develop into an established sect or denomination."[12] More recently, Larry Shinn, in his discussion of the Hare Krishnas, noted, "A critical juncture in a charismatic community's history is the death of its founder."[13] This truism concerning leadership succession derives from the earlier discussion in Weber of the problem of transferring the informal charisma attached to a founding person or persons to a formal, routinized structure.

Among scholars, while little has been written on the succession question, the strongly held opinion remains that the death of a leader is a crisis event of major proportions for a new religion. The dearth of written material on this point may be due to the virtual nonexistence of incidents of succession problems. In recent years, for example, we have witnessed the death of the founder-leader of the Church of Scientology, the Way International, the Worldwide Church of God, the Church Universal and Triumphant, the International Society for Krishna Consciousness, the Alamo Christian Foundation, the International Buddhist Meditation Cen-

ter, the Zen Center of San Francisco, and ECKANKAR, to name but a few prominent examples. Each group passed through a brief period of mourning, analogous to that commonly acknowledged by older, more established churches following the death of a beloved bishop or respected leader. In each case, there was a relatively smooth transition to a previously designated leadership, though there were certainly some power struggles.

The defunct nonconventional religious groups listed in *EAR3* were examined to see if their demise could be tied to the founder's death. The largest percentage of defunct groups died after only a few years, long before the death or even retirement of the leader. Among recently defunct groups, correspondence has been continued with their founders. Others survived their leaders' death only to die after several generations of vital life. We are currently watching the Shakers die out completely. Of 125 defunct groups, less than 10 showed any relationship between their founder's death and their demise. These groups were all quite similar in that they were organized as personal ministries of a single person who, for doctrinal and/or personal reasons, refused to mobilize followers as a church. Margaret Laird, for example, carried a distrust of organization with her upon leaving the tightly organized Church of Christ, Scientist. Psychiana's founder briefly organized local groups but soon disbanded them. Unable to find a suitable successor, he allowed the movement to die with him. These few groups that died with their leader

12. Yinger, *Religion, Society and the Individual*, p. 155.

13. Larry D. Shinn, "The Future of an Old Man's Vision: ISKCON in the Twenty-first Century," in *Future of New Religious Movements*, ed. Bromley and Hammond, p. 24.

were all organized as personal ministries and possessed a strong antidenominational bias. They were not groups that failed simply because of succession problems.

One might think that if the natural expected death of a leader would not be traumatic, then the unexpected death of a leader by assassination certainly would. In one case, that of the Bishop Hill community in Illinois, whose leader, Eric Jannson, was shot by a disgruntled member, this seems possibly to have been the case. In numerous other cases, however, the groups survived and either still exist or survived for many generations. The Mormons have experienced the largest number of leader assassinations: Joseph Smith, James Jesse Strang, Joseph Morris, Joel LeBaron, to mention a few. But, except for the Morrisites, who died out in the mid-twentieth century, these Mormon groups have survived to this day.

Three reasons can be offered as to why succession is a minor to nonexistent problem. First, we can point to Max Weber's concept of the routinization of charisma. The routinization of charismatic authority should properly occur during the leader's lifetime, so that by the time of his or her death, the organization has completed the shift of focus. For example, the initial stages of the transfer of authority from L. Ron Hubbard to somewhat anonymous church officials of the Church of Scientology can be seen to have occurred as early as 1966, when Hubbard resigned all official positions in the church. While he informally continued to play an important role, his charismatic authority had already largely been transferred to his writings and to the organization by the time of his death a few years ago.

Second, the problem of succession was largely the product of an inaccurate picture of nonconventional religions. Cults were pictured as ephemeral ahistorical products that arose only in the immediate past, without significant roots in previous religious traditions. Such is not the case. Overwhelmingly, nonconventional religions are merely individual examples of a larger religious tradition. From their tradition, be it Hindu, Buddhist, Islamic, or the occult, the group has inherited models for transferring authority through a succession of leaders, as in the dharma transmission among Buddhists, the institutionalization of mediums as pastors among Spiritualists, or a succession of elected corporate officers as adopted by most occult groups over a century ago.

Adding to the distorted picture of nonconventional religions has been the inappropriate superlative language used in describing charismatic leaders. Echoing the rhetoric of the anti-cult movement, scholarly observers have frequently ascribed almost superhuman abilities to religious founders as they interpret the allegiance, devotion, and respect of group followers to be an intense dependent relationship. I would suggest that while a highly dependent relationship between founder and followers sometimes exists, it is never total, even though it can occasionally contribute to the performance of illegal actions and even, on very rare occasions, under exacting circumstances, lead to a follower's death. Fieldwork on contemporary nonconventional religions corroborates the many accounts by ex-members that reveal patterns of doubt in individual members and ongoing critical review of leaders by the members of supposedly totalistic groups. In the case of the Unification Church, the Church of Scientology, and the Hare Krishnas, continued internal critical review has forced major changes in both structures and practices. We might also make note of those groups such as the Process Church of the Final Judgment and the Alive Polarity Fellowship who removed their charismatic leader-founder from office when that leadership proved unacceptable.

Third, even if we grant that at one time succession might have been a problem for first-generation religious groups, such is no longer the case simply because of the imposition of new legal demands upon new religions. Increasingly over the last two generations, during which time over half of all currently existing religious bodies have been formed, tax laws have forced almost all of them to organize or reorganize on a corporate model and, as a not-for-profit corporation, to place major legal powers—that is, the real powers—especially title to property, in the hands of a stable board of directors. While it is possible to exist as a religious organization without so incorporating, it is most difficult, and few groups follow that option, even for a short period.[14]

Given the corporate stable legal structure apart from any charismatic

leader, upon the leader's death or retirement, the group's board of directors immediately assumes its assigned role and oversees the smooth transfer of authority. To date, no treatment of the significant, powerful, but largely hidden role of boards of directors has found its way into the discussion of the life of nonconventional religions. Similarly, no treatment of the implications for religious groups of the subtle restructuring of American religion as a result of government fiat has found its way into church-state discussions.[15]

UNCONVENTIONAL RELIGION AND SOCIAL UNREST

No issue has been so discussed and seemingly found so much agreement among social scientists as has the assertion of the connection between social turmoil and the emergence of new religions. While this assertion has been frequently made by religious sociologists and anthropologists throughout the century, it reappeared frequently in discussions of the new nonconventional religions in the West because of the early connection made between new religions and the disturbance associated with the counterculture. Thus, as many observers juxtaposed the emerging religious situation of the 1970s beside their vivid encounter with the campus-centered turmoil and the street

14. Laws analogous to those governing not-for-profit corporations in the United States also operate in most other Western countries.

15. For a more complete discussion of the issue of succession, see J. Gordon Melton, "Introduction: When Prophets Die: The Succession Crisis in New Religions," in When Prophets Die: The Postcharismatic Fate of New Religious Movements, ed. Timothy Miller (Albany: State University of New York Press, 1991), pp. 1-12.

people of the 1960s, the social upheavals of the 1960s offered themselves as the immediate and logical explanation of the religious ferment. Thus Tipton could speak of "getting saved from the sixties."[16] Possibly Anthony, Robbins, and Schwarz summarized the position best when they wrote, "The emergence of new religions can be interpreted as the effects of a widespread perception in certain western societies on the inadequacy of scientific-technical rationalism alone to orient contemporary social life."[17] This perception, it can be argued, lies behind what emerged as political radicalism in the 1960s and now continues in some of the new movements that can be viewed as the surviving remnants of the 1960s counterculture in modern societies. Wuthnow, writing in the mid-1980s, defined the period of the most vigorous new religious movement activity as the period from the 1960s to 1973, noting that "the Vietnam War which brought the religious and cultural unrest to a climax did not end until 1973."[18] The big story of this era was the rise of new religions, which grew until 1975 or 1976 and then went into a period of stability and decline. Beckford saw the new religious movements in the West as directly tied to the period of social turmoil—

the years of the early 1960s through early 1970s—and concludes simply that "rapid social change in the twentieth century is associated with the rise of a large number of new religious movements. They are both a response to change and a means of contributing to it."[19]

If the emergence of the noticeable number of nonconventional religions is but an overflow from the social unrest of the 1960s, then we should be able to expect (1) that the number of new groups formed should show a distinct relationship to the era of greatest social unrest and (2) that the recruitment and growth of those groups so formed should show a distinct decline as distance from the tumultuous time increased.

The exact opposite seems to be the case, however. As Table 1 reveals, a marked rise in the number of new religions began in the 1950s (with 88 new groups reported as opposed to only 35 in the previous decade). The number of new groups showed a marked increase in the 1960s (175) and through the 1970s (216). So far, with data essentially from the first half of the 1980s, the number of new nonconventional religions being formed continues to be on the increase.

Thus, as the distance from the 1960s grows ever greater, the number of new nonconventional religions continues ever upward, and there is no indication that that rate of increase will slow in the foreseeable future. It is difficult to predict which families of religions will continue to expand, but the occult and Eastern groups show no loss of popularity.

16. Tipton, *Getting Saved from the Sixties*.
17. Dick Anthony, Thomas Robbins, and Paul Schwarz, "Contemporary Religious Movements and the Secularization Process," in *New Religious Movements*, ed. John Coleman and Gregory Baum (New York: Seabury Press, 1983), p. 7.
18. Robert Wuthnow, "Religious Movements and Countermovements in North America," in *New Religious Movements and Rapid Social Change*, ed. James A. Beckford (Beverly Hills, CA: Sage, 1986), pp. 1-28.
19. Beckford, *Cult Controversies*, p. xv.

Second, as new nonconventional religions emerge, older groups have shown an amazing staying power. Of more than 500 groups formed since 1950, less than 100 have become defunct, and 21 of those were small Neo-Pagan covens and groves, which have been quickly replaced. During this same period, while some groups have experienced significant ups and downs, most of the older groups have shown a pattern of continued high-level recruitment of new members, net growth, and geographical spread. The most successful have developed centers in Europe, Asia, the Caribbean, and South America.

Contrary to expectations, the pattern of growth shown by nonconventional religions treated in this study reveals no relation to social unrest or lack thereof and provides significant disconfirmation of the social unrest theories. The pattern of growth also provides additional disconfirmation of the image of nonconventional religions as ephemeral religious phenomena confined to the margin of culture.

Besides the overall pattern of religious growth, special note should be made of the growth of specific kinds of religious groups. Asian religious groups have shown a remarkable growth since the late 1960s. During the 1970s, they were a major reference point for social unrest theorists. However, it is to be noted that their growth began in the 1950s, with the emergence of Buddhism among soldiers who experienced life in Japan after World War II, which accounts for the emergence of Buddhism in America a decade earlier than Hinduism. More rapid growth began after the passing of the new immigration laws in 1965, which for the first time allowed many Asian teachers to migrate or spend long periods of time in the United States. That first burst of real growth of Asian religion has continued unabated as immigration continues.

The growth of Spiritualist and Ancient Occult Wisdom religions began immediately after World War II—wars have usually spurred Spiritualist activity—and new groups developed steadily through the 1960s. Slowing during the 1970s, they again revived, with the New Age Movement, and in the 1980s they reached new levels of acceptance in America.

Neo-Paganism, a form of popular magic religion, was imported to the United States in the mid-1960s. It emerged before the end of the decade and has enjoyed two decades of steady growth. It also seems to have a bright future, in spite of forces in the culture that continue to confuse it with Satanism.

Additionally, the overall growth pattern of new nonconventional religions within North America fits comfortably into the overall growth pattern of religion in general.[20] During the twentieth century, Christianity has shown a steady rate of growth, more than twice that of the population. The problems of a few of the large, older, prominent denominations, which have experienced a period of decline over the last few decades, were more than compensated

20. For documentation on the overall growth patterns of mainline religion in America, see Edwin Gaustad, *Historical Atlas of Religion in America* (New York: Harper & Row, 1976).

for by the growth of Roman Catholicism, the Southern Baptists, the Assemblies of God, and a number of
other denominations that experienced a period of rapid expansion. At
the same time, there has been a
steady decade-by-decade appearance
of new Christian denominations, the
number of which grew from approximately 150 in 1900 to more than 600
by 1980. The appearance of new
Christian sects continued unabated
through the 1980s and also gives no
indication of slowing or stopping.

The overall growth pattern of both
conventional and nonconventional
religion in America during the twentieth century suggests that religion is
an independent force active in the
world of economics and politics and
must be considered in its own right,
not as a mere child of economic forces,
social unrest, and/or ephemeral
shifts of political mood. I suggest that
in the modern world, while the larger
social climate may temporarily alter
the immediate program of religious
groups—thus creating variations in
such things as recruitment tactics
and social priorities—lead to adjustments in theological rhetoric and emphases, and change public perceptions of religious activity, religion as
a whole continues on its own course
in spite of either the social climate or
the monetary expansion or decline of
any particular group.

A NEW PERSPECTIVE ON NONCONVENTIONAL RELIGION

If the model of nonconventional
religions as a set of small, ephemeral,
deviant, weird, and largely irrelevant religions on the margin of culture is inadequate and the major

building blocks of that perspective
unsubstantiated by the data, what
perspective does most adequately fit
the data? A more global model should
be developed that, first of all, sees
North America and the West as participants both in the almost universal
growth of religion around the world
and in the immense diffusion of the
older religions from their traditional
geographical bases. During the twentieth century, Christianity has continued its penetration of customar-
ily non-Christian lands, but its mobility has now been matched by
Hinduism, Buddhism, Sikhism,
Jainism, Baha'ism, Zoroastrianism,
Islam, Sufism—all the world's religions—which have become equally
mobile through the migration of missionaries and adherents. As noted
earlier, most of those groups that
have been labeled cults in the West
are simply representative denominations of these older religious traditions that are rapidly being established in the Western nations, are
adapting to Western culture, and are
initiating programs of recruitment in
their new host countries.

Second, as the older religions have
extended their following globally, the
West spawned and/or revived several
additional alternative religious traditions that during the last half century have matured, shown an amazing growth potential, and are now
being exported around the world
along with Christianity. Many of
these new traditions, created in nineteenth-century America, include the
Metaphysical tradition, which grew
out of the thought and work of such
people as Ralph Waldo Emerson,
Mary Baker Eddy, and Emma Curtis

Hopkins; the occult tradition, which reemerged through the likes of Andrew Jackson Davis, Madame Blavatsky, and Pascal Beverly Randolph; the Mormon tradition, which began with Joseph Smith; and the Adventist movement, initiated by William Miller. Each of these traditions represents a new gestalt in American religious life. Moreover, apart from the truth claims of any particular religious group, that is, by any objective scholarly standard, each of these traditions is just as valid and each possesses just as sophisticated a body of religious wisdom as do the several mainline Christian traditions or Judaism.

Third, just as Christianity, in spite of the decline of several of the older denominations, has experienced a steady growth in North America for the past century, a growth in both the numbers of adherents and the number of new denominations, so the new religions have experienced a steady growth during the same period of time. The rate of that growth was significantly increased in 1965 by the passing of new immigration law that allowed a host of new Asian teachers into the country and the subsequent growth of several hundred new Eastern-based religious bodies. The addition of new religions should continue at an even higher rate given the immigration law of 1990, which increases limits on immigration from Asia by 60 percent annually. While what we have thought of as alternative and nonconventional religions show no sign of becoming the majority in North America, they have established themselves as significant and stable minorities and are bringing about a new pluralistic religious environment in which each urban area will have a medley of all of the world's major religions and many of its lesser ones.

ANNALS, *AAPSS*, **527**, May 1993

The Rise and Fall of
American Televangelism

By JEFFREY K. HADDEN

ABSTRACT: Religious broadcasting has been an integral part of American culture since the very beginning of radio. Over the decades, religious broadcasters have periodically generated considerable controversy as they have used the airwaves to transmit unorthodox spiritual and political messages. The decade of the 1980s has been the most tumultuous and political thus far in the history of religious broadcasting. Televangelists forged a coalition that provided critical electoral support for Ronald Reagan and George Bush while also playing a significant role in defining the social agenda of the decade. Toward the end of the decade, however, religious broadcasting appeared to self-destruct in the wake of financial and sexual scandals that rocked several major ministries. Still, religious broadcasting not only persists, but some ministries thrive and some televangelists continue to influence the American political scene. This article examines the rise and fall of televangelism and explores the prospects for the continuing influence of broadcasters in American religion and politics.

Jeffrey K. Hadden is professor of sociology at the University of Virginia at Charlottesville. He has written extensively on religion in America and, most recently, several books on religious broadcasting, including Prime Time Preachers *and* Televangelism: Power and Politics on God's Frontier.

THE sacred texts of Christianity command the followers of Jesus to preach the Gospel to every living creature on earth (Mark 16:15). Evangelical[1] Christians take this commandment seriously, and many among them view the development of radio and television as instruments sent by God to help them fulfill this "Great Commission." It is no accident, therefore, that from the beginning of broadcasting, evangelicals have expressed greater enthusiasm for utilizing the airwaves than have the so-called mainline or liberal Protestant traditions.[2] In the early years of network broadcasting, evangelicals did not fare well in the battle for scarce air time, but for the last two decades they have virtually dominated the airwaves of both radio and television to the near exclusion of mainline traditions.

This article examines several dimensions that are critical for understanding the rise and fall of American televangelism. First, it provides an overview of the early years of broadcasting with the objective of providing insight as to how and why evangelical broadcasters became marginalized. Second, it examines four essential processes that contributed

1. The concept "evangelical" is here used to include the wide spectrum of conservative Christian traditions that are known by and call themselves "fundamentalist," "Pentecostal," "charismatic," and, simply, "evangelical."
2. The concepts of liberal and mainline Protestantism are employed broadly to include those denominations or traditions that opted in the late nineteenth century for a modern worldview characterized by social concern and a commitment to shaping this world, in contrast to the evangelical worldview that stressed individual salvation and other-worldliness.

to the ascension of evangelicals to a position of dominance in religious broadcasting. While evangelicals still dominate religious broadcasting, their perceived, if not actual, influence has diminished in recent years. The third part of this article identifies underlying factors that have contributed to undermining the strength, scope, and perceived legitimacy of religious broadcasting.

Notwithstanding the demise of several once-prominent religious broadcasters, and much evidence that other major ministries have suffered significant audience and revenue losses, religious broadcasting—both radio and television—persists, even thrives. The final section of the article seeks to examine the structure and resources of religious broadcasters with an eye toward understanding the seemingly paradoxical developments of recent years. Is it possible that the phoenix of conservative religious broadcasting may yet rise from the ashes of its own self-destructive tendencies?

THE EARLY YEARS:
FROM THE MARGIN
TO DOMINATION

Two decades passed from Guglielmo Marconi's discovery of wireless communication until the first successful voice transmission by Reginald Fessenden that was beamed to ships at sea off the coast of Massachusetts on Christmas Eve of 1906. The first radio broadcast was also the first religious broadcast, as Fessenden transmitted sacred music and read from the New Testament.

Pittsburgh radio station KDKA, owned by Westinghouse Electric, commenced regular broadcasting with the returns of the Harding-Cox presidential election on 2 November 1920. Two months later KDKA produced the first remote broadcast, a Sunday evening service from the Calvary Episcopal Church.

Following quickly on the heels of the Westinghouse experiment, broadcasting exploded across the country. By 1922, there were 382 radio stations, and the number had grown to 732 by 1927.[3] The early years of broadcasting were stormy as "stations competed for the airwaves all across the frequency band, drowning one another in [a] bedlam of squeaks, whistles, and disjointed words."[4]

From early on, religious broadcasters contributed to the "frenzied frequency free-for-all"[5] as they attempted to position themselves to compete for the hearts and minds of the nation. Aimee Semple McPherson, a flamboyant radio evangelist, who insisted that she could not be bound by the government's "wave length nonsense" when she offered prayers to the Almighty, was one of the more testy of the religious figures. Herbert Hoover, then Secretary of Commerce, attempted to shut down McPherson but discovered he did not have the authority. The Radio Act of 1912 had simply not antici-

pated the problems of regulating this new communications medium.

Father Charles E. Coughlin, a Roman Catholic priest, was the first religious broadcaster to attract a mass audience. Beginning on a single station in Detroit in 1926, Coughlin went national on CBS radio in 1930, and by 1932 his audience was estimated at 45 million weekly.[6] Over time, his message became increasingly political. Coughlin's frequent attacks on Franklin D. Roosevelt angered the President and aroused fear on the part of many that this parish priest was a dangerous demagogue.

In the end, Coughlin did not succeed in building his loyal radio audience into a powerful social movement army. He did succeed, however, in persuading CBS of the wisdom of not selling air time for religious broadcasting. For a while, it appeared that all the networks were moving in that direction. As much as several of the burgeoning networks could have used the revenues, the headaches caused by evangelical broadcasters were seen as greater than the financial gain. Gradually, evangelicals were squeezed from network broadcasting. The mainline religious traditions became the beneficiaries of a policy of sustaining, or free, air time granted in modest portions.

In 1944, the Mutual Broadcasting Company, the only network selling air time, announced policies that made it extremely difficult for evan-

3. Dennis N. Voskuil, "The Power of the Air: Evangelicals and the Rise of Religious Broadcasting," in *American Evangelicals and the Mass Media*, ed. Quentin J. Schultze (Grand Rapids, MI: Zondervan, 1990), p. 71.

4. Ben Armstrong, *The Electric Church* (Nashville, TN: Thomas Nelson, 1979), p. 24.

5. Kimberly A. Neuendorf, "The Public Trust versus the Almighty Dollar," in *Religious Television: Controversies and Conclusions*, ed. Robert Abelman and Steward M. Hoover (Norwood, NJ: Ablex, 1990), p. 73.

6. This estimate is reported in a variety of sources, but I have been unable to locate a primary source. Like the audience estimates of many contemporary televangelists, this figure is almost certainly an exaggeration. Other indicators, however, suggest that Coughlin did, indeed, have a very substantial following.

gelicals to buy time. That same year, 150 evangelical broadcasters formed the National Religious Broadcasters (NRB). Their first official business was to hire a Washington-based communications attorney.

Almost from the beginning, NRB had some success in gaining network air access for members. The really significant breakthroughs, however, commenced in 1956, when James De-Forest Murch became executive director of NRB. Murch moved the site of the organization's annual meetings to Washington and aggressively took the case of evangelical broadcasters to the Federal Communications Commission (FCC), to the Congress, and to the broadcasting trade industry. Perhaps Murch's greatest success was convincing Sol Taishoff, editor and publisher of *Broadcasting*, that evangelicals had a legitimate complaint. Taishoff became a champion of NRB's campaign to purchase broadcast time. This time frame corresponded to the rapid expansion of television across the country, and efforts to purchase air time for religious broadcasting spread to this medium as well.

Precariously situated on the margin during the first quarter of a century of network broadcasting, evangelicals began to make significant strides in their effort to purchase air time. By the end of the 1960s, the airwaves substantially belonged to evangelical broadcasters.

Evangelical dominance of the religious airwaves has persisted now for more than two decades. The scandals of the late 1980s clearly tarnished the reputation of these broadcasters, and their total audience shrank ap-

preciably. In the wake of the scandals, a cable network for mainliners was launched, but this development appears not to have had much impact on the dominant position of evangelicals.

HOW EVANGELICAL
DOMINANCE WAS
ESTABLISHED AND SUSTAINED

Three interrelated factors are critical to explaining how evangelicals gained dominance in broadcasting. Once this dominance was obtained, rapid technological developments in the delivery of television contributed to the solidification of evangelicals' superior access to the airwaves.

*Theology and
free-market principles*

At the heart of the evangelicals' success in monopolizing air time is a confluence of theology and the free-market principles of broadcasting in the United States. On the one hand, evangelicals believe passionately in the commandment to take the message of Jesus Christ to all. On the other hand, broadcasting in America, almost from the onset, has been an instrument of a free-market economy. As we have noted, there were early efforts to exclude evangelicals from broadcasting. This notwithstanding, the right to buy air time or sponsorship has been a critical market principle of broadcasting in the United States from nearly the beginning. Furthermore, few restrictions have been placed on broadcast content.

Evangelicals, like automobile and personal-hygiene manufacturers, have a product to sell and the airwaves are a marketing instrument. The evangelicals' product is Jesus Christ and his gift of eternal salvation for all who will accept.

In commerce, a proportion of the cost of doing business is advertising. What distinguishes evangelical broadcasters from the hucksters of all sorts of other products is the point at which the cost of advertising is paid.

When a consumer buys a new automobile, for example, a portion of the projected cost of that product is earmarked for advertising and is built into the price, albeit as a hidden cost.

Evangelicals ask satisfied customers to pay for the air time. If viewers feel spiritually enriched or committed to helping this particular program in its quest to win others to Christ, they are asked to help pay for the broadcast. Many radio and television ministers readily admit that they would prefer not to have to devote air time to fund-raising, but most see it as a necessary part of doing the Lord's work.[7]

The structure for paying for religious broadcasting thus is a little precarious. It is hard to imagine General Motors asking its customers to send in a check to cover the advertising after they have purchased a new automobile. Given this comparison, it is

7. Cynical viewers typically challenge the motives of religious broadcasters, seeing the religious broadcast itself as an instrument for the self-aggrandizement of the televangelist and his cronies. This, of course, is the subject for another article. For some relevant reflections, see Jeffrey K. Hadden and Anson Shupe, "Elmer Gantry: Exemplar of American Televangelism," in *Religious Television*, ed. Abelman and Hoover, pp. 13-22.

not surprising to note that television preachers do occasionally have to lean on their viewers to send in donations. This can be likened, on the one hand, to high-pressure sales techniques in commercial advertising. On the other hand, there is a likeness to the high-pressure techniques of revivalism. In the revivalist tradition, the individual must acknowledge God's saving grace as a condition of salvation. Applying a little pressure to get the unsaved to accept Christ is an old and honorable revival tradition. In sharp contrast to evangelicals, most mainline Protestant and Catholic traditions are not so heavily committed to proselytization. Furthermore, they find the thought of begging for money on the air to be quite repugnant. Thus they repudiate both the motives and the methods of evangelical preachers.

As already noted, the early days of broadcasting saw the mainline traditions relying heavily on sustaining time as a means of gaining air access. As we shall see, that avenue eroded rapidly after an FCC public service ruling in 1960.

Given that mainline traditions have effectively excluded on-air solicitation of funds, they have either to bankroll the cost of air time with their own resources or seek commercial sponsorship. In the early 1980s, the United Methodist Church envisioned the purchase of a major metropolitan television station with the idea of using profits from that enterprise to develop religious programming. A nationwide fund-raising drive failed miserably.

In the early days of television, Bishop Fulton J. Sheen had a commercial sponsor. Subsequently, a life insurance company sponsored a gospel music program. But commercial sponsorship does not appear to be a likely option. In an increasingly pluralistic culture, commercial sponsorship of particular religious programs would likely be viewed as partisan and unhealthy for business.

FCC ruling on public service time

In 1960, the FCC ruled that there was no intrinsic relationship between sustaining time and public service time. This meant that local station owners could sell time to broadcasters and still get credit for public interest broadcasting.[8] All over America, station owners gradually began selling Sunday air time to evangelicals.

This uncoupling of public interest broadcasting from free air time left the mainline traditions totally at the mercy of the networks and local stations. The mainline denominations continued to argue that they were entitled to sustaining time, but, in the face of the FCC ruling, this argument carried little weight. For a

___

8. Public service broadcasting has always been a responsibility that comes with the granting of a license to broadcast. FCC guidelines as to what constitutes public service broadcasting are general rather than explicit. Prior to 1960, it was always understood that sustaining, or free, time for religious broadcasting constituted public service broadcasting. As long as there are people standing in line to buy air time for religious programming, and as long as that paid programming is considered public service broadcasting, there is no incentive to give away air time.

while, networks continued to produce sustaining time programs featuring mainline preachers, but local stations are not obliged to run network-produced programming. With evangelicals clamoring to get on the air, and offering top dollar to do so, more and more, local stations dropped network programs to carry paid programming. For the most part, the mainline traditions could not afford, or refused, to pay for air time. Eventually, the networks suspended production of programming featuring mainline traditions.

This resulted in a situation that was totally felicitous to evangelicals. They had never quarreled with station owners about being charged for air time. Indeed, they were more than willing to pay. Their goal was to get on the air. Networks were not willing to sell time, but local stations were. By the mid-1960s, evangelicals were buying lots of air time. For the next two decades, evangelicals seemed to have an insatiable appetite, buying up all the time they could get. The gradual disappearance of sustaining time left evangelicals with virtually no competition, except between themselves.

Mainline ambivalence

A third factor that has contributed to the dominance of the airwaves by evangelicals has been an ambivalence toward broadcasting on the part of mainline traditions. Liberal Protestantism's ambivalence goes beyond religious broadcasting. Many liberal Protestant spokespersons have expressed leeriness about the efficaciousness of radio and television in modern cultures. While evangelicals clamored for an opportunity to get on the air, mainliners debated and reflected deeply on the meaning and implications of radio and television.[9]

John W. Bachman, a member, and quasi-official spokesperson, of a National Council of Churches study commission on the effects of radio and television, described American broadcasting as a "giant" that had the potential of becoming a "monster," although it was "more likely to degenerate into a buffoon." For the church "to enter into any sort of meaningful relationship with [broadcasting] is to become engaged in a struggle which will try the soul."[10]

From the earliest days of radio, right on through the 1980s, this profound ambivalence—occasionally bordering on outright condemnation—can be found in articles appearing in the liberal Protestant publication *Christian Century*.

In the final analysis, evangelical broadcasters won the battle for the airwaves by default. Once free time was withdrawn, the mainliners were never serious players. While a few liberals view evangelical broadcasters as sufficiently dangerous to warrant suspension from the airwaves by

regulation or, if necessary, by law, this is not likely in the offing.

Technology contributes to evangelical dominance

The ascending dominance of the airwaves by evangelicals came at a time of rapidly developing technologies that were skillfully used by evangelicals to help solidify their dominance. First came the videotape, a magnetic recording device that permitted rapid reproduction of multiple copies of a program. Before videotape, broadcasters had to make multiple copies of movie film.

The time and cost of producing many copies of film make it impractical to ship copies to every station on which a program is aired. Thus a few copies were made and shipped from one station to the next.[11] This made the presentation of timely materials virtually impossible. A given station might be airing an Easter celebration in July or a Christmas celebration in March. Coordinating fund-raising campaigns or announcing forthcoming events was, at best, awkward. The technology of the videotape made it possible to air the same program at the same time in hundreds of cities. Timeliness of programming contributed significantly to effectiveness.

Satellite transmission further enriched the mix of delivery capabilities, including live broadcasting. Even more important to the development of religious broadcasting was the creation of broadcasting networks.

---

9. In 1958, the National Council of Churches of Christ formed a blue-ribbon Study Commission on the Role of Radio, Television, and Films in Religion. While a final report was never published, a book by commission member John W. Bachman (*The Church in the World of Radio-Television* [New York: Association Press, 1960]) was viewed by the commission secretary as representing the views of commission members.

10. Ibid., p. 174.

11. This process of shipping film from one station to another was called "bicycling."

In 1977, Pat Robertson led the Christian Broadcasting Network (CBN) into a bold new adventure when he leased a satellite transponder to beam religious programming into households all over the nation around the clock via the rapidly emerging cable delivery systems.

Robertson's pioneering effort was quickly emulated by Paul Crouch with the Trinity Broadcasting Network (TBN) and Jim Bakker with the PTL Network (PTL). These broadcasters were actually ahead of the delivery capabilities of the new technology. It would be yet another decade before the nation was effectively wired for cable transmission. During the 1980s, both Robertson and Bakker utilized the dual delivery of satellite transmission to cable systems and commercial station syndication.

In summary, three intertwined factors contributed to the evangelicals' ability to gain a dominant position in religious broadcasting: (1) the confluence of their proselytizing theology and the free-market economy, (2) the uncoupling of public interest and sustaining time broadcasting, and (3) the ambivalence of mainline Protestants toward broadcasting. An advantage gained, the technological developments of videotape, satellite delivery, and broadcasting networks facilitated the ability of evangelicals to retain their position of dominance.

ANATOMY OF THE FALL

The period from the late 1960s through the first years of the 1980s witnessed unprecedented growth in religious television. The average number of Americans viewing a religious television program soared from approximately 5 million in the late 1960s to almost 25 million by the mid-1980s.[12] The ancillary projects of the televangelists, including cathedrals, colleges and universities, religious theme parks, and total-living communities, also grew at a phenomenal pace.

All of this growth appeared to come to an abrupt end in the late 1980s in the wake of the scandals that commenced in 1987, when Jim Bakker announced he was stepping down as head of PTL and Heritage USA in anticipation of the *Charlotte Observer*'s publishing details of a tryst Bakker had had with a church secretary some years earlier. This, of course, was only the tip of the iceberg of scandalous behavior committed by Bakker and other televangelists.

Contrary to popular perceptions, the scandals were not the beginning of a deeply troubling period that still besets religious broadcasting. While the scandals seriously damaged whatever legitimacy the religious broadcasting industry had, they were more symptom than cause. NRB has taken significant steps to try to deal with the symptoms, but the underlying problems persist and will likely continue to haunt religious broadcasters for a long time.

12. These numbers represent a sum of the average number of viewers for all syndicated programs based on quarter-hour estimates. The data were assembled by the author from Arbitron ratings. The total cumulative audience would be substantially larger. For a discussion of audience, including the debate about audience size, see Jeffrey K. Hadden and Anson Shupe, *Televangelism: Power and Politics on God's Frontier* (New York: Henry Holt, 1988), pp. 142-59.

Three underlying factors have contributed to the disarray that religious broadcasting finds itself in today. First, religious broadcasting has experienced a classic case of competition and market saturation. Stated in the simplest terms, there were simply too many religious broadcasters for the potential market. Second, the religious broadcasting industry is essentially unregulated. Federal agencies have long been hesitant to regulate it, and the religious broadcasters do not seem to understand the perilous implications of failing to regulate themselves. A third underlying factor that has rendered the fate of religious broadcasting precarious has been the insatiable urge on the part of some broadcasters to mix religion and politics to the point that the two become virtually undifferentiated.

*Competition and
    market saturation*

In 1970, there were 38 syndicated religious programs.[13] That number grew to 65 in 1975 and remained in that range until the end of the decade. During the second half of the decade, however, many syndicators significantly increased the number of stations on which they were aired. The leading broadcasters appeared on 150 to over 300 stations in the United States, and several had significant outlets in foreign countries.

13. All of the audience data presented in this article, unless otherwise indicated, were assembled by the author for the month of February from Arbitron publications. My thanks to Shelley Cagner of Arbitron for assistance. Arbitron and Nielsen operationally define "syndication" as broadcasting in five or more markets.

The appearance of three 24-hour-a-day religious television networks near the end of the 1970s spawned another cycle of rapid expansion. Initially, CBN, TBN, and PTL aired only religious programming. The rapid creation of three competing networks created a demand for new religious television programming—lots of new programming.

Much of the new programming was of fairly low quality, but the religious network structures created the opportunity for many preachers, and would-be producers of other types of religious programming, to try their hand. Those who were good, and some who were not so good, soon commenced to purchase air time on commercial television stations.

During the first year of the 1980s, the number of syndicators leaped from 66 to 96, a growth of 45 percent in a single year! Thereafter, the number of syndicated programs ranged between 90 and 100 until the scandals of 1987 and 1988.

With a growing number of religious programs available in most markets, individual syndicators had to hope for significant growth in the total audience in a given market or a greater amount of viewing by those who already regularly watched religious programming. In fact, neither obtained. Instead, most broadcasters experienced a decline in the average number of viewers per station.

Two principles guided the televangelists' purchase of air time. First, they sought to buy time slots that would deliver larger audiences.[14] Sec-

14. From marketing research, including assessment of their own mail response, they

ond, they sought to get into as many markets as possible. This proved to be a felicitous development for local station managers. With demand for air time exceeding supply, many stations were not adverse to encouraging bidding wars between religious syndicators. This, of course, drove the cost of doing business even higher and eventually led to the demise of some major ministries.

For example, in 1975 Rex Humbard appeared on 175 stations and had an average audience of 9589 households per station. Over the next decade, competition for viewers and the rising cost of air time forced Humbard to cut back on the number of stations on which he appeared. By 1985, the year Humbard left the air, the number of stations on which he appeared had declined to 112 stations, a loss of 36 percent. Even more dramatic, the average number of households viewing Humbard per station had dropped 40 percent, to 5786. The loss of stations plus the declining number of viewers per station resulted in a 61 percent loss of audience over the decade.

Jerry Falwell suffered a similar but even more dramatic fate. In 1975, Falwell was on 123 stations, with an average of 5154 viewers per station. Over the next five years, Falwell nearly doubled the number of stations on which he appeared, but the average number of viewers dropped by 16 percent, to 4331. Falwell's average number of viewers per station

dropped gradually over the decade, with an accelerated dip after the scandals. When Falwell was forced to drop all but half a dozen stations in 1990, his average number of viewers per station had dropped 55 percent and his total audience had fallen 70 percent over the decade.

While some markets generate higher per capita revenues than others, there is overall a strong positive correlation between audience size and revenues. Competition within any given market simultaneously resulted in a decline in the average audience size of individual broadcasters even as the great demand for air time drove the cost of air time yet higher.

Aggressive direct-mail and tele-marketing solicitations helped provide a respite against impending financial disaster for some ministries, but others were too overextended to adjust quickly enough to rapidly changing market conditions. Such was the case for Humbard in 1985 and Falwell in 1990.

The scandals, of course, exacerbated the problem. In 1986, the year before the scandals hit the world of televangelism, Arbitron measured 15.1 million households tuning into religious broadcasting during an average week. By February of 1992, that figued had dropped to 9.5 million, a decline of 37 percent.

Unregulated industry

Since the scandals that commenced in 1987, religious broadcasters have deservedly been the subject of intense public scrutiny. At the

---

learned that the station, time slot, and program immediately preceding can have important impacts on audience size.

heart of the problem is the fact that religious broadcasting is a substantially unregulated industry. This reality must be viewed, however, in part, in the context of commercial radio and television in the United States. In no other country does broadcasting operate with so little interference by government. In one sense, thus, religious broadcasters merely operate within a minimally regulated industry.

But this is only one dimension of the issue. There is a deeper and more troubling problem. At the core of this problem is the perception on the part of broadcasters that they are entitled to special treatment that precludes regulatory interference. First, they see themselves as having a heavenly mandate to spread the Gospel. Radio and television are the instruments for that mission. For many broadcasters, there is a sense that their personal calling is unique and involves a special relationship with their heavenly Father. Given this special relationship, neither government nor peer regulation seems appropriate. How could either government regulators or fellow broadcasters discern the mission and agenda that God has set for them personally?

In addition to rejecting the general principle that others should regulate their broadcasting activities, religious broadcasters further perceive themselves as accountable to God. Regulation, thus, is both inappropriate and unnecessary and, therefore, unwelcome.

Most broadcast ministries would further argue that they are accountable to a board, or a church, or both.

In reality, however, a large proportion of broadcast ministries have boards with a composition consisting heavily of family members and employees. Sometimes board members are representatives of other ministries who benefit from the generosity of the broadcast ministry. In a word, the composition of the boards of many broadcast ministries falls short of comprising persons who are in a position to offer solid terrestrial guidance.

To this needs to be added the fact that the heads of most broadcast ministries are charismatic and, thus, effective in persuading boards to approve their projects. After the PTL scandals broke, we learned in considerable detail of Jim Bakker's ability to enthrall board members with his dazzling plans to build a Christian theme park beyond the imagination of any previous mortal. The minutes of PTL board meetings detail the absence of much governance at all.

What is known about other broadcast ministries suggests that dominance by a charismatic leader is fairly typical. Seldom do hard-nosed business considerations temper the enthusiasm of these leaders. Indeed, autobiographies abound with proud statements of how broadcasters were able to prevail upon their boards to go along with their ambitious projects. Usually, moreover, there is at least a hint of attribution to God for the success. In short, projects are presented as God's projects.

The task of governance in organizations headed by charismatic leaders who perceive themselves to be the instruments of God's will is, at best, difficult. It was not until the late 1970s that religious leaders themselves began to take seriously the task of collective governance and accountability.

In 1979, under considerable threat of congressional regulation, evangelical parachurches[15] formed the Evangelical Council for Financial Accountability (ECFA). This was an important step toward self-governance. ECFA had some considerable success in bringing parachurches under its wing, but the organization lacked adequate resources to investigate noncompliance.

Further, ECFA was not successful in attracting many religious broadcasters. This was disappointing, given that religious broadcasters were high on the list of parachurch organizations that were of concern to the congressmen who had encouraged self-regulation.

In January 1987, two months before the PTL scandal broke, the governing board of the National Religious Broadcasters approved the creation of a broadcasters' regulatory agency to be called the Ethics and Financial Integrity Commission (EFICOM). While the scandals gave NRB the leverage to strengthen the ethics code, it was two years before EFICOM formally went on line. In the interim, an ad hoc action of the NRB Board expelled Jimmy Swaggart but declined to conduct a full investigation when charges were brought against Paul Crouch, head of TBN.

In January 1989, NRB gave member organizations three months to comply with EFICOM standards or be booted out of NRB. By early 1992, there were still a substantial number of NRB members who had not joined EFICOM, and considerable doubt remained as to when, or even whether, full compliance would be achieved. In the interim, it appeared that a significant number of organizations would be dropping their NRB affiliation rather than be formally ejected.[16]

Whether NRB's own integrity or perhaps even its viability will be on the line for lack of member compliance with EFICOM standards remains to be seen. Even if the organization does get by this crisis, major broadcast ministries remain outside the reach of NRB.

So long as religious broadcasters remain outside a strong orbit of self-regulation, televangelists will continue to confuse their own ambitions with God's plan. And so long as this is the case, we can expect hard-hitting investigative reporting, the likes of ABC's *Prime Time Live* coverage of three television ministries based in Texas. Each time a scandal comes to light, the dark shroud of illegitimacy will be cast upon the entire religious-broadcast industry.

It is possible that NRB will take stronger measures to regulate its members and actively seek to stigmatize those outside its orbit. Such a development, however, seems problematic. It is not so much a matter of

---

15. A parachurch is a religious organization that is freestanding, that is, independent of governance by denomination or major church bodies.

16. For a discussion of the status of EFICOM, see "NRB Moves Slowly to Enforce Ethics Code," *Christianity Today*, 9 Mar. 1992, p. 59.

the organization's not having the stomach for hardball as it is members' uneasiness about being regulated. While the scandals created a crisis mood that resulted in many members' feeling they had no alternative but to go along with EFICOM, many felt put upon in doing so. In their hearts, they see themselves as being both accountable to and right with their God, and they would prefer to leave it to others to take care of their own accountability.

Mixing religion and politics

The mixing of religion and politics on the airwaves has a long history in America. As noted in the introduction, Father Charles E. Coughlin was a troubling presence in American politics during the 1930s and into the early 1940s. His bellicose attacks on communists, socialists, international bankers, Jews, labor union leaders and, finally, President Franklin Roosevelt led many to fear Coughlin more than Germany's Hitler. Coughlin was finally driven from the air in 1940 as broadcasters in large numbers failed to renew his contract, invoking a National Association of Broadcasters' code of ethics that barred "controversial" speakers, a code that was effectively written to deal with the disputatious Coughlin.

While Coughlin had been the most formidable religious broadcaster pursuing a political agenda in America until the 1980s, there had been many others. Carl McIntire and Billy James Hargis, two tactless fundamentalists, both had substantial radio ministries during the 1950s.

Both unrelentingly attacked politicians who were "soft on communism" and religious leaders who preached "spiritual apostasy." There were others, some preachers and others lay leaders—for example, Gerald B. Winrod, Frederick C. Schwartz, Dean Clarence Manion, Dan Smoot, and Edgar Bundy—who dressed their right-wing political messages in religious clothing and utilized the airwaves to promote their causes. These persons were particularly annoying to liberals, but none of them ever approached the potential political threat that Father Coughlin mounted.[17]

There was evidence from as early as the mid-1970s that several television preachers were moving toward political agendas. It was not until 1980, however, that this became evident to the press and the general public. Two events that year raised the consciousness of the nation.

In April, Pat Robertson cosponsored a mass rally called "Washington for Jesus" that attracted perhaps a half-million participants, one of the largest crowds ever to assemble on the Mall. While Robertson and other leaders claimed they came to Washington merely to pray, the rally and promotion activities leading up to it teemed with political tactics and messages.[18]

17. For an illuminating and sober assessment of the Christian Right from the Great Depression through the Cold War, see Leo P. Ribuffo, *The Old Christian Right* (Philadelphia: Temple University Press, 1983).

18. Robertson, along with other radio and television broadcasters, used his programming to enlist participants. The rally demonstrated the potential for evangelicals to utilize the infrastructure of Christian radio, television,

In August, a star-studded cast of televangelists joined in a National Affairs Briefing in Dallas that was highlighted by the appearance of presidential candidate Ronald Reagan, who endorsed the political agenda of the television-preacher-led New Christian Right movement.

Evangelical Christians voted in large numbers for Reagan, and the politically minded televangelists wasted no time in stepping forward to claim credit for delivering this large voting bloc. The perception that conservative television preachers contributed significantly to the election of Ronald Reagan sent shock waves of fear through the rank and file of liberals in America. New organizations, like People for the American Way, were formed to do battle with the religious Right. President Reagan did little to alleviate that discomfort as he openly courted the televangelists, addressing the annual NRB meetings, selecting the annual meeting of the National Association of Evangelicals to deliver his "evil empire" speech, and regularly inviting Christian Right celebrities to the White House.

Reagan's close association with the religious Right clearly did not hurt his popularity. At the same time, the trek of televangelists into the world of politics did not enhance their popularity among their established constituencies. Further, it did not result in drawing new constituencies into their orbit. The evidence of audience size suggests they probably paid a price for involvement in politics.[19]

When Jerry Falwell became highly visible as the leader of the Moral Majority, he experienced no increase in the number of households viewing his *Old-Time Gospel Hour* program. Given that he quickly moved from low to very high national visibility and name recognition, one might have expected that mere curiosity would have resulted in some discernible increase of viewers.

Between 1985 and 1988 Pat Robertson lost 52 percent of his audience. The televangelism scandals almost certainly had an impact on Robertson's audience ratings, as they negatively affected his bid to challenge George Bush for the Republican nomination for the presidency. But Robertson's audience ratings began to show a significant decline from 1985, which corresponds to the beginning of public discussion of a presidential bid.

Between February 1985 and February 1987, *The 700 Club* suffered a 21 percent audience decline.[20] There

19. Most of the politically minded televangelists operate within legally permissible boundaries, at least most of the time. But the very fact that they have come to view their faith as inseparable from politics has positioned them beyond the range of permissible activity as far as many potential constituencies are concerned. They may have adequate resources to operate quite comfortably, at least for a while. But when hard times beset them, they will have extreme difficulty in establishing rapport with potential constituents whom they have already alienated. An equal, if not even more important, implication is the fact that they contribute to negative public perceptions that have tarnished their cathode-ray colleagues who resolutely avoid politics.

and religious presses to mobilize political participation.

20. The PTL scandal did not break until late March of 1987.

are too many interacting factors to assess the independent impact of each. What is clear is that Pat Robertson's move toward the political arena, like Jerry Falwell's rather sudden high visibility in politics, did not lead to an increase of viewers.

Robertson's political campaign probably recruited some constituency from outside his loyal television audience, but this group was not mobilized as viewers or financial supporters of his television ministry. Furthermore, there is evidence to suggest that some of his already established constituency had difficulty accommodating the political with the spiritual messages.

Public opinion polls have demonstrated that a large proportion of the American population is evangelical and generally supportive of conservative social and economic agendas.[21] But this support for issues does not necessarily translate into support for preachers who, through their broadcast ministries, place themselves at the head of political and social movements. Many people have serious reservations about spiritual leaders' also being political leaders.

It seems reasonable to postulate, thus, that the more aggressive a religious broadcaster becomes in pursuing a public political role, the narrower the base of support for his religious broadcasting role. The reason for this seems fairly clear. An aggressive political role almost certainly leads to a greater specificity of political doctrines. The greater the

specificity, the greater the probability of articulating views at variance with those of constituents.[22]

When a preacher-politician expresses political views at variance with those of his constituents, cognitive dissonance will be created. The greater the dissonance, the greater the probability that constituents will withdraw support. Thus, unless a television preacher builds an audience base from the start with a clearly articulated political position, to become politically active along the way is almost certain to narrow the support base.

The implications of this seems clear. First, as they got deeper into politics, Falwell and, later, Robertson almost certainly lost some of their audience that had been their financial-support base. The high level of competition during this time frame provided a wide variety of options for viewing and the reallocation of financial support.

In the minds of many, the involvement in politics served to delegitimize not only the ministry in question but religious broadcasting more generally. The financial and sexual scandals contributed further to the cognitive dissonance that many viewers were already experiencing. Some people changed channels, but others turned their television sets off.

In summary, the decline and fall of religious broadcasting is only partially the result of the shame brought upon the industry by greed and sleaziness. Jim Bakker and Jimmy Swaggart brought disgrace to reli-

21. John H. Simpson, "Moral Issues and Status Politics," in *The New Christian Right*, ed. Robert C. Liebman and Robert Wuthnow (New York: Aldine, 1983).

22. This is probably an important reason why politicians become increasingly vague as they move closer to elections.

gious broadcasting. Ambition to be television preacher stars brought more competition than the market could absorb. And the insistence on linking highly particularistic political agendas with theological doctrine narrowed the base of potential support.

The phoenix is a legendary bird of antiquity that is consumed by fire and then miraculously reborn out of the ashes of its own immolation.

Evangelical religious broadcasters were nearly wiped off the air during the late 1930s and 1940s. This resulted from determined efforts of networks, broadcast associations, local station owners, and mainline Protestant leaders to rid the airwaves of their presence. But in another sense, their demise was self-inflicted. They were a noisy, unpredictable, and sometimes unruly element capable of offending large numbers of people and stirring up prejudice and hatred toward religious, cultural, and racial minorities.

From near extinction, they rose to secure a position of dominance in religious broadcasting for more than two decades. In the last years of the 1980s, sex and money scandals, competition in a saturated market, and political partisanship all contributed to another fall that, even more than the demise of the 1930s and 1940s, appears to be self-inflicted.

By most available indicators, the religious broadcasters appear to have taken a terrible tumble. Several former giants of the industry are no longer on the air. The leader of one ministry is in prison; another faces apparent imminent bankruptcy of a university that earlier appeared to be an enduring tribute to its founder and the success of his religious broadcast. Audience sizes and contributions are down sharply, and rising costs have threatened to drive yet other prominent figures from the airwaves. In the midst of all this bad news, there have emerged yet new unsavory characters, the likes of Robert Tilton. Surely this beleaguered industry cannot once again rise from the ashes of its own fire.

As difficult as it may be for outsiders to comprehend, there is evidence of structural strength from which rebirth and renewal might emerge. There are two primary structural elements that make survival a realistic prospect. The first is the broadcasting network structures. The second is a steady growth in the number of full-time religious stations in metropolitan areas across the country.

Both of these elements are possible because of rapidly changing technology. During the decade of the 1980s, the nation was substantially wired for cable television. That task will effectively be completed during the current decade even as more sophisticated delivery systems are in the offing. With cable came a greatly expanded availability of channels.

Pat Robertson's Christian Broadcasting Network was the first and is financially the most successful of the religious networks. Over the decade of the 1980s, Robertson restructured the network to present family entertainment programming. He also succeeded in greatly expanding his cable outlets. By the end of 1991, the Family Channel reached 92 percent of all cable households and 59 percent of all households in America, market shares that rank it among the largest cable systems in the country. The Family Channel broadcasts *The 700 Club* and related programming daily and offers a substantial outlet for religious programs on Sunday.

The increased number of channels on cable television has resulted in significant expansion of three other religious channels: TBN, Eternal Word Network (EWN), and Vision Interfaith Satellite Network (VISN).

TBN is by far the most viable of these three. Founder and owner Paul Crouch has aggressively bought up small powered television stations in addition to working hard to expand coverage on cable systems. TBN produces a substantial amount of its own programming, which is Pentecostal in character, and provides an outlet for syndicators.

EWN was founded by a Roman Catholic nun, Sister Angelica from Alabama, and VISN is a collective effort of 28 mainline Protestant, Jewish, Roman Catholic, and Eastern Orthodox groups. Neither is well capitalized. In the fall of 1992, VISN began sharing broadcast time with the American Christian Television System (ACTS), a Southern Baptist network that was founded in the early 1980s.

These three networks provide an enormous quantity of air time for religious broadcasting. Much of the broadcasting is not of very good quality. Neither Arbitron nor Nielsen has the capability to measure the audience size of these networks. Most certainly, the average viewing audience is not very large. At the same time,

however, the cumulative audience is likely considerable.

If these networks survive, it is reasonable to expect that the passage of time will see eventual improvement in programming quality. Furthermore, if they can extend their presence on cable systems and hold those gains, they will gradually experience audience growth.

The second important structural outlet for religious programming is the local religious television station. The 1990 *Directory of Religious Broadcasting*, published by NRB, reports a growth of religious television stations from 25 in 1980 to 339 in 1990. This includes low-power stations. A large proportion of these stations are independent. If financially successful, they are likely to increase their radiated power in the metropolitan communities where they operate. The local station may choose to affiliate with a religious network, sell time to syndicators, create its own programming schedule, or some combination thereof.

In addition to the religious networks and local religious stations, religious broadcasters are also finding outlets on other cable networks. Black Entertainment Network, for example, currently sells a substantial amount of time to religious broadcasters. This can be expected to decline in direct proportion to the network's financial success with its primary mission, but other networks might later serve as an outlet for religious broadcasting.

It is difficult to assess what the future will bring in terms of options for syndicators to buy air time on major very high frequency stations.

If the loss of market shares to ultra-high frequency stations and satellite-delivered cable systems is precipitous, then the cost of air time may stabilize, even decline, and permit religious syndicators to again expand syndicated broadcasting.

While the total measured viewing audience of religious programs is down sharply since the scandals, the structure for rebuilding is in place. If rebuilding occurs, we will most certainly see new faces, as the first-generation titans are aging or have already fallen.

As for the role of televangelists in building and holding together a conservative political coalition in America, the 1992 presidential campaign brought renewed evidence that such televangelists are still around. The Republican National Convention saw Pat Robertson addressing the convention in prime time, and Jerry Falwell and D. James Kennedy were prominently visible.

After the Houston convention, and 12 years to the day that Ronald Reagan addressed the National Affairs Briefing in Dallas, Bush returned to the site and again rallied this right-wing religious constituency. Along the campaign trail, Bush went to Virginia Beach to address Robertson's Christian Coalition, a group vowing to achieve working control of the Republican Party by 1996.

Whatever may eventually happen to the televangelists and the political ambitions of some of them, it is still premature to attempt to write the final chapter.

ANNALS, *AAPSS*, **527**, May 1993

Fisher Kings and Public Places:
The Old New Age in the 1990s

By CATHERINE L. ALBANESE

ABSTRACT: The New Age is best seen as a new spirituality with pervasive ties to a large general American culture rather than as a narrowly defined movement with mostly theosophical roots. In fact, the New Age is an expression of American nature religion, intimately tied to a nineteenth-century past that blurred distinctions between spirit and matter. This nature religion carries considerable moral weight and, especially with its emphasis on healing as reconciliation, contains a social ethic. It also reveals ties to Protestant America by pointing toward evangelical ideas of disharmony and sin and by the ambiguities of its millennial preoccupation. Finally, its social ethic means a willingness to engage in public discourse on themes of environmentalism and related concerns. Thus the new spirituality demonstrates an ease in the "naked public square," which Christianity and civil religion have not been able to inhabit comfortably in our time.

Catherine L. Albanese is professor of religious studies at the University of California, Santa Barbara. An American religious historian, she is the author, most recently, of Nature Religion in America: From the Algonkian Indians to the New Age *(1990) and* America: Religions and Religion *(second edition, 1992).*

READERS of the *New Age Journal* presumably know something about the New Age in the United States. In the recent survey "Spirituality and the Family," conducted by the journal, respondents provided a collective profile of their religious past and present. Two-thirds had come from homes in which both parents shared the same religious background, and, in childhood, just 14 percent were introduced to teachings outside the Jewish or Christian tradition. However, fully 95 percent acknowledged that they had explored spiritual alternatives, and 62 percent told the *New Age Journal* that they had "followed a spiritual teacher." Meanwhile, for only 30 percent of survey respondents did a relationship with their childhood religious tradition continue. Of those who were raised Protestant, 11 percent claimed to practice within the denominational boundaries that had shaped their early years. Among Catholics, 25 percent still practiced their original faith. "In general," the article summarized, "our respondents have replaced the religions of their youth with practices ranging from Pagan to Unitarian, 'metaphysical' to 'spiritual,' nondenominational Christian to Buddhist." Still, although no respondents described themselves as atheists, "none" was the most popular survey answer to a question about which religion was observed.[1]

If the survey revealed a strong distaste for organized religion among many, it also showed a preference for

theological ambiguity: respondents were more comfortable claiming belief in "something" than claiming belief in God.[2] This conceptual yeastiness is most to the point here, for the expansive, fuzzy theology of survey respondents suggests the catchall nature of the New Age. It is possible to underline the theosophical forces that shaped it, as J. Gordon Melton does, or to stress its ties to the esoteric tradition of the West, as does Robert Ellwood, Jr. Alternatively, we might, with Mary Farrell Bednarowski, adopt the implicit definition assumed by New Age teacher David Spangler, who declared that believers "espoused explicitly the idea of an emerging planetary culture based on human transformation."[3] Each of these views tells us something useful, and each illuminates the movement from a somewhat different perspective. But the evolving nature of what is called New Age suggests the difficulties of characterizing it. Indeed, it might be preferable to avoid the term because, already, it carries connotations that may weigh negatively for some or suggests a provenance that does not fit for others.

THE OLD NEW AGE IN AMERICA

Besides the embarrassment or discontent of the would-not-be New

2. Ibid., p. 55.

3. J. Gordon Melton, "New Thought and the New Age," in *Perspectives on the New Age*, ed. James R. Lewis and J. Gordon Melton (Albany: State University of New York Press, 1992), pp. 15-29; Robert Ellwood, Jr., "How New Is the New Age?" in ibid., pp. 59-67; Mary Farrell Bednarowski, *New Religions and the Theological Imagination in America* (Bloom-

1. Drew Kampion and Phil Catalfo, "All in the Family," *New Age Journal*, 11:54-55 (July-Aug. 1992).

Ager, there are solid intellectual reasons for moving past the term. In truth, the new age has been reigning over American religion ever since, in the late eighteenth century, a congressional committee settled on a design for the Great Seal of the United States. With its Latin phrase *novus ordo seclorum*, the Great Seal of 1782—visible today on the reverse side of a dollar bill—proclaimed a "new order of the ages." The unfinished pyramid and mysterious eye that stood above the proclamation told of the complicity of the Founders with the alternative mystical tradition of the West. Mediated to them through Freemasonry and its deistic beliefs, this tradition formed the noncontroversial social background for the lives of most of the Founders.

The nation's Founders did not particularly elaborate on the tradition's esotericism and emphasized, as much or more, its ethic of honest and upright dealing with one's fellows in a fraternal social network. But the world they came from, if elite, was only thinly separated from a popular world of belief and practice. Here, Christian theology lived side by side with astrology, witchcraft, folk magic, and legendary lore stressing patterns of connection between an overarching natural cosmos and a human social world. Historians have given us brief but tantalizing glimpses of this religious world, and what they have shown suggests that the proper and approved universe of orthodox Christianity was but the shoreline of a spiritual continent.

Moreover, the astounding success of Mormonism, with its meteoric rise in the 1830s, points toward a rich magical background of peepstones, dowsing tools, communicating salamanders, and numinous buried treasure.[4]

Novus ordo seclorum, in sum, was a spiritual Pandora's box, and its new age of the spirit was to be an age of theological ferment, religious democracy, and sectarian multiplication. By the end of the nineteenth century, the new age of American religion was still, for contemporaries, just beginning or beckoning from over a near horizon. Adventists had denominationalized after an earlier millennial excitement that predicted the end of the present world and the Second Coming of Christ in 1843 and then 1844. Dispensational premillennialists, ancestors of twentieth-century fundamentalists, held that they were living in the last moments of the penultimate age, or dispensation, and they expected the new era of the millennium imminently. Their spiritual cousins, who would form the Pentecostal movement in the early twentieth century, felt that they were already experiencing a new time through the fire and tongues of the

---

4. For colonial popular religion and occultism, see Herbert Leventhal, *In the Shadow of the Enlightenment: Occultism and Renaissance Science in Eighteenth-Century America* (New York: New York University Press, 1976); David D. Hall, *Worlds of Wonder, Days of Judgment: Popular Religious Belief in Early New England* (New York: Alfred A. Knopf, 1989); Jon Butler, *Awash in a Sea of Faith: Christianizing the American People* (Cambridge, MA: Harvard University Press, 1990), esp. pp. 67-97. For the magical provenance of early Mormonism, see D. Michael Quinn, *Early Mormonism and the Magic World View* (Salt Lake City, UT: Signature Books, 1987).

ington: Indiana University Press, 1989), p. 15; David Spangler, *Emergence: The Rebirth of the Sacred* (New York: Dell, 1984), p. 167.

spirit. Meanwhile, the New Thought movement proclaimed its radical break with an old religious era, and members of the Theosophical Society expected the dawn of a new age with the arrival of a world teacher.

THE NEW AGE
AS NATURE RELIGION

Seen in this context, the New Age movement does not look terribly new. Even further, if we move past its mood of expectation and anticipation —a mood that links it to so much that has gone before in American religious history—there are other grounds for deconstructing the New Age. In brief, if examined in terms of its intrinsic belief and religious practice, the New Age movement, or, as I shall call it provisionally hereafter, the new—in the sense that it was less visible and less self-conscious before—spirituality, is a version of American nature religion. As such, its central theological proposition is a modern-day expression of the theory of correspondence. In this way of thinking, human society is a small-scale version of a grand cosmological design, so that "as above, so below" becomes the general rubric for understanding. And if the microcosm of the human world reflects a superordinate macrocosm, the message is clearly connection. The macrocosm is, of course, greater in size, but the microcosm is made of the same stuff as the universe itself. To say this another way, the worlds of matter—that is, nature—and spirit are continuous.

Antebellum nineteenth-century religious movements including Swedenborgianism, mesmerism, spiritualism, Transcendentalism, and also Mormonism eagerly conflated material and spiritual worlds. In so doing, they elevated nature to a moral principle, an arbiter and guide for virtuous living. Spirit became a more refined version of matter; matter, a congealed expression of spirit. None of this was above the natural or, to use the theological language of the Christian church, supernatural. Rather, the energy of the spirit suffused earthly existence. This meant, in practical terms, that nature became the rule writ large to which humans should conform. So harmony with nature, with the macrocosm in which the abiding forces of the spirit could be found, was enjoined.

Thus matter possessed its own kind of priority. As a manifestation of the spiritual energy in the universe, it spoke of power to shape and change. It argued for mastery of the yet unmanifest, for the ability to create or re-create in accordance with the plan of spirit—or thought or mind—as found in human life. Paradoxically, the injunction to be in harmony with an enveloping macrocosm could be turned inside out. It could become the command to control, to reorder reality according to human design.

After the Civil War, the spiritualist reform movement that came to birth in the Theosophical Society continued to advance these themes. Formed initially, in 1875, to penetrate "the esoteric philosophies of ancient times," it aimed to "collect and diffuse knowledge of the laws which govern the universe."[5] In these aspi-

5. For this reading of the Theosophical Society as a spiritualist reform movement, I am indebted to Stephen Prothero at Georgia State

rations, early theosophists proclaimed a nature religion that merged harmonial themes with occult directives to mastery and control through knowledge. From other quarters, the New Thought movement recapitulated the merger. Mind cure and prosperity went hand in hand for those who argued for the role of thought in constructing and reconstructing matter. On the other hand, New Thought also enjoined harmonial themes. Misfortune came when people cut themselves off from the divine flow of Goodness and Supply. The human task was, therefore, to open mind and heart to the divine shower of blessings, to conform to the universal law of Good.

HEALING AS MORAL MEANING:
THE SPIRITUALITY
OF THE FISHER KING

If we skip over the decades from the beginning of this century to its end, we find a new spirituality that, since the late 1960s and early 1970s, has recapitulated the substantive and moral capital of this nineteenth-century nature religion. Not that the nineteenth century provides the only, or the exclusive, source of the new spirituality. A full account would highlight the role of humanistic psychology and parapsychology, of Eastern and Native American religious forms, of astrology and environmental concerns, of holistic healing, and even of quantum physics. But the nineteenth century shaped the grid or template; its basic way of appre-

hending moral meaning continues in late-twentieth-century nature religion. Each new source that has been appropriated has blended unobtrusively; each has appealed for its harmonial themes and, simultaneously, for its promise of personal and social empowerment. Likewise, each has appealed because it has delivered a world in which matter and energy (read "spirit") could be easily transformed one into the other—because matter and energy were ultimately one.

In this context, we need to look especially at descriptions of the new spirituality that emphasize healing. In movement literature and language, attention to healing is pervasive, and even a cursory glance at pulp periodicals such as the Los Angeles *Whole Life Times* or its equivalent in other cities underlines its importance. Advertisements and notices that form the bulk of the information announce the availability of a remarkable range of healers and their services, while short articles, which form the other major category of material, as often as not focus on issues of healing, too. Beyond the printed page, only a few conversations with movement participants are needed to notice that healing is a preoccupation, even an obsession, and that healing involves more than the physical body. The language of healing, in fact, forms a major component of the religious discourse community that is united in its commitment to the new spirituality.[6]

University; quoted in Bruce F. Campbell, *Ancient Wisdom Revived: A History of the Theosophical Movement* (Berkeley: University of California Press, 1980), p. 28.

6. For the New Age movement as a religious discourse community that emphasizes healing, see Catherine L. Albanese, "The Mag-

One way to reflect on the meaning of healing within this loosely joined community is to return to the England of medieval legend in tales of King Arthur and his Knights of the Round Table.[7] Here it is the archetypal Grail story of Parcifal, or Perceval, that will most instruct. The background for Parcifal's journey in search of the Grail is the disabling illness of one known as the Fisher King, who rules over Parcifal's land. The king's sickness is the direct and immediate cause of a blight upon the land: even as the king wastes away, so does his domain.

Hence the task of the hero Parcifal is to heal the king through his (Parcifal's) encounter with the Grail and, by implication, to heal the land as well. In variations, with Gawain and Galahad alternately as heroes, the main features of the legend take different shapes and yield different results. But in its classic form the quest for the Holy Grail intends a twofold outcome. It is meant to benefit first the king and then the land.[8]

RE-MEMBERING THE PEOPLE, RE-MEMBERING THE LAND

The symbiosis between king and land and the priority given to the healing of the king offer an allegory

for the moral quest within the new spirituality. The health of the king, the empowered and active self, is intimately bound to the health of the land, that is, to the health of the human community and the environment. But the health of the individual—the well-being of the king—of necessity must come first. Moreover, as the moral earnestness of the Grail legend suggests, healing is a metaphor for a work that, as we have already noticed, goes beyond the physical. New spirituality authors say that relationships must be healed, that forgiveness and reconciliation must work to end separation and dis-ease. They warn that physical sickness is ultimately an expression of sickness of the spirit.

Take, for example, the channeled document known as *A Course in Miracles*. "Healing is a thought by which two minds perceive their oneness and become glad," the *Course* announces. "Remember that the Holy Spirit interprets the body only as a means of communication," it instructs, and "healing is the result of using the body solely for communication." This means, in the parlance of the *Course*, a state that banishes all separation and unforgiveness. New spirituality teacher Louise Hay, strongly influenced by the *Course*, writes that "we may not know how to forgive, and we may not want to forgive; but the very fact we say we are willing to forgive begins the healing process." Again, directly quoting the *Course*, she tells readers, " 'All disease comes from a state of unforgiveness,' and 'Whenever we are ill, we need to look

ical Staff: Quantum Healing in the New Age," in *Perspectives on the New Age*, ed. Lewis and Melton, pp. 68-86.

7. It is perhaps significant that one of the most popular New Age novels—Marion Zimmer Bradley's *Mists of Avalon*—embroiders Arthurian themes, from a Wiccan and feminist perspective. See Bradley, *The Mists of Avalon* (1982; reprint ed., New York: Ballantine Books, Del Rey Book, 1984).

8. For this insight and its development, see Jessie L. Weston, *From Ritual to Romance*

(1920; reprint ed., Garden City, NY: Doubleday, Anchor Books, 1957), esp. p. 21.

around to see who it is that we need to forgive.' "[9]

For Hay and other movement participants, holistic healing means just that: the healing of the person whole and entire. Moreover, for many, as in the archetypal illness of the Fisher King, healing involves not merely the human community but the environment as well. It is not only a re-membering of people, a reuniting of members of the group through the sharing of common memory and anticipation of a common goal. Healing is also a re-membering of the land, a gathering together of its forces and resources so that age-old patterns of relationship between species perdure and flourish. Healing is likewise an anticipation of ecological wholeness for the land. Thus a social ethic arises from the new spirituality and is perhaps its strongest point of linkage with a broader American culture.

SAVING THE EARTH
AS SOCIAL ETHICS

To cite one example, consider the message of John Robbins and his EarthSave Foundation. Heir to the Baskin-Robbins ice cream fortune, Robbins chose to leave family interests and values to pursue a vision of his own. When his *Diet for a New America* was published in 1987, it was widely noticed by reviewers and was also nominated for a Pulitzer Prize. The book was a serious argument and an impassioned tract in

favor of a natural foods diet that promoted vegetarianism. But what set it apart from other, more circumscribed accounts that advanced a vegetarian life-style was the way it framed its message. Read carefully, Robbins's work urged strong movement in a vegetarian direction without calling outright for a total embrace. More important here, Robbins joined concepts of animal rights and suffering on factory farms with issues regarding preventive health measures and themes of environmental pollution and sustainable—organic—agriculture.

In short, Robbins's "new direction to America's diet-style" arose out of a philosophical stance that stressed linkage. Significantly, the stance was a careful and considered reflection of new spirituality themes. The book was filled with the results of comprehensive research that, in meticulous statistical terms, documented the case for the new diet-style. But the impetus for the book, it was clear, lay in a mystical vision of relationship to the land and to other humans. The book was a call, as it were, from a new Parcifal for the healing of the rulers and, simultaneously, the healing of the earth. Like so many Fisher Kings, in a democratic society the people and their corporate, industrial, and political leaders controlled, for Robbins and those who agreed, the fate of the land.

"At the present time, when most of us sit down to eat, we aren't very aware of how our food choices affect the world," Robbins wrote. "We don't realize that in every Big Mac there is a piece of the tropical rainforests, and with every billion burgers sold another hundred species become ex-

9. [Helen Schucman], *A Course in Miracles* (Tiburon, CA: Foundation for Inner Peace, 1985), pp. 66, 140, 142; Louise L. Hay, *You Can Heal Your Life* (Santa Monica, CA: Hay House, 1984), pp. 13-14.

tinct. We don't realize that in the sizzle of our steaks there is the suffering of animals, the mining of our topsoil, the slashing of our forests, the harming of our economy, and the eroding of our health. We don't hear in the sizzle the cry of the hungry millions who might otherwise be fed. We don't see the toxic poisons accumulating in the food chains, poisoning our children and our earth for generations to come."[10]

Quoting both the biblical Ecclesiastes and the Native American Chief Seattle, Robbins went on to tell readers that "the earth itself will remind us, as will our children, and the animals and the forests and the sky and the rivers, that we are part of this earth, and it is part of us. All things are deeply connected."[11] As significant for its argument, the book sought to elicit an activist stance. Readers were directed to a series of organizations that work toward one or another of the goals espoused in the book. Most of all, they were directed to Robbins's own EarthSave Foundation, an educational enterprise over which he presides from Santa Cruz, California.

The EarthSave Foundation's newsletter—also titled *EarthSave*—carries on its masthead the notice "Helping the Earth to Heal." A typical issue contains articles and information regarding sustainable agriculture, vegetarian diet, the dangers of food irradiation, the development of a holistic, nutritional medicine, and even movement poetry. EarthSave sponsors ed-

ucational tours and speeches by Robbins, offers a short list of advocacy publications—by Robbins and kindred authors—and products, and encourages wilderness trips and learning experiences in which new spirituality practices—meditation, yoga, chanting, group sharing, and the like—are incorporated into an overall frame that stresses the importance of nature as the ground for both physical and spiritual wholeness. EarthSave also sustains ties to a series of local action groups and a support network in various parts of the nation and in Canada.[12]

In sum, if John Robbins and EarthSave are representative of the new spirituality—and I argue that they are—they tell us that a strong social ethic is emerging as a major component. This ethic might be called an activist form of mystical endeavor, for it supports transformational work in society as an outgrowth and manifestation of transformation of the self. Working for environmental reform, for peace, for feminist values, and for communitarian and economic causes that favor small-group values and natural lifestyles, those who embrace the new spirituality have thereby stayed in touch with the social, political, and economic texture of their times.

Still further, movement people regard their immersion in transformational activity as a work of healing. Inheritors of the moral ambiguity of the nature religion of the past, they both promote harmonial values and suggest themes of empowerment and

10. John Robbins, *Diet for a New America* (Walpole, NH: Stillpoint, 1987), p. 379.

11. Ibid., pp. 380, 381.

12. See, for example, *EarthSave*, 3(2, 3) (Spring and Summer 1992).

control. (Robbins's twin message of return to more "natural" agricultural styles and of wresting control of food production and consumption from corporate and industrial interests that have gone awry is one example.) But in the metaphor of healing that the new spirituality favors, it has at hand its own therapeutic attempt at resolution.

THERAPEUTIC SPIRITUALITY AND A NEW CAST OF ANCESTORS

Healing, as *A Course in Miracles* told it, is a work of reconciliation predicated on communication. As such, healing in the new spirituality assumes a harmony of forces, a homeostasis that represents the balancing of physiological, emotional, and spiritual powers. But healing also means the power and the freedom to act in decisive and effective ways. So healing, besides being harmonial, is also about having the vital force to take control of self and to leave one's imprint on a larger environment.

To summarize, the harmony ethic appears to give priority to nature. But since, as manifestations of nature, humans also embody its ultimacy, in theological language the divine force resides within each human being. Harmony and control have managed to pull off a partnership, and the new spirituality advocate has found a cosmic loophole to avoid cognitive dissonance. Such a description appears to align the new spirituality with Asian religious forms, Native American religions, Western revitalizations of paganism, and the like. But scrutinized more closely, even this description hints of other sources and other ancestors.

Indeed, the harmonialism of the new spirituality may in some ways be a cover. It may mask the more pedestrian Anglo-American roots of the seemingly exotic flower. Behind the holistic discourse of empowerment and life energies may be well-disguised fears of the old evangelical disharmony that is sin. Read from one point of view, of course, the language of empowerment is a kind of naive gloss on a more sinister discourse about power that preoccupies philosophers and critics in a postmodern world. But one does not need the cannons of postmodernity to fire on the gun-shy of the new age. If proponents of the new spirituality often look Pollyanna-like or appear, in ostrich fashion, to be hiding their heads in sand, the forced ignorance may be a willed refusal to accept an evangelical critique.

It is well nigh impossible to establish such a case directly. All the same, the prevailing evangelical Protestantism of the world from which the new spirituality grew suggests as much. A kind of conspiracy of optimism may be one response to a deep cultural sense of guilt and sin, a concomitant need for visible perfection as assurance of regeneration and sanctification, and an active struggle to forget the evidence of imperfection in the new-model evangelical self. A discourse about power—cast as the personal empowerment of those oppressed by society and its lingering beliefs about original sin and guilt—can function as a covert response to old cultural tales of confinement. It is not difficult to read Ralph Waldo Emerson's opening salvo in his own Transcendental gospel, *Nature*, in this late-twentieth-century version of nature religion. "Our age is retrospective," he wrote. "It builds the sepulchres of the fathers." But there was, for Emerson and his followers, a new and better way. "The sun shines to-day also," he proclaimed. "There is more wool and flax in the fields. There are new lands, new men, new thoughts. Let us demand our own works and laws and worship."[13]

Similarly, contemporary spiritual venturers, raised, as the *New Age Journal* informed us, very much in touch with a Judeo-Christian world, have turned in a different direction. But it needs to be recognized that the turn is incomprehensible without seeing what was turned from. Original sin lurks at the borders of the new fields and lands. Guilt, obligation, and Christian duty peek through the new spiritual wool and flax in the fields. The protests of original innocence and blessing are too strong to make sense without the long matriculation in an evangelical schoolhouse.[14] The insistence on the joys of physicality and sexuality, the rewards of massage and bodywork, the importance of touch and contact in relationship all tell of a past in which such themes were denied or underplayed.

13. Ralph Waldo Emerson, *Nature*, in *The Collected Works of Ralph Waldo Emerson*, vol. 1, *Nature, Addresses, and Lectures*, ed. Alfred R. Ferguson and Robert E. Spiller (Cambridge, MA: Harvard University Press, Belknap Press, 1971-), p. 7.
14. A particularly apt illustration of a similar theme from a Roman Catholic perspective is Matthew Fox, *Original Blessing: A Primer in Creation Spirituality* (Sante Fe: Bear, 1983).

In sum, the assurance of innocence and the free play of guiltless power argue for a culture of concealment, a spirituality created to hide the wound that the evangelical past bestowed. The Fisher Kings of the late twentieth century are, ironically, replicating their mythical ancestor in one more significant way. The Fisher Kings of the late twentieth century, like the king of the legend, are unhealed healers, and they have caught their disease from their culture.

DOORSTEP OF THE
MILLENNIUM OR EDGE
OF THE APOCALYPSE?

A hidden discourse about power is not the only ambivalence within the new spirituality that is related to Protestant Christian themes. The optimism that slogans like "Create your own reality" evidences is, even in the conscious culture of the movement, never total. Forced and strained as it often appears under scrutiny, sometimes it disappears entirely. Nowhere is this more apparent than in speculations about the millennium that proponents of the new spirituality may expect. Movement people exhibit an ambivalence about the millennium to come that is as deep or deeper than the ambivalence about power. It is not clear, in this contemporary form of nature religion, whether participants anticipate a golden age of harmony and understanding, akin to postmillennial mainstream Protestant ideas, or a great ice age—literally—of cosmic destruction and painful purification, which is not far from the doomsday of a fundamentalist premillennialism.

Consider, as one example, the macrobiotic community's preoccupation with scientific evidence to support the environmental theory of not a dire future of global warming but, even more devastating, the return of an age of ice. Nowhere has the argument been more forcefully pursued than in the pages of the now-defunct periodical *Solstice*. There, rallying behind the work of John Hamaker in *The Survival of Civilization*, editor John David Mann told readers in 1987 that there were two climatological theories that modeled the future. The first, the greenhouse theory, could be subsumed under the second, or cooling, thesis; under the cooling thesis, the greenhouse triggers "a more comprehensive, more drastic and far more sudden shift in the Earth's climatic stability."[15]

Instead of the "mild cause for concern" that would be generated by the greenhouse theory, wrote Mann, the cooling model posited "the likelihood of a catastrophic shift from interglacial to glacial conditions." This shift would occur "within the next 5 to 20 years" and demanded a series of steps to slow or to reverse the process. Among the chief of these should be small-scale efforts to remineralize local soils through the use of rock dust. The energy with which the magazine and others in the macrobiotic community promoted soil remineralization programs suggested that disaster could, indeed, be reversed by their work and that the earth itself

could be healed. And the ambivalence persisted: Mann's magazine was quick to notice news that supported the cooling theory, announcing, for example, a November 1987 iceberg "twice the size of Rhode Island" that had "broken off the Ross Ice Shelf in the Antarctic" and noting that the iceberg joined "four others floating at various points around the Antarctic."[16]

At the same time, the Institute for a Future advertised a new video, *Stopping the Coming Ice Age*, and macrobiotic mail-order food suppliers later began to add rock dust to their catalogue items. With a combination of apocalypticism and hope, *Solstice* continued to track developments, arguing that whether global warming or greenhouse-to-glaciation were embraced, "the set of appropriate responses is practically identical." There was, however, one exception required by the adoption of the Hamaker scenario, and that was soil remineralization. "Broadcasting finely crushed gravel dust would seem to be the critical link in the climate equation, the 'philosopher's stone' for geopolitical alchemists seeking to change global disaster into golden opportunity."[17]

15. John D. Hamaker and Donald A. Weaver, *The Survival of Civilization* (Burlingame, CA: Hamaker-Weaver, 1982); John David Mann, "The Cooling, Part 2," *Solstice: Perspectives on Health and the Environment*, no. 9, p. 36 (Dec. 1987).

16. Mann, "Cooling, Part 2"; idem, "Bread from Stones: The Cooling, Part 3," *Solstice: Perspectives on Health and the Environment*, no. 10, cover, pp. 6-9, 50, 52-54 (May 1988); "Hints of an Ice Age?" ibid., no. 9, p. 35 (Dec. 1987). See also "A Rock Dust Primer," ibid., no. 10, pp. 48-49 (May 1988).

17. See "The Imminent Ice Age and How We Can Stop It," advertisement by the Institute for a Future, *Solstice: Perspectives on Health and the Environment*, no. 10, inside front cover (May 1988); "Hopeful Signals on Climate Change Policy," ibid., no. 35, pp. 60, 61 (Mar.-Apr. 1989).

Despite their ambivalence about which future they would ultimately embrace, *Solstice* and others in the macrobiotic community understood their interest in a hypothetical ice age in terms of general macrobiotic theory. They saw connections between the microbiology of individuals—specifically, their diet—and the macrobiology of, in the words of the foremost American macrobiotic teacher, Michio Kushi, "one peaceful world."[18] Their interest in soil remineralization—to grow the organic food thought to maximize human biological potential—was in keeping with their cosmological theory of balance between yin and yang forces and their commitment to a social ethic in these terms. But their apprehensions of woe and disaster, shared, too, by Kushi, were continuous with American evangelical theories of millennial upheaval, for we have already seen historical American forms of millennialism within the Protestant camps of Adventists, dispensationalists, and Pentecostals. Getting into position to heal the earth meant standing on the edge of Armageddon's crisis.

FISHER KINGS AND COMMON SPEECH IN THE PUBLIC SQUARE

Meanwhile, outside the macrobiotic community, others in the new spirituality movement told their tales of coming earth changes and purifications that would be painful for earth and its inhabitants. Even so, they preached their gospel of personal and social transformation that would yield a golden age. For many who disdained the Protestant evangelical and fundamentalist communities, the plains of Armageddon were clearly coming into view, and for still the same people, a postmillennial hope akin to that of the liberal Protestant community meant an optimism about change that was maximal. Yet these ambivalences were not the most important points of connection with a larger American Protestant world. As late-twentieth-century Protestants struggled alongside others to find a language to speak their deepest commitments in public and found that, as Robert Bellah and his sociological colleagues argued, they lacked one, new spirituality people were moving past them.[19]

With what many would regard as unpromising beginnings in individualistic mystical themes, their metaphor of healing as reconciliation had led them to a concern for healing relationships with others. From there, in a move that fit their mentality as nature religionists, they had turned to a cosmological concern for healing the earth and reconciling the human community with it. In so doing, they had also aligned themselves with evangelical and social gospel themes that invoked a sense of collective moral responsibility. In particular, they had found a common voice to speak in that hypothetically empty place that Richard J. Neuhaus has called the "naked public square."[20]

18. See Michio Kushi with Alex Jack, *One Peaceful World* (New York: St. Martin's Press, 1987).

19. Robert N. Bellah et al., *Habits of the Heart: Individualism and Commitment in American Life* (Berkeley: University of California Press, 1985), esp. pp. 20-21.

20. Richard J. Neuhaus, *The Naked Public Square: Religion and Democracy in America* (Grand Rapids, MI: William B. Eerdmans, 1984).

Their provisional successes could be measured by the growth of green politics and green products, by the movement of environmentalism, antinuclearism, and feminism from the alienated fringes of American public life closer and closer to its center. By the early 1990s, no major political leader could afford to ignore the environment, and at least lip service had to be paid to environmental concerns. Neither—for a variety of reasons, many of them outside my scope here—could the nuclear industry look toward a bright future of proliferating facilities for heating homes and irradiating food. Nor, after Clarence Thomas and Anita Hill and after the public troubles of the Kennedy household and of Mike Tyson, could feminist talk be simply disdained.

Earth Days became corporate fashion, and environmental summits had to be noticed. Bumper stickers that enjoined loving one's mother under a picture of Earth were acceptable, even middle-of-the-road. To speak of healing the planet was good public discourse, and so was language about energies and vibrations and about thinking globally but act-ing locally. In fine, the new spirituality had become pervasive and powerful. Far more than a set of theosophical ideas and activities that could be assessed through the enumeration of individuals who subscribed to this or that belief or who endorsed this or that specific practice, it had become a mood, an atmosphere, a way of talking and being talked to. Nature religion had become a prime candidate for performances in public. And if both Christianity and civil religion had left the public square naked—if, as Robert Bellah and his colleagues said, no common language from the Protestant biblical and Enlightenment past was still supplying the terms for public moral discourse— perhaps there was a new collective voice to be heard. Perhaps, to the chagrin of some and the delight of others, new spirituality people were talking to the body politic and moving comfortably into its central square as the old religious and philosophical establishment was leaving. Perhaps, for a generation of Fisher Kings, mysticism and moral discourse were becoming public partners, at least for the time.

Health and Spirituality
as Contemporary Concerns

By MEREDITH B. McGUIRE

ABSTRACT: One theme of particular importance in contemporary U.S. religion and quasi-religion is health and healing. Groups as diverse as Pentecostal Christians and New Age groups, women's spirituality groups and New Thought churches are promoting non-medical approaches to health and healing. Indeed, to many contemporary Americans, health and healing appear to be salient metaphors for salvation and holiness. Religious and quasi-religious attention to health is adamantly holistic in the belief that spiritual, emotional, social, and physical aspects of well-being are fundamentally interconnected. To understand the significance of this widespread focus on health and healing, we need to look beyond the religious groups themselves and appreciate some twentieth-century structural and cultural changes in the meanings of the body, the self, and the nature of well-being.

Meredith B. McGuire is professor of sociology and anthropology at Trinity University, San Antonio, Texas. She is the author or coauthor of several books in the sociology of religion and in medical sociology, including most recently Health, Illness and the Social Body, *written with Peter E. S. Freund. She is past president of the Society for the Scientific Study of Religion and the Association for the Sociology of Religion.*

MANY Americans from a broad spectrum of religious backgrounds hold health and well-being as central spiritual concerns. Holiness, physical and emotional health, spiritual growth, salvation, and sense of well-being are intertwined in an adamantly holistic linkage of mind-body-spirit. While such linkages have never been absent from the American religious scene, in the last decades of this century many diverse religious and quasi-religious movements promoting a mind-body-spirit holism have flourished.

Interestingly, this attention to health and spirituality is widespread in precisely those sectors of American society that conventional wisdom suggests would be secularized and likely to use only rational approaches to healing and health maintenance. Educated, economically comfortable, middle-class and upper-middle-class urban and suburban dwellers are choosing beliefs and practices that link health and spirituality. For example, a well-to-do Catholic suburbanite exclaimed, " 'Health, wholeness—all these words to me are Scripture and salvation. It all goes together. A healthy person to me would be one that was whole in spirit, soul, mind and body.' "

An avid practitioner of Zen (Buddhist) meditation and various New Age spiritualities stated, " 'I think of health at every level: a healthy mind, a healthy spirit, as well as a healthy body. So that [a] person would have to have energy, alertness, enthusiasm, a love of life, a love of people, a love of themselves.' "

Similarly, a member of a psychic healing circle explained,

"I think that [truly healthy persons] are very spontaneous and flexible and I think they have more options that they experience. I think they have a sense of aliveness and feeling of being in the flow. . . . They are feeling connected to a larger purpose and connected with other people. . . . Sensitivity is an important part of being healthy. I would also say that being in power, feeling powerful in your life, feeling responsible for your life is a very important part of it."[1]

Some of this linkage of health and spiritual concerns is expressed in churches, synagogues, and other regular religious settings; some expression occurs in new religious and quasi-religious movements, and some occurs among the unchurched and officially nonreligious. Analysis of this widespread, but rather amorphous, linkage of health concerns and spiritual concerns suggests some of the ways religion or spirituality is a vital part of many Americans' lives.

HISTORICAL AND CROSS-CULTURAL CONTEXTS

Health and well-being are very much religious or spiritual concerns in traditional societies—including Western religious traditions. We are not surprised that a Central American peasant makes an arduous pilgrimage to the shrine of a saint known for healing. We acknowledge that indigenous religions of such peoples as the !Kung of the Kalahari, the Qollahuaya of the Andes, and the

1. Quoted in Meredith B. McGuire, *Ritual Healing in Suburban America* (New Brunswick, NJ: Rutgers University Press, 1988), pp. 39, 97, 136. Descriptions of contemporary religious healing groups used in this article are documented in this book.

Navajo of the southwestern United States all closely connect the spiritual, emotional, social, and physical well-being of individuals, families, tribes, and entire social and ecological environments. Why, then, do we find it surprising to witness modern Western movements linking health and spirituality?

Anthropological studies of health and healing in diverse cultures show that health is a cultural ideal and varies widely over time and from culture to culture. Religions have traditionally been important sources of cultural ideals, providing images, rituals, and symbols for linking the individual to a larger reality. For example, religions often give special meaning to body symbolism, such as blood, milk, hearts, hands, and eyes. In most instances, these images, rituals, and symbols simultaneously involve the body, emotions, cognitions, and spirit. Thus expressions of illness can serve as idioms of suffering, distress, and dissent.[2] Many cultures understand the illness of the individual body as an expression of social discord. Likewise, the individual body can serve as a referent for a culture's pattern of the relationship between the individual and society. For example, participants in the several days and nights of a Navajo chant—frequently done for healing—can attune their individual experiences, through ritual action, to accomplish the culturally valued sense of harmony between the individual, social group, and environment.[3]

Social structural changes

Two aspects of modernization have, however, challenged the synthesis of health and spirituality: institutional differentiation and rationalization. Institutional differentiation is the process whereby arenas of human action have become separated into functionally specialized institutions. Health, healing, and well-being were traditionally interwoven with other institutional domains, especially religion and the family, but Western medicine has gradually become differentiated from these other institutional spheres. The differentiation of medicine involved the development of a distinctive body of knowledge, a corps of specialists with control over this body of knowledge and its application, and public acknowledgment, or legitimacy, of the authority of medical specialists. Although the roots of this differentiation date from the Enlightenment, biomedicine did not achieve much legitimacy or effective control over the domain of health and healing until this century.[4]

Biomedicine claimed control over the health and curing of physical bodies; a separate science claimed the health and well-being of minds; and

2. Nancy Scheper-Hughes and Margaret M. Lock, "Speaking 'Truth' to Illness: Metaphor, Reification, and a Pedagogy for Patients," *Medical Anthropology Quarterly*, 17:137-40 (1986); idem, "The Mindful Body: A Prolegomenon to Future Work in Medical Anthropology," *Medical Anthropology*, 1:6-41 (1987).

3. James V. Spickard, "Experiencing Religious Rituals: A Schutzian Analysis of Navajo Ceremonies," *Sociological Analysis*, 52(2):191-204 (1991).

4. Eliot Freidson, *Profession of Medicine* (New York: Dodd, Mead, 1970); Paul Starr, *The Social Transformation of American Medicine* (New York: Basic Books, 1982).

religion was relegated to the sphere of the purely spiritual. To a certain extent, many religious groups cooperated in this differentiation, relinquishing all but token ways by which religion addressed bodily and emotional concerns. Many established Christian denominations, for example, criticized those religions that preached religious answers to believers' material concerns—such as illness, unemployment, or scarcity of resources for subsistence—as superstitious, as less pure forms of spirituality than their own.

Institutional differentiation has produced extensive internal specialization in modern Western medicine, due in large part to the growth of large-scale, bureaucratic settings for the learning and practice of medicine and to pervasive paradigmatic assumptions of biomedicine itself, which will be discussed further later in this article. One by-product of institutional differentiation is that modern medicine focuses on diseases—conceptually linked with discrete pathologies—rather than on sick persons. This differentiated model of medicine limits any religious response to peripheral, albeit valuable nonhealing roles, such as comforting the dying or helping chronically ill persons to cope with their conditions.

Rationalization, a second aspect of modernization, refers to the application of criteria of functional rationality to social and economic life. In the division of labor, rationalization promotes bureaucratic forms of organization and an emphasis on efficiency, standardization, and instrumental criteria for decision making, as exemplified by the modern hospital. Another aspect of rationalization is an emphasis on rational ways of knowing, such as use of empirical evidence for explaining natural phenomena without reference to nonempirical categories of thought. A by-product of such rationalization is medicine's focus upon technology and technique for transforming rational knowledge into rational mastery.

Rationalized biomedicine assumes a mind-body dualism, in which physical diseases and their causes are presumed to be located strictly within the body.[5] Accordingly, the body can be understood and treated separately from the person inhabiting it. A related biomedical assumption is physical reductionism, the idea that illnesses can be reduced to disordered bodily—for example, biochemical or neurophysiological—functions. These assumptions exclude social, psychological, spiritual, and behavioral dimensions of illness. As a result of these assumptions, the medical model views disease as localized in the individual body, almost as a property of the sick person. Another feature of rationalized biomedicine is its intense pursuit of mastery and control over the body—for instance, by therapeutic regimens, surgical and pharmaceutical interventions, or technological developments and techniques. Although rationalized biomedicine has considerable achievements to its credit, in part due to these very characteristics, these paradigmatic assumptions have also

5. Deborah Gordon, "Tenacious Assumptions in Western Medicine," in *Biomedicine Examined*, ed. M. Lock and D. R. Gordon (Dordrecht, Netherlands: Kluwer, 1988), pp. 19-56.

constricted medicine's ability to meet many health needs. Today's spiritual healing movements are one expression of the dissatisfaction with the limitations of compartmentalized, rationalized medicine.

American cultural developments

Contemporary U.S. society promotes a particularly high expectation of individual health; optimum health is one of the culture's strongest values. Furthermore, there is a widespread presumption that optimum health is—in principle—achievable. This belief is due partly to a modern image of the body and emotions as malleable, controllable, permanently revisable. A corollary belief—actively marketed by health professions—is that scientific knowledge and technology have expanded the scope of potential control such that all human bodily or emotional experiences are best mediated by experts. Thus normal human experiences, such as pregnancy and childbirth, grief, anxiety, death, anger, menstruation, eating, exercise, and sex, have been redefined as health problems and medicalized.[6]

At the same time, however, U.S. cultural—and political—values are highly individualistic. Illness is located within the individual alone, and the individual is generally held responsible for his or her own health:

6. Irving K. Zola, *Socio-Medical Inquiries: Recollections, Reflections, and Reconsiderations* (Philadelphia: Temple University Press, 1983), p. 261. See also Peter Conrad and Joseph W. Schneider, *Deviance and Medicalization: From Badness to Sickness* (St. Louis: C. V. Mosby, 1980).

one must eat right, exercise, get the right amount of sleep, manage daily stresses correctly, avoid unhealthy environmental conditions and risks, and actively resist unhealthy foods, drink, drugs, sex, feelings, and activities. In a capitalist society, the healthy person is one who consumes correctly. As a result of these high expectations surrounding a greatly valued ideal, health has become a salient metaphor for salvation even for nonreligious Americans. Indeed, if we were to ask, "From what do you most want to be saved/delivered/protected?" many religious and nonreligious people alike would be likely ·to name illness.

CONTEMPORARY RELIGION-HEALTH LINKAGES

Many modern religious and quasi-religious movements are asserting a holism of mind, body, and spirit. Their images involve mind, body, and spirit not merely as related parts but as fully interpenetrating, mutually informing, integrated aspects of each person's very self. The enormous diversity within and between these movements linking religion and health is itself evidence of a growing pluralism both of patterns of religiosity and of ideas about health, healing, and well-being.

Some contemporary healing movements, such as the charismatic or Pentecostal movements within several Christian denominations, draw their beliefs and practices primarily from a single religious tradition. They view their movements as a renewal or reform, true to that tradition.

Many other contemporary healing movements, such as New Age groups, are eclectic; they borrow images, myths, symbols, rituals, and healing practices from such diverse sources as Asian religious traditions, Christianity, the Western occult traditions, nature religions, Native American and other indigenous traditions, recent psychotherapeutic approaches, and the human potential movement. They seek to break with both the biomedical establishment and official religions, but their eclecticism, while often somewhat experimental, is not random or frivolous. Some eclecticism is guided by a central underlying idea, such as the nature and use of healing energy, which believers hold as an alternative to the biomedical model. Another basis of eclecticism is a group's critique of the extant traditions. Most women's spirituality groups, for instance, reject the hierarchical ideology embedded in the Judeo-Christian tradition, among others, so they frequently appropriate and transform myths and symbols from their own and other traditions into altogether new meanings and images. Although, historically, numerous religions have arisen as amalgams of pieces of multiple religious traditions, both the scope of eclecticism and the degree of individual freedom to choose components for personal spirituality appear to be unique to these modern movements.

In addition to the avowedly religious movements, many quasi-religious movements also make a connection between health or well-being and spirituality as a key part of their beliefs and practices. Alcoholics Anonymous and various related 12-step programs are one such approach; similarly, the recent men's movement offers rituals and myths to address problems of well-being in the face of contemporary difficulties with manhood.

Most of these present-day movements do not reject medicine; indeed, members regularly consult doctors and use hospitals. They do, however, view medicine as largely inadequate or insufficient, because it does not treat the whole person and because it addresses only the superficial—that is, purely physical—symptoms and causes of illness. As a result of their central linkage of mind, body, and spirit, these religious and quasi-religious groups differ from the biomedical model in some important ways.

Causes of illness

While not rejecting medical explanations of disease causation, spiritual healing movements typically consider medical causes to be insufficient explanations for illness. Other causes of illness emphasized by some groups include emotions, attitudes, life-style choices, discord and disorder, social situations—for example, stressful workplace or unsatisfactory social roles—economic distress, environmental pollution, and spiritual weakness. Some groups hold that spiritual conditions—such as sinfulness, evil in the world—are ultimate causes of illness, although physical, emotional, and social factors might be proximate causes. Due to their alternative interpretations of illness causality, then, these groups have alternative, nonmedical ways of addressing believers' health concerns. These religious groups also have alternative answers to the question, In what ways are individuals responsible for their own or others' sickness or well-being? Like the medical imputation of responsibility, these interpretations indicate evaluations of and normative prescriptions for good or health-promoting patterns. Both medical and spiritual approaches to responsibility carry a moral tag.

Source of power to heal

Just as nonmedical approaches to healing vary widely in their understanding of causes of illness, so, too, do they have different ideas about the source or sources of healing power. For example, groups with intricate beliefs about how emotions are linked with physical illnesses are likely to have similarly complex ways for trying to change or mobilize emotions to promote healing. There appear to be two primary conceptualizations of the source of healing power: transcendent and imminent.

Images of a transcendent healing power are familiar in Western religions, especially Christianity and the Western occult tradition. Accordingly, a supreme being possesses extraordinary powers, which can be tapped, as through prayer, or channeled, as, for example, through intercession of a saint. This linkage of religion and health is, thus, based upon taking seriously belief in God's power to affect the material—as well as spiritual, emotional, and social— well-being of believers.

Imminent sources of healing— those found within oneself or one's immediate experience—imply a very different approach to well-being and healing. Typically, these conceptual-

izations are based upon the belief that the individual mind-body-spirit has natural self-healing capacities, which need to be developed, strengthened, or unblocked. Often borrowing from Eastern religious traditions, many of these approaches also emphasize a larger cosmic source of energy or life force, which presumably flows through all persons, enabling individual well-being as well as formation of genuine social bonds. Based upon this conceptualization, then, individual health and well-being come primarily from looking within—to keep this life force flowing and to tap it for self-healing power.

Religious and quasi-religious groups that make these kinds of mind-body-spirit linkages are, thus, an expression of dissent from the medicalized conception of health and healing. They also represent some patterns of modern religiosity that are distinct from American modes of religiosity characteristic at the turn of this century.

MODERN RELIGIOSITY AND WELL-BEING

It is difficult to gauge the extent of influence of social movements that emphasize a mind-body-spirit linkage because people often adopt some of their perspectives without actually joining a group of believers. Furthermore, adherence to any of a number of these movements overlaps with other religious commitments. For example, a person might be an active member—or even a leader—in the local Methodist church while simultaneously engaging in Tibetan meditation, Shiatsu massage, crystal healing, and psychosynthesis.

The importance of the linkage of health and spiritual concerns lies in (1) what it shows about contemporary dissatisfaction with rationalized biomedicine, (2) what it suggests about the place and organizational forms of religion in modern societies; and (3) how it reflects the nature of self-identity in the context of modernity.

Organizational forms of contemporary religion

Although other organizational forms of religion, especially denominations, perdure, the organizational forms that dissenting groups take are especially important for interpreting the situation of religion today. Contemporary spiritual healing groups, for example, have adopted forms of social organization that are particularly well suited to the structural location of religion in modern societies. In pluralistic modern society, no single religious perspective can be taken for granted. Religious commitment and personal spirituality are essentially voluntary. Dissenting movements that promote a religion-health linkage tend to adopt one of two characteristic organizational responses to pluralism: sectarian retrenchment or cultic celebration of pluralism.

The sectarian response to the modern world is the creation and maintenance of strong boundaries around the group's truth, such as firm moral norms and rigid adherence to doctrinal orthodoxy. The group maintains boundaries by avoiding outside communication media, by socializing mainly with other believers, by marrying within the religion, by educating children separately, or even by withdrawing into a physically separate economic and social subsociety. For example, most fundamentalist Christian groups employ some of these strategies.

A corollary of these firm boundaries is intense authoritarianism; there is only one truth, presented authoritatively by group leaders. The individual's religious role is, ideally, diffused throughout all aspects of everyday life. Indeed, in modern society, one point of sectarian dissent is that the social structure does not honor or encourage the application of religion to other spheres of life. Sectarian religious forms preserve religious purity and effectiveness by shoring up the supports of belief—typically, in a transcendent sacred reality—by a close-knit enclave of fellow believers, protected from the threats of "the world."

The cultic pattern, by contrast, turns pluralism, individualism, and freedom of choice, characteristic of the modern world, into religious virtues and advantages in a spiritual realm focused on an imminent sacred reality.[7] For example, a meditation center or healing circle might attract a number of participants who indi-

7. Unfortunately, since the 1960s, the mass media have misapplied the term "cult" to a wide range of unfamiliar religious movements—most of which are actually sects, as characterized previously—giving the concept a pejorative connotation of deviance. The sociological concept of cult is neutral, describing a loose association of persons with an eclectic, individual religiosity. Historically, most religion probably has been cultlike, since the consolidation of effective authority and control of doctrine and ritual, characteristic of official religions, is relatively recent, unevenly achieved in all parts of society, and waning in most contemporary societies.

vidually are pursuing many different paths for their physical-emotional-social-spiritual well-being. They may be unified only by their common value of spiritual approaches to well-being. While the group may offer instruction on various spiritual healing approaches, members are free to choose which paths to try for themselves. Cult-type groups have loosely defined boundaries; doctrine is typically absent or minimal and membership is voluntary and tolerant of competing allegiances. Like the sectarian response to modern society, cultlike healing groups are critical and dissenting, but their dissent is typically less virulent because of their pluralistic tolerance of competing approaches.

Historically, sects have been off-shoots of official religious groups, whereas nonofficial religion has tended to spawn cults. One reason for this organizational pattern is that nonofficial religion itself is seldom a coherent, authoritative, organized belief system; adherents are often loosely affiliated, drawn together only by vaguely similar perspectives or parallel beliefs. Cultic religious groups emerge from the amorphous background of nonofficial religion, and they are inherently precarious organizationally, because cultic adherence is highly individualistic and eclectic. Because of their tolerance and loose boundaries, contemporary adherents often participate in several such religious groups—as well as in ordinary Jewish or Christian denominations—at the same time. Although specific cultic organizations tend to be short-lived, nonofficial religions are highly adaptable, so

their beliefs and practices have considerable durability.

The emphatic linkage of health and religion has a very different significance in each type of religious group. In the sect-type groups, to assert the relevance of religion for the well-being of body and emotions represents a dissent from modern society's secularized approach to health and well-being. Even though many sectarian responses to modernity are reactionary reaffirmations of traditional norms, patterns of identity, and beliefs and practices, for believers to employ these traditions in the context of modern society requires considerable effort. None of these beliefs and practices can be taken for granted in a complex pluralistic society. The social organization of sectarian religious groups is one effective way they can sustain their dissent.

In the cult-type groups, the linkage of health and spirituality often reflects a very different kind of dissent. Nonofficial religions are particularly likely to reflect the concerns, albeit often poorly articulated, of those excluded from power in society. Historically, women, minorities, disabled persons, colonized peoples, and mentally or sexually different individuals have held more esteemed positions in nonofficial religions, even while they may have simultaneously belonged to official religions.

Contemporary linkages of health and spirituality in the context of cultlike nonofficial religions and quasi-religions are, therefore, sometimes assertions of alternative definitions of self-identity. For example, the women's spirituality movement promotes an image of healthy gender identities that is radically different from the larger society's gender expectations. Similarly, cult-type religiosity among blacks—as in the spiritualist churches—and Mexican Americans—as in popular devotions to folk saints—employs healing rituals to assert alternative values and alternative self-identities. Thus these groups not only dissent at the level of ideas but also dissent by continually working to accomplish the transformation of their selves toward the alternative ideals of well-being.

Interestingly, these cult-type spiritual healing groups most closely resemble what, in 1898, Emile Durkheim prophesied would be the future form of religion:

As societies become more voluminous and spread over vaster territories, their traditions and practices . . . are compelled to maintain a state of plasticity and instability which no longer offers adequate resistance to individual variations. These latter, being less well contained, develop more freely and multiply in number; that is, everyone increasingly follows his own path.[8]

Durkheim further predicted that modern religions would focus on the enhancement of the human personality because this would be all that members of such diverse societies would have in common. Whereas traditional religions located the sacred outside the individual, reflecting, according to Durkheim, the self-consciousness of the whole social group, modern religions would express and

dramatize social relations but locate sacred power within each individual.[9]

The nature of self-identity

As Durkheim predicted, the sheer multiplicity of available spiritual paths, together with the near impossibility of enforcing any societywide orthodoxy, has made religion an essentially voluntary, individual choice in modern societies. Indeed, most significant components of an individual's identity have become dramatically more voluntary than ever before conceivable.[10] I am free to consider and choose my mode of spirituality, whether I will identify with a religious group, and how I will express that involvement. I am also able to decide whether I want to make an ethnic or national identity a significant part of my self—and I can choose which ethnic connections to claim and how I want to perform them. I can decide the extent and quality of my marriage and kinship identities. I am even relatively free to choose my gender identity—who am I as a woman?

With the linking of health and spiritual concerns, health becomes an idealization of a kind of self, healing is then part of the ongoing process by which that self is accomplished, and well-being is the individual's resulting subjective experience. Al-

8. Emile Durkheim, "Individualism and the Intellectuals," trans. S. Lukes, *Political Studies*, 17:26 (1969).

9. Frances Westley, "The Cult of Man: Durkheim's Predictions and New Religious Movements," *Sociological Analysis*, 39(2):135-45 (1978).

10. Anthony Giddens, *Modernity and Self-Identity: Self and Society in the Late Modern Age* (Stanford, CA: Stanford University Press, 1991).

though many groups address the problem of modern self-identity by emphatically reaffirming traditional norms and role expectations, many others promote a reflexive transformation of self. Some alternative healing approaches, for instance, encourage individuals to choose the quality of their own bodily and emotional experience, as well as their own definition of well-being and paths to achieving it.[11] In the context of pluralism and voluntarism, perhaps the contemporary linkage of religion and health may also be understood as one form of identity work by which the individual pursues the ongoing project of constructing his or her self.

11. Cf. Hans P. Dreitzel, "The Socialization of Nature: Western Attitudes towards Body and Emotions," in *Indigenous Psychologies: The Anthropology of the Self*, ed. P. Heelas and A. Lock (New York: Academic, 1981), pp. 205-23.

ANNALS, *AAPSS*, **527**, May 1993

Toward the Year 2000:
Reconstructions of Religious Space

By WADE CLARK ROOF

ABSTRACT: As we approach the year 2000, there will be much reflection about the nation's religious and spiritual condition. In this article, three domains of American life are singled out as examples of how religious space is being reconstructed by the large portion of the population known as baby boomers. The first is the new religious pluralism of the nation's inner cities, reflecting a global order. Hispanics, Asian immigrants, and people of color are creating new solidarities and forging new religious voices. The second is a shift in institutional alignments between family and religion. These changes have provoked new spiritual concerns arising out of changing family patterns. The third is the new spirituality, generally of the postwar generation, with its emphasis on personal choice, faith exploration, and more holistic ways of thinking. What happens in these spaces will greatly influence the religious trends of the 1990s and of the early years of the next century.

Wade Clark Roof is J. F. Rowny Professor of Religion and Society at the University of California at Santa Barbara. He is author or editor of numerous books and essays on religion in America, the most recent being A Generation of Seekers: The Spiritual Journeys of the Baby Boom Generation.

ALREADY in the early 1990s there is a mounting awareness of living in the last days—the last days of a century and, even more, of a millennium. And year by year, as the decade unfolds, we will no doubt feel even more of a gravitational pull toward the year 2000. Even if that benchmark does not result in millennial madness, some great outburst of religious energies, it most certainly will be a time of considerable reflection and reassessment for Americans. Questions such as "Who are we?" and "Where are we headed?" will be standard fare for commentators as they assess the country demographically, politically, economically, globally, and, most assuredly, in a deeper religious and spiritual sense as well.

Still seven years before that benchmark, I am not going to offer any premature general assessment; however, I take this opportunity to describe what I believe to be some important trends helping to shape the American future. Over the past five years I have had an unusual opportunity afforded me by the Lilly Endowment, Inc., to explore religious trends broadly of the postwar baby-boom generation. With the help of my research assistants, I have talked to hundreds of young Americans over the telephone, visited dozens of them in their homes, conducted group interviews in churches and synagogues, gone to New Age festivals and seminars, sat through countless church services, observed and informally interviewed people wherever I could—on airplanes, in classes, at bars, in ticket lines at the movies.[1]

Based on all of this, I have some general observations about what is happening in the 1990s, best described by a simple rubric: reconstructions of religious space.

Sidney E. Mead once wrote that, if we are to understand religion in America, we must understand that it took shape in relation to a people's movement through space and that space has overshadowed time in creating the ideals most cherished by the American mind and spirit.[2] Mead spoke, of course, about white settlers for whom there was never enough time to spare but for whom there was a plentiful supply of space. Vast physical spaces invited people to pack up and move, to keep on the go; however, there were also two other types of space: social space and inner space. Those settling the continent had largely broken the binding ties of habit, custom, and tradition, and thus they set out to create new social space, opening up possibilities for what we would later call social mobility. And inner space and experience— the psychological realm William James called "the sphere of felicity"— beckoned those who like Emerson and others dared to journey inward, to make spiritual movement. Space for Americans, at least for the dominant cultural groups, has meant freedom to move, whether physically, socially, or inwardly. This being so deeply embedded in the American ex-

1. I was funded by the Lilly Endowment, Inc., for a study of the baby-boom generation, born after World War II. The book reporting this research is *A Generation of Seekers: The Spiritual Journeys of the Baby Boom Generation* (San Francisco: Harper San Francisco, 1993).
2. Sidney E. Mead, *The Lively Experiment: The Shaping of Christianity in America* (New York: Harper & Row, 1963), chap. 1.

perience, the year 2000—whatever else it may mean—is likely to present us with reconstructions of space, in the many senses of that term.

The term I use—"reconstruction"— suggests that I prefer to move beyond the customary arguments on the decline of religion among sociologists, in favor of what I take to be a more insightful, more nuanced interpretation of religion in America. My approach is in keeping with a newer sociology-of-religion paradigm gradually emerging that is more historically informed and that privileges themes of voluntarism and innovation, the continuing vitality of American religious culture, and supply-side rather than exclusively demand-side explanations of change.[3] It presupposes the viability of religion as an energizing force despite changing forms rather than secular assumptions of shrinking plausibilities. Hence in this article I look for embryonic and holistic forms of religion, often unstable and sporadic but that appear to be filling in spaces opened up by broad-scaled changes in what is increasingly called a postmodern world. The focus especially is on cultural and psychological themes, which provides, I think, clues of the shape of the religious in the years ahead.

THE NEW
RELIGIOUS PLURALISM

Let us begin with something quite simple, yet quite complex: the coun-

3. See R. Stephen Warner, "Work in Progress toward a New Paradigm for the Sociological Study of Religion in the United States," *American Journal of Sociology*, vol. 99 (Mar. 1993).

try's new religious pluralism. By "new" pluralism, I do not mean simply a declining Protestant population, a growing Catholic population, and fairly stable Jewish and religiously unaffiliated populations, although these are all interesting and important trends of religious analysis. Nor am I referring to the declining old-line Protestant hegemony over the culture or the fast-growing evangelical and fundamentalist faiths or even the more amorphous New Age spiritualities that have attracted so much attention in recent times—all significant trends as well bearing upon the country's future religious makeup. What I have in mind is something far more simple: the changing mix of peoples and cultures in this country that began to emerge in the 1960s. A new religious and ethnic demography began to appear about that time that seems to have permanently altered the nation's religious landscape. Its full impact, in fact, is just now beginning to become apparent in many American cities; indeed, it took the Los Angeles riots of 1992 to jolt many of us into an awareness of this new style of pluralism.

Let me cite the case of San Jose, California, a city not all that unusual on the West Coast. In the early 1960s, it was a city predominantly of whites, of Catholics and WASPs, plus a sprinkling of African Americans and Latinos. But two decades later the demographic mix had changed dramatically with a massive influx of young immigrants from Laos, Vietnam, Mexico, El Salvador, Nicaragua, Colombia, Sri Lanka, the Philippines, India, and the Pacific Islands. By then, the Hispanic and Asian populations were sizable, as were the many differing ethnic traditions of Christianity and of Buddhism and Hinduism. The local telephone directory tells much of the story: it takes 14 pages to list the Vietnamese surname Nguyen but only 8 pages for Smith.[4] Alternatively, consider Boston, Massachusetts, on the other side of the continent. The 1990 census showed this city to be a major center for refugees and immigrants, not Irish and Italians as was once the case but Salvadorans, Brazilians, Haitians, Guatemalans, Cambodians, and Cape Verdians. From 1980 to 1990, the rate of increase in immigrants to the city was staggering; there were an estimated 100,000 undocumented immigrants in 1990 alone, mostly people of color, Asians, and Hispanics.[5] Boston is a repository for the Atlantic Rim as cities in California are for the Pacific Rim.

It may well be that by the year 2000, as historians look back on the American Century, the Immigration Reform Act of 1965 will be remembered as the twin and equal of the Civil Rights Act of 1964. The Civil Rights Act sought to institutionalize equality—to redefine, if you will, the historical social space of blacks and whites—while passage of the immigration act opened the gates to a massive population movement that, slowly, is reshaping American culture. In 1965, legislators expected neither Latin American immigration on the scale we have come to know nor, much less, Asian immigration to play so vital a part in the country's future. Impoverished conditions in so much of Africa and in South America, combined with the disruptions of war in South Asia, the rumbles of war in Central America, and, of course, a global network of multinational corporations, created a backdrop that, once the legislation passed, led to massive population shifts. Stated differently, what happened was a significant fast-forwarding in the globalization of American life: the bringing together of many differing peoples and cultures into a new, reconstructed space, sustained, of course, by a changing political and economic world order. It has created a new global ethnic mix for America, new alignments of religion and ethnicity, and, as Jack Miles points out, a "new American dilemma" of young blacks and browns pitted against one another in fierce competition for dead-end jobs.[6]

What does all this mean for religion? For one thing, it means that these new residents of America's inner cities—most of whom are poor and unskilled—have been thrust together in a common fate. A reconstructed space opens up possibilities of greater exposure to religions and cultures that are qualitatively different from the earlier mixes of immigrants in the cities—far more diverse culturally, ethnically, and religiously. Even members of the same tradition—for example, Muslims—discover in today's urban centers just how diverse they are and worry about ethnic and nationality divisions threatening their unity as they move toward becoming the second-largest

4. See *Los Angeles Times*, 1 Aug. 1992.
5. See *Boston Globe*, 18 Feb. 1991.

6. Jack Miles, "Immigration and the New American Dilemma," *Atlantic*, vol. 220 (Oct. 1992).

faith in the country. But it also means something more: this new global context encourages new-style, multiethnic religious communities in places like San Jose and Boston where groups of differing backgrounds gather—for example, Catholics to celebrate the Eucharist in a variety of languages—and then discover each other's holidays, festivals, saints, heroes, and day-to-day problems. Inner-city Catholic schools are increasingly multicultural, multiracial, and multireligious, open not just to Catholics but also to Protestants, Muslims, Hindus, and sectarian faiths of many varieties. The schools and parishes hold workshops in language training, ethnic history, and child care and health and, in a nod to this new pluralism, conduct what they call "discussions" on other religions. Boundaries are being redefined, often in ways signifying that social and religious space is becoming more complex, as we saw during the Los Angeles riots when Vietnamese American Buddhists responded to attacks on their stores differently from the way Vietnamese American Catholics did. Faith and social location seem to have meshed together in new ways, reshaping once again American-style pluralism.

The result is not just greater exposure to a multicultural and multireligious world but also, some say, greater religious vitality. Casual observation suggests that multiethnic parishes are among the most alive within American Catholicism today; an example is St. Brigid's parish in the riot-torn South Central area of Los Angeles. Here, one can find Southern Baptist hymns and African mu-

sic; red, black, and green African American freedom flags hanging over the altar; and a portrait of Dr. Martin Luther King, Jr., under the stained-glass windows. The choir dresses with African *kufi* hats, as do many in the congregation. People of color from many nationality backgrounds come together, creating what C. Eric Lincoln and Lawrence Mamiya call a "black sacred cosmos," a shared world of meaning and belonging.[7] When asked if this is a Catholic church, the pastor replies, "This is just as Catholic as Rome, but we're allowed to use the culture of the people."[8]

Using "the culture of the people" is not new, of course, to African Americans and other minorities, but what is striking is the openness and forthrightness about these new solidarities today. Similar accounts can be told about the emerging *mestizo* cultures in Hispanic parishes. Those religious communities that are most vibrant allow for separate groups to have what religion in America has always provided: "free social space," as Sara Evans and Harry Boyte say in their intriguing analysis of the sources of democratic change in America.[9] Religion continues to bring people together and to mobilize group action. At the hands of innovative religious leaders—for example, the Reverend Cecil Murray of the First

7. C. Eric Lincoln and Lawrence H. Mamiya, *The Black Church in the African American Experience* (Durham, NC: Duke University Press, 1990).

8. *Los Angeles Times*, 23 Feb. 1992.

9. Sara M. Evans and Harry C. Boyte, *Free Spaces: The Sources of Democratic Change in America* (New York: Harper & Row, 1986).

African Methodist Episcopal Church in Los Angeles—old religious structures still have power, solidifying religious as well as political and economic philosophies—for example, the Reverend Murray's plan for "trickle-up" urban development—and channel energies in the direction of gaining control over community institutions. Yet at the same time, this refuge of free association and group organizing now occurs in a larger space of multicultural tolerance and respect for one another's traditions. Today, in inner cities across the country, groups are experimenting to find ways of working together and reshaping the alignments of ethnicity and religion. There are both continuity and change, a good example of religion's structural adaptability, and also new visions of unity forged out of the racial and ethnic regroupings created by a new world order. In such times of regrouping, there is more than simply cultural blending; there is also what Timothy Smith describes as a "theologizing experience."[10]

It should also be noted, however, that there can be religious anomalies in a global world. An example is that within old-line, white Anglo-Saxon Protestantism—the aging WASP institutions—there is a pattern of new recruits who are immigrants from the Third World countries. As one might expect, the styles of faith and practice for these two constituencies are strikingly different despite their often having a common denominational heritage. People whose families were converted by missionaries one, two, or possibly three generations ago in places like Korea and China have migrated to this country; they decide to affiliate with a religious institution and often seek out the same faith traditions that they left behind. What they find here typically is a pale form of faith compared to the missionary-style evangelical religion they remember from their childhood; often they create an all-ethnic United Church of Christ or Presbyterian congregation that stands out as really different from other congregations in the same tradition. There is more than a little irony here, considering that what little growth there is within liberal Protestantism in the late twentieth century is now coming from this more conservative offspring of the nineteenth-century missionary movement. In this instance of a reconstructed social and religious space, as Barbara Brown Zikmund points out, "more and more members of mainline liberal Protestant denominations literally do not understand the liberal traditions of their church."[11]

NEW PATTERNS OF FAMILY AND RELIGION

Next we turn to a different type of reconstructed space: the changing linkages between family and religion. Here I rely more heavily on the larger constituency of white, mostly middle-class baby boomers, that sector of the generation that has been at

10. Timothy L. Smith, "Religion and Ethnicity in America," *American Historical Review*, 83:1175 (Dec. 1978).

11. Barbara Brown Zikmund, "Liberal Protestantism and the Language of Faith," in *Liberal Protestantism*, ed. Robert S. Michaelsen and Wade Clark Roof (New York: Pilgrim Press, 1986), p. 189.

the center of gender, family, and life-style changes that have engulfed this country since mid-century.

This is a generation with many firsts—the first generation to grow up on television, the first generation to be identified as a mass-marketing audience by modern advertising, the first generation to grow up with the birth-control pill. Growing up in the era of postwar affluence and optimism, they had high hopes and expectations, but they also experienced wars, assassinations, long gas lines, racial injustice, environmental destruction, and the threat of nuclear annihilation. Demography and history thus combined to shape a generation who as young adults still today are very self-conscious and aware of how they differ from their parents' generation. The 1992 presidential election offered a vivid confrontation between these two generational cultures: Bush, the aging Cold War warrior, over against the youthful Clinton, who throughout the campaign was hounded by charges of dodging the draft during Vietnam; wife Barbara, the homemaker, mother, and grandmother, and Hillary, the career woman with her own opinions; and a campaign rhetoric saturated with themes of patriotism, use of drugs, views on abortion, and, of course, "family values."

It is not surprising that family values have surfaced in today's cultural wars. The massive changes in family life since mid-century, more so than in any other realm, continue to arouse the religious Right and to mobilize groups seeking to restore a Norman Rockwell America. Cultural changes evoke strong anxieties, especially when they touch upon such intimate realms as sexuality and family arrangements. My purpose here is not to describe these family changes; the situation of singles living alone, cohabiting singles, single parents, childless couples, blended families, gay and lesbian couples, and all sorts of extended-family arrangements is well known. No one watching television today is likely to mistake *Murphy Brown* or *Different Strokes* for reruns of *Ozzie and Harriet*. And without question, the implications for organized religion and for religious socialization within the family are substantial.

In the older, white bourgeois Protestant family that came to be the normative nuclear family, religious and family symbolism were closely intertwined—indeed, one might say families created religious space. The family was an extension of the church, the place where faith and practice were lived out. Grace at meals, family prayers, and family celebrations all helped to pass along the tradition. The mainline churches relied heavily on intact families with children to replenish them. Penny Long Marler's research shows that, among other demographic changes, declines in nuclear family units have contributed most to the decline in Protestant church membership since 1950, leading her to conclude that "as the family goes, so goes the church."[12]

Today, the family-religion connection is radically altered in a time

12. Penny Long Marler, "Lost in the Fifties: The Changing Family and the Nostalgic Church," in *Work, Family and Religion: New Patterns among Institutions*, ed. Nancy Ammerman and Wade Clark Roof (forthcoming).

when almost one-half of all boomer marriages fail, when 75 percent of boomer women are in the paid labor force, and when many second marriages blend together children of differing religious backgrounds. We would expect considerable erosion in the norms surrounding the family-religion connection, but the extent of the changes is perhaps greater than realized. In our young-adult survey, the question was asked, "Is it important to you to attend church/synagogue as a family, or should family members make individual choices about religion?" The point of the question was to see how far contemporary norms of individualism had invaded the family sphere, traditionally a stronghold of shared religious worlds. Our findings show a young-adult population only slightly more inclined to the family-oriented norms: 55 percent indicating a desire for families to have a shared faith, 45 percent saying members within families should make their own choices. Among conservative Protestants, family togetherness as a theme is more pronounced, yet, even here, a third of born-again boomer Christians endorse the individualistic response. Two factors more than any others influence this type of individualism: work and family type. Full-time working women emphasize individual choice. So also do the divorced and separated and, not surprisingly, those without children.

But there is also another side to these changes. While the individualistic types are the least committed to traditional faith and practice, it should not be overlooked that they are the ones leading the way in creating new religious space within families. Historically, people on the margins of religious institutions—and women especially—have been innovators. Today, there are signs of a deep ferment once again. Such people start support groups, organize new programs for children, and look for more creative ways to do things; if the established religious institutions cannot accommodate them, they often turn elsewhere. They are the lay equivalents to entrepreneurial religious leaders, drawing off the same supply-side spirituality that Americans have long been known for and that encourages expressive spirituality and pragmatic and changing religious forms.

Even among interfaith and blended families, where traditional religious socialization is greatly eroded, there are new developments. One is synagogues that are now setting up forums to deal openly with interfaith marriages. A topic often deemed taboo in Jewish circles has emerged as an opportunity, especially in synagogues with large boomer constituencies, for exploring new, enriched religious styles. Another example is the trend for grandparents in all the faiths to take more active roles in helping to socialize the children. My research suggests that the grandparent connection is far more important than has been suggested in the past: even when grandparents are physically removed and cannot assume direct responsibilities, there appears to be a growing respect for the types of religious and spiritual styles they represent, on the part of both boomer parents and their children. When checked into further, this often means an appreciation for simplicity, integrity, commitment, and living in accordance with one's beliefs—all primitive religious and spiritual values in keeping with currents flowing today toward holistic, experiential, and often syncretistic meaning systems.

The changed worlds of work and family have created new opportunities for the infusion of religious and spiritual values. Career women with families especially quest after new religious formulations. Juggling the demands of work while keeping marriages going and raising children, many women do not fit into the older gender-based groups as found in the religious establishment, which were created in an earlier time—hence so many new women's support groups. These groups empower and envision, renew and revise, or reconstruct significant spaces in women's lives. This reconstructing is occurring across religious sectors—in evangelical Protestant churches, in mainline Protestant and Catholic churches, and outside the established religions altogether.

This reconstruction is not limited to women. An integral part of such reconstruction is the creation of new family rituals. Manuals are available in the self-help section of bookstores to assist families in resacralizing family experiences, whether enriching marriages, building bonds between mothers and daughters and fathers and sons, celebrating a family's happy moments, or dealing with its crises. Close analysis of this literature reveals frequent reference to space—"finding space," "sharing space," "creating space," all, of course, imply-

ing psychological reconstructions. Moreover, this literature is replete with resources from various religious traditions to assist people to enhance their lives and their relationships. Put simply, as boomers have been remaking family life, so have they been redefining religious space in the family.

These reconstructions of family and religion show up in unexpected places and even in paradoxical ways. In her study of Orthodox Jews, for example, Lynn Davidman tells of young, boomer-age women—career women in New York City who have achieved considerable success in their jobs—who are attracted to a faith that to radical feminists would seem very stifling. Inquiring further, she discovers that a major reason is that they are looking for a private sphere in which they do not have to be "out there" asserting themselves. Wanting to be married and to have families, these women, Davidman says, find the "clear delineation of separate roles for men and women . . . a welcome contrast to the blurring and confusion about these roles in secular society."[13] They want clarity in gender definitions, though not necessarily all the old sexist meanings: the women turning to Orthodox Judaism still wanted men who would help with the child care! Definitions of Orthodox Judaism are undergoing redefinition, and so too are the spaces between the genders and between parents and children.

13. Lynn Davidman, "Women's Search for Family and Roots: A Jewish Religious Solution to a Modern Dilemma," in *In Gods We Trust*, ed. Thomas Robbins and Dick Anthony (New Brunswick, NJ: Transaction, 1990), p. 392.

Similar observations are made about working-class women who turn to evangelicalism. Judith Stacey and Susan Gerard write that such women's "turn to evangelicalism represents . . . a strategy that refuses to forfeit, and even builds upon, the feminist critique of men and the 'traditional' family" and provides them with "effective strategies for reshaping husbands in their own image."[14] To say that evangelicalism and feminism do not mix is to spin fiction contrary to the "brave new families" that Stacey observes. In both of these contexts—career-minded Jewish women and working-class evangelical women, very different religiously and socially—we see evidence of a new balance that blends elements of contemporary feminism and individualism with a more traditional conception of gender roles.

NEW FORMS
OF SPIRITUALITY

Finally, we look more generally at religious and spiritual trends today. Again I draw from the experiences of a generation of young adults, for whom space—both physical and psychological—figures prominently now and for whom it was prominent in the past: they were crowded into classrooms growing up; they were aware that colleges and universities expanded to accommodate them; they have known since childhood that

14. Judith Stacey and Susan E. Gerard, " 'We Are Not Doormats': The Influence of Feminism on Contemporary Evangelicals in the United States," in *Uncertain Terms: Negotiating Gender in American Culture*, ed. Faye Ginsburg and Anna L. Tsing (Boston: Beacon Press, 1990), pp. 112-13.

market researchers play to their consumer tastes and the pollsters to their opinions. Now, with many of them facing mid-life, their quests and concerns are very much before the whole society.

To start with, it is not so much that this generation is less religious than their parents, although on some indicators that may well be the case. Far more important is how they are religious. For sure, this is a religiously diverse generation: one-third have remained fairly loyal to the faiths in which they grew up; among the two-thirds who dropped out as youths, about 40 percent of them are involved again in some kind of religious group, but the majority of the dropouts have no meaningful, ongoing connection with a church, synagogue, temple, or mosque. Better put, what they have are revised interpretations about religion, more along the line of looking to religious institutions to provide services in times of personal or family need. Even those most estranged from religious institutions still look to them for what the French call *rites de passage* at times of birth, marriage, and death, or as some wag in this country puts it, at times of "hatching, matching, and dispatching."

Several themes are important for grasping boomer religious styles, all interpretable as a result of the reduced institutional space. Perhaps the most striking is that of choice. Canadian sociologist Reginald Bibby's apt phrase "religion a la carte" summarizes the highly selective way boomers involve themselves in religion.[15] Especially, educated, middle-class boom-

15. Reginald W. Bibby, *Fragmented Gods* (Toronto: Irwin, 1987).

ers, from all religious backgrounds—Protestant, Catholic, Jewish, Muslim—look upon religion much the same way they look upon choice of life-style and consumption patterns. One rejects a fixed menu and picks and chooses among religious alternatives. Personal growth is at the basis of such choice: one participates in a congregation or cultivates a New Age spirituality, or does both as is not so uncommon, much for the same reason as one is involved in a 12-step recovery group—"if it helps you," as we heard repeatedly in our interviews with boomers. Choice and growth are articulated less among evangelical boomers, of which there are many, yet, even here, one uncovers evidence of the fusion of psychology and faith as well as the trend toward "menu diversification," or the increased options made available for styles of religious involvement in megachurches.

A second theme is the high degree of faith exploration. Boomers grew up exposed to the world religions; they remember the Beatles' turning East. As they move in and out of religious involvement, they check out various religious and spiritual possibilities and construct, or reconstruct, their own personal form of spirituality, drawing from a variety of sources. When we asked our interviewees if they should explore the teachings of various religions or stick to a particular faith tradition, less than a third said stick to one tradition. Sixty percent said one should explore other possibilities. Consequently, it should come as no real surprise that multi-layered meaning systems are commonplace—that is, pastiche styles of belief and practice, combining elements from such diverse sources as Eastern meditation, Native American spirituality, psychotherapy, ecology, feminism, Jungian psychology, as well as more traditional Judeo-Christian beliefs.

But there is more than just greater choice and faith exploration—themes conjuring up notions of fads and fashions in a consumer religious economy. One senses a strong reaction to modernity's highly differentiated world, which bifurcates body and spirit, public and private, institution and life. The craving for holism spills over into renewed appreciation for connections with all of life—with the environment, with animals, with people both globally and locally. There is renewal of power as found in relations over against that of dominance and destruction, in earthborn rather than skyborne energy. There are spiritual rediscoveries, such as appreciation of the body and its ties with nature—for example, "women's mysteries" as related to monthly cycles. Among men, too, at least some men, there is an awareness of breaking out of old notions of manhood and exploring new aspects of their identity. There is a profound searching, but not so much that of navel gazing, as was often alleged in the past, as a quest for balance—between self and others, between self-fulfillment and social responsibilities. Especially among the older members of this generation, one finds a discernible "ethic of commitment," as pollster Daniel Yankelovich termed it some years ago.[16]

16. Daniel Yankelovich, *New Rules: Searching for Self-Fulfillment in a World Turned Upside Down* (New York: Random House, 1981).

In the culture at large, questions of faith and spirit seem to have gone public: television programs, novels, magazine stories, and newspaper articles now give serious attention to the spiritual and religious questions of a generation that grew up suspicious of the faith and morality handed down to them by their elders. Popular culture is saturated with spiritual concerns but with a distinctive 1960s and 1970s twist. "The religious search that seems to be emerging," writes Craig Dykstra, "is not a nostalgic revisiting of a safe, comfortable, sentimental religiousness. . . . Rather the search is for a truer, healthier suspiciousness, one that can smoke out deceit, oppression, violence, and evil . . . and tell it for what it is." Then Dykstra goes on to identify what I believe is a powerful existential force behind this generation's spiritual quests. He writes, "To support the suspiciousness, there must be something that is not suspiciousness itself, something that is not so ultimately suspicious it must finally suspect itself."[17] For many, what is beyond suspiciousness is called God; for others it is a Higher Power, a Life-Force, or some other symbolic expression of ultimacy and significance.

This attention to spirituality is not limited to the United States. In many European societies, the young adults are the carriers of a postmodern spirituality. Political scientist Ronald Inglehart documents a "culture shift" toward postmaterialist values of peace, egalitarianism, environmentalism, and quality of life in a dozen

or more advanced industrial societies during the post-World War II years.[18] Cross-cultural research that my collaborators and I have undertaken shows a heightened interest in spirituality and faith exploration despite declines in institutional religion, and both are closely related to this shift in values.[19] In fact, the real impact of the postwar generation on religion may yet lie ahead. In the United States, especially, there is reason to expect continuing spiritual vitality. Between now and the year 2000, year by year, the thirtysomething population turns into the fortysomething population. Boomer demography thus assures a large supply of young adults passing through mid-life transitions well into the next century. If developmental psychologists are correct about identifying these years as the peak time of reflection and realignment of loyalties, then we can expect a heightened religious and spiritual ferment for some years to come.

Finally, a word about group involvement. If the previous description implies a free-floating, privatized, and disembodied spirituality, then a more balanced perspective is in order. Spiritual energies do express themselves in highly personal and diffused forms, but we should not overlook the social groups and movements that are a part of this generation. It is easy to miss the social aspects, since so much of religious and

17. Craig Dykstra, [Editorial], *Theology Today*, 46:127 (July 1989).

18. Ronald Inglehart, *Culture Shift in Advanced Society* (Princeton, NJ: Princeton University Press, 1990).

19. Wade Clark Roof, Jackson W. Carroll, and David A. Roozen, *The Post-War Generation and Religious Establishment: Cross-Cultural Perspectives* (forthcoming).

spiritual rhetoric today is cast in psychological terms: as journey, as recovery, as growth. But this rhetoric is deceptive because a narcissistic and addictive culture simply makes it easier for us to talk about ourselves even if it is in groups where the talking occurs; indeed, we might even go so far as to say that the psychological is the mode of the religious in middle-class American culture today.

The fact is that boomers and millions of other Americans find support in small groups across the country today. Everywhere there are small groups—fueled in great part by both the self-help movement and the meta-church movement within evangelical and charismatic megachurches. If there was one thing that really struck me in my research on young adults, it was the vast array of small groups organized around people's experiences, feelings, and inner states. The perennial human concerns—for sharing, caring, and belonging—are as real today as ever before, but they find expression in new and varied ways. The concerns themselves often are more important than where people actually find them: women explore their own spirituality in Goddess groups but also in home churches; many people, both men and women, find support in adult-children-of-alcoholics meetings and in other 12-step groups but also in evangelical prayer groups; there are meaningful group experiences and, often, bonding experiences—whether among those spending a week working with Habitat for Humanity or among those exploring the meaning of visualization and dream analysis; there is community and celebration

on Jesus Day but also on Earth Day. In all of this, what seems most essential is that people find ways to forge a link between individual experience and religious and spiritual teachings, and, in so doing, they often find community.

If the belonging dimension for boomers is easily missed in contemporary analysis, the same holds for much of American religion. It is a time of the "new voluntarism," as William McKinney and I suggested in 1987, and of a shift from "collective-expressive" to "individual-expressive" identities, as Phillip Hammond has recently suggested.[20] Yet we must be careful here. When McKinney and I proposed the phrase "new voluntarism," we had in mind a further development in the historical course toward greater individual autonomy in religious matters. There are two aspects to this process, and how one reads them and the weights accorded one with respect to the other colors one's interpretation. Greater voluntarism in religious life involves liberation from ascriptive bonds and thus presumably a weakening of group ties; but it also implies something more—enhanced personal religious and moral responsibility and, it should be underscored, the possibility for new forms of belonging and community organized around people's deeper expressive concerns. Historical and sociological studies that fail to grasp the latter in their rush to

20. Wade Clark Roof and William McKinney, *American Mainline Religion* (New Brunswick, NJ: Rutgers University Press, 1987); Phillip E. Hammond, *Religion and Personal Autonomy* (Columbia: University of South Carolina Press, 1992).

pronounce religion's collapse or to lament the country's excessive religious individualism miss, it seems to me, the cutting edges of what is happening religiously in the 1990s.

I offer two brief illustrations:

1. Despite all that is said about "new voluntarism" and the shift to "individual-expressive" identities since the 1960s, national polls since then show no significant declines in religious involvement. They show no gains either, despite all that has been said about an evangelical revival. Whatever the shifts of culture and of religion during this period, they seem to have made little difference in actual rates of participation. There was an increase in the number of dropouts from organized religion in the 1960s and 1970s, but it has stabilized—a pattern that, as Andrew M. Greeley explains, was due largely to life-cycle characteristics of the large boomer population at the time, and not a long-term shift in religious patterns.

2. Consider the great amount of religious switching that occurs in the United States: well over a third of Americans change religious affiliations over the course of a lifetime. The cynical interpretation is that this shows how superficial and impermanent religious loyalties are or that religion is simply a mirror of social interests and belonging. But the data suggest otherwise: people who switch do so largely for moral and religious reasons. Often, their reasons are expressed psychologically—"to find a place where I am comfortable," as one person told us, which in her case meant Bible-preaching and pro-life

stands. Religious switching in the 1990s contributes to the restructuring of American religion and is helping to create more clearly defined boundaries between groups. Here, it seems the "new voluntarism" and "individual-expressive" trends are making a difference in lifting up the choice factor in religious—and nonreligious— identification and participation.

What then is really my point? My point is that with the breakdown of ascriptive loyalties, there is more, not less, potential for religious and spiritual expression. The way is opened up for people to give expression to their personal and expressive concerns, or to their more genuinely religious and spiritual values. The United States today is moving in the direction not so much of a melting pot as a centrifuge, to use Francis Fitzgerald's metaphor, which suggests a new sorting out of groups, still on the basis of language, nationality, color, ethnicity, and class, but increasingly on dimensions of gender, sexual orientation, and life-style.[21]

As one cultural layer after another is stripped away in the centrifugal process, we get closer to the experiential and the inner realities of the religious. In all sorts of settings, one observes the centrality of experience, whether in the casual evangelical setting of jeans, cotton sweaters, drums, and guitars where members brag about not being "churchy" or in the emotional and heart-felt participation one senses at the Metropolitan Community Church, whose members are finally free to acknowl-

21. Francis Fitzgerald, *Cities on a Hill* (New York: Simon & Schuster, 1981).

edge who they really are. What the "new voluntarism" amounts to is another leap forward in the centrifugal process, regrouping and reposturing in ways that offer a positive definition of who people are and give expression to fundamental identities.

We have barely begun to see where all this new religious freedom might lead. One thing I think we will see is new emergent forms of community, perhaps of many differing kinds. It is simply not true, for example, that boomers are not interested in community or commitment: they were galvanized in youth into strong social solidarities and passionate concerns and are still capable of them. What is true is that existing social institutions do not always give expression to their concerns. Hence they often turn to small groups and interaction rituals—both within and outside of organized religion. As one person told us: "It's not that they are anti-commitment. . . . rather they are weighing what commitment means." I sense this reaching out to commit, a yearning for connections and the importance of sacred and expressive values. The yearning comes through in many ways: in the concern about family and for deeper personal relationships; in the questioning of instrumental values in favor of a closer relationship to the land, the mountains, and the oceans; in quests of simple values such as harmony, peace, and a holistic conception of life; in untapped idealism and reverential thinking as expressed in the ideal of community. When Bill Clinton calls for a "new covenant," for example, he gives voice to that ideal of community.

CONCLUSION

Given what I have described here about reconstructions of groups, institutions, and lives, I am not as concerned as Robert Bellah and his associates are in their book *Habits of the Heart* and its sequel, *The Good Society*, about the corrosive effects of individualism on religious belonging.[22] Their analysis suggests a sort of parallelism, almost a zero-sum game, as if individualism is the antithesis of institutional commitment. I think a more fruitful approach would be to recognize more nuanced patterns of individuals and institutions and to acknowledge that social rituals and institutions are social constructions —if these constructions mediate self-transcendence, people find meaning with them, and if they do not, then people turn to other institutions or modalities. There are many reasons why rituals and institutions may or may not be satisfying for people, but a fundamental one concerns whether they affirm and extend the self. Clearly, as we approach the year 2000, not only is there a good deal of weighing what commitment means but also a sorting out of institutions and forms to give expression to people's deepest commitments.

One final comment bears upon today's psychoreligious culture. Narcissism as a psychological condition is a frequent target of attack, yet it is arguable that this effort is misplaced. Serious searching of inner space, as

22. Robert N. Bellah et al., *Habits of the Heart: Individualism and Commitment in American Life* (Berkeley: University of California Press, 1985); idem, *The Good Society* (New York: Alfred A. Knopf, 1991).

the great spiritual teachers and countless saints and mystics have taught us, often leads to outer commitments. Rather than look upon the narcissistic self as the source of the problem of expressive individualism, perhaps a better solution lies in recognizing the close association between narcissism and religion and in capitalizing on the current signs of a transformed narcissism in contemporary culture.

The notion of a transformed narcissism and its emphasis upon shame, as opposed to guilt, as a religious response holds considerable promise. As described by psychologist Heinz Kohut, transformed narcissism is a mature form of narcissism with features compatible with the positive, reinforcing role of religion: for personal creativity, for a person's need for affirmation, for expressiveness, for the wisdom arising out of a sense of one's own limitations.[23] Shame draws attention to unmet potential, of falling short not just in the eyes of others but in one's own eyes. We can

go even further and speculate that such psychology may well be essential to the continuing role of the sacred in a highly secular society. A person's freedom to develop his or her own talents, flexibility and adaptation to new life conditions, confrontation with one's own mortality, a sense of irony and the capacity to laugh at it, and asking how one's own creativity may contribute to the well-being of others may all be critically important to sustaining a sense of the sacred in the future.

Indeed, it could be, as psychologist Donald Capps ventures to suggest, that the rise of the narcissistic self is gradually bringing about a new conception of the divine in the place of traditional theism—God as the "accessible Self."[24] Should that turn out to be the case, we can say in the coming years that we have taken a deep voyage into inner space, perhaps leading to the biggest reconstruction of all—new metaphysical space.

23. Heinz Kohut, "Forms and Transformations of Narcissism," in *The Search for the Self: Selected Writings of Heinz Kohut 1950-1978*, ed. Paul H. Ornstein (New York: International Universities Press, 1978), vol. 1.

24. Donald Capps, "Religion and Psychological Well-Being," in *The Sacred in a Secular Age*, ed. Phillip E. Hammond (Berkeley: University of California Press, 1985), pp. 237-56.

Book Department

INTERNATIONAL RELATIONS AND POLITICS

ALLISON, GRAHAM and GREGORY F. TREVERTON, eds. *Rethinking America's Security: Beyond Cold War to New World Order.* Pp. 479. New York: Norton, 1992. $24.95.

The transition from the stability of the Cold War to the uncertainty of the future is already a cottage industry. This volume brings together experts from a variety of disciplines and provides a compendium of authoritative assessments of where we have been in U.S. foreign and security policy and of the directions in which we are likely to go. Notable current and former policymakers are included in the collection along with academics, journalists, and other public policy influentials. The result is an informative and readable collection of papers that professional students of defense and security as well as other readers will find thought provoking and delightfully controversial.

Allison and Treverton's introductory essay is cast in the framework of a "secu-rity portfolio review" analogous to corporate portfolio appraisals. The idea is to see where resources have been concentrated in the past within the broad domain of U.S. security concerns and to estimate whether this pattern ought to continue in the future. Allison and Treverton evaluate U.S. security policy during the Cold War years as one of "mixed incoherence" and note that policy was heavily militarized. Nonmilitary dimensions of security received relatively little attention from policymakers, nor did the same nonmilitary aspects of security get very much money. Only about one-fifth of the entire security effort in budgetary terms, and even less in terms of personnel committed, went into foreign assistance, diplomacy, energy, economic assistance, and other activities that were not directly military but security related. Moreover, according to Allison and Treverton, the U.S. Cold War nonmilitary security effort was widely dispersed; those effects that it might have had were mediated through many different agencies and programs. In short, Cold War security policy was Pentagon policy, and Pentagon priorities emphasized the containment of Soviet military power through conventional and nuclear deterrence.

On the other hand, according to Allison and Treverton, although investments in economic security were small compared to investments in military security, economic security expenditures paid great dividends. The creation of transnational monetary regimes after World War II, including the General Agreement on Tariffs and Trade, the International Monetary Fund, and the World Bank permitted unprecedented economic growth, which in turn fostered the development of a security community in Europe. The editors also observe that diplomacy is inexpensive compared to military measures, and during the Cold War years as well as subsequently, diplomacy has been found to provide substantial benefits for insubstantial costs.

Ernest R. May traces the expansion and retraction of U.S. concepts of national security through history. May notes that the concept of an "empire for liberty" had strong idealistic resonance among U.S. policymakers during both world wars of the twentieth century and that it continued to influence U.S. behavior during the years of Cold War. Throughout American history, business and other leaders have argued that U.S. economic strength was an important component of national security, but definitions of economic strength related to security have not been consistent. Although U.S. military power has been acknowledged to rest to some extent on national economic growth and productivity, rankings of states in terms of their gross national products would produce some anomalous great-power ratings. May shows that Washington and Lincoln epitomized two very different presidential standards for identifying the domestic attributes of national security. One standard explicitly connects improved domestic political cohesion and

welfare with a higher probability of success in the conduct of foreign relations. The other standard assumes that success in foreign and defense policy will be a by-product of domestic tranquillity and productivity.

U.S. Under Secretary of Defense for Policy Paul D. Wolfowitz outlines the Bush administration defense strategy. He notes that planning for a new strategic environment began in 1989, long before the Soviet Union actually collapsed but well within the envelope of a changed U.S. threat perception after four years of Gorbachev. According to Wolfowitz, Bush strategy called for reduced forward deployments, especially in Europe, and an emphasis with regard to ready forces on mobility for regional crisis response. Although Desert Storm showed that regional crises can require very large forces, under the Bush plan U.S. Department of Defense planning for fiscal years 1991-96 would reduce Army strength to 12 active divisions, Air Force holdings to 15 tactical fighter-wing equivalents, and the Navy to a fleet of 451 ships, although the Navy would retain 12 operational aircraft carriers and one training carrier. Since this chapter was written, Bush had taken further unilateral initiatives to reduce the numbers of U.S. tactical nuclear weapons worldwide and had offered to engage in bilateral strategic arms reductions with Russia well below the levels already agreed to in the Strategic Arms Reduction Talks. Defense outlays as a proportion of gross national product were expected to decline to about 3.6 percent in fiscal year 1996.

Contributors offer several alternate visions of the new world order. John Mearsheimer argues the neorealist position in favor of the continued importance of state actors and power politics after the Cold War. Charles A. Kupchan and Clifford A. Kupchan argue for a "concert-based collective security" arrangement for Europe, in which a security group of major powers under the aegis of the Conference on Security and Cooperation in Europe takes responsibility for regional peacekeeping. Charles Krauthammer challenges the conventional wisdom that the bipolar world will give way to multipolarity. Instead, according to Krauthammer, the "unipolar moment" has arrived for the United States: the United States is an unchallenged superpower with various powers of the second rank, economically important but militarily impotent, trailing behind. General William Odom notes that U.S. military advantages in large-scale conventional operations such as Desert Storm will not necessarily deter insurgencies and internal wars. Rejecting both isolationism and pax Americana, Odom favors a U.S. strategy for managing regional balances of power. Other interesting views of world order or disorder are contributed by Richard N. Gardner on practical internationalism, by John H. Barton and Barry E. Carter on the role of international law, by Michael Doyle on the concept of a liberal international community, by George Ball on the Arab-Israeli conflict, and by Alan Romberg on U.S.-Japanese relations.

Perhaps the most originally contentious chapter in the collection is by David Hendrickson, who contends that the outcome of Desert Storm, although a brilliant military victory, represented a political and moral liability. The United States, Hendrickson maintains, deliberately followed a strategy designed to minimize the number of American casualties and to avoid protracted war. This strategy dictated the use of overwhelming firepower for the purpose of mass slaughter of Iraqi ground forces. Although U.S. political guidance sought to distinguish between military and other targets, in practice, the military targets included virtually the entire social infrastructure of Iraq. In addition, according to Hendrickson, the exertions of war were not followed by a better peace: neither liberty

nor order prevailed in Iraq in the aftermath of U.S. and allied intervention. The author points to the potential dilemma: an expanded U.S. role in international peacekeeping by means of military intervention raises the imperial flag without necessarily bringing in its train imperial responsibility for postwar civil peace. Both liberal and conservative internationalists, and especially "unipolarists," should note the potential risks of imperial swordsmanship without imperial policy.

STEPHEN J. CIMBALA

Pennsylvania State University
Media

BROOKER, PAUL. *The Faces of Fraternalism: Nazi Germany, Fascist Italy and Imperial Japan*. Pp. viii, 397. New York: Oxford University Press, 1991. $69.00.

How do nations govern themselves without monarchy? Political scientists may well characterize the twentieth century as a combat of three "isms" to resolve this dilemma. They are generally identified as democratic capitalism, communism, and national socialism or fascism.

In *The Faces of Fraternalism*, Paul Brooker masters a wide-ranging original exploration of one of these "isms," with a comparative study of Nazi Germany, Fascist Italy, and the 1930s' imperial Japan. He focuses on the very similar and highly unusual social policies of these three regimes. He uses the term "fraternalism" to describe their unique social policy of attempting to instill in a modern society the primeval type of social solidarity found in clans and tribes and known to sociologists as mechanical solidarity.

Brooker begins by describing the regimes' social origins and then explains how their fraternalist social policy arose from a desire to prepare their societies for the rigors of a total war like that of 1914-18. The central chapters' dense prose demonstrates that these regimes were convinced that the liberal idea of individual liberty was not compatible with the pursuit of the national or racial fraternity that they sought, and they were quite prepared to sacrifice individual liberty in favor of their nationalist or racist version of the ideal of fraternity, leading to bankruptcy and destruction.

This fine, scholarly work indicates clearly that, while the three social policies were not cut of the same cloth, they were more alike than different, ideological kin springing from similar sources and with similar messages to the world. Indeed, these movements were multifaceted and contained the paradoxes that were the stuff of fascism: order and disorder, appeal to the masses and a conscious elitism, action and stagnation, heroism and corruption, revolution and preservation of the existing social order, purposefulness and ambiguity. In short, they were a volatile blend of illusion and reality, the twin qualities being helplessly intertwined, largely incapable either of separation or of identification. These movements shared a common reservoir of frustrations and hatreds. All of them were easily recognizable as products of a world in crisis, itself the product of war and its legacy of political, social, and economic upheaval.

The book is cinematic, with a series of tables that graphically ranks and compares the achievements and failures of the three regimes. Of the three, Japan seems obviously the most successful in both inculcating mechanical solidarity in its society and strengthening its society to face the rigors of total war. The fanatical, self-sacrificing, and often suicidal commitment of the Japanese people in the closing years of World War II in the defense of the Emperor and the homeland does suggest a very high level of social solidarity, markedly higher than in Italy or Germany.

This fresh volume will help the student of contemporary history to comprehend fully the forces that led the world into World War II. More than that, however, it is an especially valuable book at the present time of alienation and the politics of frustration—all the ingredients of the past surges are with us again.

GERALD L. SBARBORO

Circuit Court
State of Illinois
Chicago

NIXON, RICHARD M. *Seize the Moment: America's Challenge in a One-Superpower World*. Pp. 322. New York: Simon & Schuster, 1992. $23.00.

TWINING, DAVID THOMAS. *Strategic Surprise in the Age of Glasnost*. Pp. vii, 309. New Brunswick, NJ: Transaction, 1992. $39.95.

Most now acknowledge that the collapse of the Soviet Union has brought with it both good and bad news. The good news is that the evil empire has collapsed and brought with it a diminution of the possibility of major wars. The bad news is that internal instability within the former Soviet Union and the remnants of its former empire may lead to serious problems for world peace. Further, the disintegration of the Soviet empire has international implications for Third World areas as well as for former Soviet client states. This new international landscape and the changed power balance are the backdrops for the themes of both books.

Richard Nixon views the world broadly, while David Twining focuses specifically on strategic conflict and self-deterrence as these pertain to the United States and the USSR. Focusing on the changes brought about by the collapse of Gorbachev's Soviet Union and the emergence of the United States as a solo superpower, Richard Nixon's wide-ranging analysis covers the regions from Europe and the Pacific to the Muslim world and the Southern Hemisphere. His analysis identifies the internal problems facing various regions as well as how these affect U.S. interests. In responding to these issues, the former president feels that a "democratic Russia working with a democratic America" could bring untold benefits to freedom and democracy throughout the world. In the final chapter, "The Renewal of America," Nixon lists a number of issues that America must address if it intends to maintain its world leadership. The overall view tends to be optimistic and includes a prescription for American leadership. The more difficult questions are how such policies and programs are to be implemented and how the support of Congress and the American people are to be ensured.

Twining provides an in-depth analysis of the possibility and likelihood of surprise nuclear attack as this pertains specifically to the United States and the USSR. He offers an excellent historical view of the various dimensions of nuclear attack as perceived by both superpowers. The analysis of changing Soviet defense strategy and doctrine during the *glasnost* period is particularly informative. Also, the Soviet change to sufficiency and political stability as the basis for a relationship with the United States is examined, as is the emerging importance of conventional forces in the Soviet Union. In this respect, Twining notes that in light of the changes in the Soviet Union, the West needs to alter its position on arms control as well as its defense programs. The turmoil with the collapse of the Soviet Union and the ouster of Mikhail Gorbachev combined with the deep problems and divisiveness within the Soviet military

appear to be the more serious issues—issues that are beyond the time frame of the book. Yet the questions raised regarding surprise nuclear attack may be useful in terms of reshaping them to fit the new security landscape. Indeed, with the proliferation of weapons throughout much of the Third World, it may be useful to review the concepts and restructure them to apply to the new security landscape.

Richard Nixon's writing has the tone of an elected leader using plain language to convince others of the relevance of his analysis and prescription. Twining's more jargon-oriented and analytically precise efforts make it heavy going for the reader; an example would be, "The possibility dimension of the surprise paradigm is now beginning to diminish." Further, while Nixon anticipates many of the changes taking place now, events seemed to have outpaced Twining's study. And even though both authors offer a conceptual basis to make some sense of the future, these must be viewed with caution. Richard Nixon's broad analysis leaves one wondering how all of what he suggests is to be done. David Twining offers good history, but one wonders about its relevance in the new world order. Nonetheless, the authors should be applauded for trying to come to grips with issues that are complex and challenging, both to policymakers and to those writing about them.

SAM C. SARKESIAN

Loyola University
Chicago
Illinois

SCOTT, PETER DALE and JONATHON MARSHALL. *Cocaine Politics: Drugs, Armies and the CIA in Central America.* Pp. vii, 279. Berkeley: University of California Press, 1991. $24.95.

Rather than the way the Iran-contra affair has generally been portrayed in the United States as an unfortunate isolated aberration, this book argues that the contra-drug connection is deeply rooted in political intrigues that extend back many years. Since the 1940s, U.S. government intelligence agencies, first in Southeast Asia and more recently in Afghanistan and Latin America, have protected many of the world's largest drug traffickers—as long as they were willing to help the United States fight its covert war against communism.

The book focuses on the role of U.S. authorities, and particularly the Central Intelligence Agency, in shaping cocaine distribution in South and Central America through the 1980s and on how the U.S. government's complicity was covered up once it became the object of congressional scrutiny. The book provides abundant evidence of how the law enforcement mandate of such organizations as the federal Bureau of Narcotics and the Drug Enforcement Administration has been subordinated to the goals of the intelligence establishment in its war on communism and suggests that Congress and the media have also generally deferred to these interests. In the process, drugs have become the common currency for espionage, paramilitary operations, and counterintelligence activities around the world.

Scott and Marshall argue that alleged Nicaraguan and Cuban involvement in drug smuggling—one of the main reasons given by the Reagan and Bush administrations for supporting the contras—is minuscule compared to U.S. involvement. Indeed, covert U.S. collaboration with corrupt governments appears to be more the rule than the exception. The consequence has been tacit U.S. government support of assassination plots, death squads, illegal arms deals, and the illicit drug trade across Central and South America at the very same time that the U.S. government purports to be fighting a war against drugs.

Because of its painstaking documentation, *Cocaine Politics* is must reading for anyone interested in developing a workable and humane drug policy. To this end, it contains a vital political message: "one of the first targets for an effective drug strategy should be Washington itself, and specifically its own support for corrupt drug-linked forces in the name of anticommunism." On the basis of the evidence they present, it is difficult to disagree with Scott and Marshall's conclusion that no approach will succeed until Washington's complicity with the drug trade is ended and until crime is taken out of drug markets; to this end, they advocate a strategy of "controlled legalization."

JOHN LOWMAN

Simon Fraser University
Burnaby
British Columbia
Canada

AFRICA, ASIA, AND LATIN AMERICA

ALEXANDER, ROBERT J. *Juscelino Kubitschek and the Development of Brazil*. Pp. xiii, 429. Athens: Ohio University Press, 1991. Paperbound, $25.00.

At a time when so much is being written and said about the prospects for democracy and market reforms around the world, Brazil's development record and the role of its leaders in designing economic, social, and cultural policy merit attention at a level beyond that of the specialist. Within this setting, it is especially fitting that Juscelino Kubitschek, president of Brazil from 1956 until 1960, be singled out for study. Not only does Robert Alexander accomplish both tasks; more importantly, through the use of political biography, he captures adeptly why Kubitschek is Brazil's most significant democratic leader and how this came about in a political environment at odds with democratic values.

To understand why all this is the case requires considering Brazil's place in the upper tier of the developing world and understanding how the life and experience of this man is intertwined with the strengths and weaknesses of modern Brazil. This is especially necessary because writing about Kubitschek entails reassessing a man whose impact on Brazil's economic, social, and political development dates back thirty years, to a time when achieving both democracy and productive markets seemed only a question of time for most Brazilians. The strength of this book is that it does all these things.

Alexander situates Kubitschek fully within the context of his era and communicates to the reader the dynamics of a modernizing Brazil. He also traces the trajectory of Kubitschek's career from his life as a young medical doctor in Minas Gerais, through his presidency, to his marginalization from public affairs by dictate of Brazil's military rulers after 1964.

Alexander makes it quite clear that Kubitschek was identified with the Vargas tradition and hence always open to attack from those who opposed the changes wrought by Vargas in modernizing the country. At the same time, in discussing Kubitschek's involvement in politics during the second Vargas presidency (1950-53) and in the uncertain political climate characteristic of Brazil after Vargas's suicide in August 1954, Alexander relates how Kubitschek had emerged as his own person in 1955 in mounting a successful presidential campaign. Thus, when Kubitschek assumed office in January 1956, he entered the presidency both as an heir to Vargas and as an innovator with a strong commit-

ment to democracy and rapid economic development.

The core of the book contains a detailed account of Kubitschek's role as president. Alexander credits Kubitschek with the creation of an environment in which Brazil's developmental potential was released and where, as a consequence, pessimism over the obstacles to be confronted was replaced with self-confidence and optimism regarding Brazil's future. This discussion takes the form of seven chapters, each devoted to a different component of the Kubitschek presidency.

The book ends with a sober assessment of what occurred in Brazil afterward and how, in the breakdown of what was an imperfect democracy, Kubitschek was marginalized and isolated by those who sought to destroy the Vargas tradition and create a very different Brazil. This aftermath entailed more than a decade in which Kubitschek was denied his political rights. Yet, writes Alexander, when he died in 1976, there was an awareness among the majority of Brazilians of the contributions he had made to his country that could not be suppressed. In Brazil's new encounter with democracy since 1985, this is a record not to be forgotten.

LAWRENCE S. GRAHAM
University of Texas
Austin

CHAN, STEVE. *East Asian Dynamism: Growth, Order and Security in the Pacific Region.* Pp. xv, 134. Boulder, CO: Westview Press, 1990. $35.00.

MILNE, R. S. and DIANE K. MAUZY. *Singapore: The Legacy of Lee Kuan Yew.* Pp. xi, 217. Boulder, CO: Westview Press, 1990. $34.00.

The merging of security studies, economics, and politics into a single area of inquiry is a relatively recent phenomenon. Steve Chan's *East Asian Dynamism* is an effort to extend the boundaries of security studies to include economics and politics in the context of the Pacific Rim countries. The main thrust of this volume is to show that the goals of growth, political order, and military strategy present a fundamental policy dilemma: they often represent competing rather than complementary targets. Furthermore, there is usually no single best policy strategy to use to attain the overall goals, and the choice between alternative strategies will itself require a trade-off between the major objectives. A high point in the book is the discussion contrasting the American approach to national security in the Pacific Rim based on superpower—military—competition with the Japanese approach, which is pursued by a more integrated strategy of military, economic, and political policies. Unfortunately, the work is flawed by conceptual ambiguities and some serious conceptional errors. For example, the glossary defines "terms of trade" as the balance of payments; defines "relative deprivation" as the perceived gap between one's aspirations and current position; and, unexplainedly, gives identical definitions for two different concepts—"voluntary export restraints" and "orderly market arrangements." These confusions show up in applying theory to events, with correspondingly dysfunctional impacts on clarity of analysis and presentation.

In an analysis that is both probing and well documented, authors Milne and Mauzy fix their attention on the underlying reasons for Lee Kuan Yew's success in guiding Singapore to a parliamentary democracy with a standard of living the envy of most other developing and even some developed countries. Factors that receive particular attention are the timing and content of Lee's political strategy, the personal qualifications of cabinet members and chief bureaucrats around Lee, and the exploitation of selected ele-

ments of Confucianism. The economic and defense dimensions of Lee's strategy are treated in separate chapters, tending to leave the reader with the impression that these were isolated facets of Lee's overall strategy, which they clearly were not. A chapter on the human costs of Lee's strategy would have provided better balance to the work. There have been significant developments since the book was published, including the election of a new prime minister and the thrust of Singapore into the position of financial capital of Southeast Asia. For a deeper understanding of current events, however, the book is an invaluable source of information.

RICHARD HOOLEY

University of Pittsburgh
Pennsylvania

DIACON, TODD A. *Millenarian Vision, Capitalist Reality: Brazil's Contestado Rebellion, 1912-1916.* Pp. xii, 199. Durham, NC: Duke University Press, 1991. Paperbound, $16.95.

The argument in this excellent book about an early-twentieth-century peasant millenarian movement and rebellion in the south of Brazil combines careful attention to historical and analytical detail with clean prose and an easy pace. Beyond its contribution to the literature on peasant politics and millenarian movements, I recommend it for illustrating to students the intense impact of capitalism on precapitalist agrarian societies. It would make a useful addition to reading lists for introductory courses on Latin American politics and history and on the politics of the developing world in general.

Diacon begins with a classic observation: the introduction of capitalism wreaks havoc in precapitalist social relations. Diacon explains that precapitalist patron-clientelism establishes strong social bonds between elites and nonelites that are both material (the exchange of labor for access to land) and spiritual (embellishing that exchange with religious meaning). Depending on whether local elites end up as partners with the capitalist "intruders"—represented in this case by a new railroad and subsequent logging and colonization enterprises—or whether these elites find their privileged social position under attack, long-standing patron-client bonds with the rural peasantry will be either unilaterally abandoned or reconstructed around a common struggle against the intruders. The Contestado rebellion—named after the region in the state of Santa Catarina in which it occurred—is largely an example of the former scenario, although elements of the latter also apply.

Using local archives and videotaped interviews with survivors, Diacon constructs a picture of the social and economic context that allowed the preachings of a wandering healer and self-styled prophet to spark a religious movement of 20,000 devotees and a painful regional civil war. Diacon establishes the changes in Contestado society wrought by land enclosures and speculation, the sale of public lands, the introduction of wage labor, and state-sponsored colonization by European immigrants. These changes wrought by capitalism led to the rapid displacement of much of the region's peasant population and to the destruction of the spiritual bonds of patron-clientelism constructed around interclass godparent ties, the sponsoring of religious festivals, and the building and maintenance of religious shrines. The destruction of these spiritual bonds created a spiritual and moral vacuum filled by a millenarian creed.

Most followers of the Contestado movement were displaced peasants. The leaders, however, were mostly landowners. Diacon explains this seeming contradic-

tion as consistent, first, with the movement's millenarian aims at reestablishing the lost morality of precapitalist patron-clientelism—albeit on a more egalitarian, religious-communal basis—and, second, with the intra-elite conflicts that found some landowners losing out to others in the new world of frontier capitalism.

WILLIAM R. NYLEN

Hilles Library
Cambridge
Massachusetts

DYZENHAUS, DAVID. *Hard Cases in Wicked Legal Systems: South African Law in the Perspective of Legal Philosophy*. Pp. xviii, 289. New York: Oxford University Press, 1991. $69.00.

Legal positivists have long argued that distinctions must be drawn between law and morality, while their critics have rejected the validity of such arguments. David Dyzenhaus opens his study *Hard Cases in Wicked Legal Systems* with an excellent discussion of judicial obligation and the rule of law. He reexamines the writings of such authorities as J. Bentham, W. Blackstone, J. Austin, H.L.A. Hart, G. J. Postema, and L. L. Fuller as well as the views of German lawyers such as Gustav Radbruch

who had rejected positivism because they thought that their experience showed that it had contributed to the subservience of the German legal profession to Nazism. As Hart understands it, Radbruch's argument is that the positivist distinction between law and morality corrupts practice precisely because it insists on a distinction between what law is and what law ought to be. (p. 14)

In an important essay, "The Model of Rules," written in 1967, Ronald Dworkin rekindled the debate. Dworkin's views center around the idea that a moral principle "is also a principle of law if it figures in a particular way in a judgement in a hard case." For positivists, there are dangers in this view: "the danger of obsequious quietism, of deference to bad laws because of the mistaken belief that laws always possess moral weight."

These issues were sharply etched for judges and the legal profession in South Africa during the years of apartheid. Dyzenhaus is correct in his statement that the rulers in South Africa succeeded in securing a judiciary that was acquiescent to "the legislative barrage . . . which make[s] it appropriate to describe South Africa's legal system as wicked." In the succeeding chapters, he examines cases in the adjudication of racial segregation, national security, dissent, common law revival, and states of emergency that he classifies as "the war against law." In dealing with states of emergencies, he concludes, judges should have resigned not because they were required to interpret apartheid laws in accordance with the official policy of apartheid but because they were no longer in a position where they could enforce and interpret a substantial part of the law. They were no longer able "to adjudicate on what is lawful in large and fundamental areas."

In the end, based on the South African situation and a study of recent English decisions mainly on state security, Dyzenhaus comes out against positivism. He concludes that a view of law should be adopted that gives the best results in practice. For him, the correct view of law should lead to morally good results and make sense of and perpetuate healthy legal practice.

This is an interesting and provocative book. Its findings are particularly important for South Africa, which is poised to make important new constitutional decisions.

PATRICK O'MEARA

Indiana University
Bloomington

FLANAGAN, SCOTT C., SHINSAKU KOHEI, ICHIRO MIYAKE, BRADLEY M. RICHARDSON, and JOJI WATANUKI. *The Japanese Voter*. Pp. xix, 497. New Haven, CT: Yale University Press, 1991. $45.00.

The reader is informed in the introduction to this book that because much that has been written on Japanese politics is of the case study variety, there is a mistaken impression that Japan is profoundly different from other democratic societies. To correct this impression and to demonstrate that Japanese voters have much in common with voters in other industrialized countries, Scott Flanagan and his coauthors have modeled this volume after Campbell et al.'s *American Voter* (1960) and voting research carried out at the University of Michigan. Their data come primarily from the 1976 elections. The authors conclude that Japan is indeed not unique, although there are important differences from Europe and the United States. It is these similarities and differences that constitute the main contribution of this book.

A key finding is that party identification is the primary predictor of voting behavior. While this is similar to the United States, the study also finds, by contrast, that voting behavior is less volatile—indeed, the Liberal Democratic Party has dominated most elections since the mid-1950s—and that many more voters can be identified as negative partisans or uninformed partisans. While this would produce lower voter turnout in a country like the United States, such a result does not occur in Japan because of the major role played by social networks in mobilizing the vote. The major role of social networks means that issues, the media, parental attitudes, and cleavages based upon religion, ethnicity, region, or social class are less likely to determine voting behavior. Rather, social networks as determined by residence, age, and occupation foster group loyalty and attitude conformity and produce a large number of mobilized voters.

This volume will be of interest more to political scientists specializing in comparative politics than it will be to Japan specialists. The book is long on methodology and short on descriptive explanation, making for a rather boring read. There are occasional needless swipes at "superficial descriptive accounts" and "folklore," evidence of what has all too often been a staple bias of behavioral researchers. Rather than appearing to be a decade and a half out of touch, the authors offer as a final chapter an analysis of the elections of 1989 and 1990. While this chapter does delve somewhat more deeply into issues, candidates, and parties, even here much of the discussion focuses on abstractions. For those interested in the theory of voting behavior, this will be a book of considerable interest; for those interested in learning more about Japanese political behavior, there may be too much theory to slog through to find it.

WAYNE PATTERSON

St. Norbert College
De Pere
Wisconsin

HALEY, JOHN OWEN. *Authority without Power: Law and the Japanese Paradox.* Pp. x, 258. New York: Oxford University Press, 1991. $37.50.

The title of this study is instructive in evaluating the main arguments delineating Japanese legal processes and the nature of social change. The author, professor of law and Asian studies at the University of Washington, considers the notion of authority to embody forms of legitimacy that members of society tend to obey. Concepts of power he defines as dealing with various capacities to coerce and influence a host of social decisions. His thesis is summarized in his introduc-

tion when he notes that "no characteristic of Japanese political life seems more remarkable or intrinsic than the separation of authority from power." Moreover, he notes that, contrary to standard analyses on this subject, Japan, as a consensual democracy, does not break up and limit the exercise of power via power sharing in its homogeneous, culturally unified society. The diffusion of coercive power, he contends, is designed and expected to "ensure the stability of the basic institutions and patterns of governance and yet also allow(s) for a high degree of political, economic and social change." These ideas are dealt with at great length, particularly the many notions of limits that the authoritarian Japanese political culture imposes on individual rights and liberties as well as the many forms of modern contractual and litigious relations and instruments that are subject to consensual relationships.

Once one accepts John Haley's many assumptions, buttressed by lengthy references to historical Chinese and Japanese political thought, then it is an easy intellectual step to appreciate that Japanese legal codes flow from a variety of basic premises drawn from Japanese political traditions. Haley cites much data on many topics to support these contentions, including civil action statistics involving family matters from 1898 to 1941, in which conciliation and the conciliator's sense of morality are the preferred means for resolving local disputes. Other evidence deals with the remarkably small number of persons passing the Japanese national legal examinations from 1949 to 1986. In the process of his complex analyses, Haley gives much deference to some questionable assertions by Japanese specialists that the "vertical structure of Japanese social organization" contributes to the "value of autonomy . . . that effectively den[ies] most Japanese freedom from organizational control without a life of substantial social and economic risk."

These and other *nihonjinron* ("in matters Japanese") rationales sprinkled throughout the text are assertive, and evidence to sustain these arguments is selectively presented.

Haley's emphasis on consensual decision making in legal and social matters eliminates the basic questions a reader may have on who decides what, in what particular way, and with what effect within the realm of politics. One could make the case for independent judicial judgment by post-World War II Japanese courts in advancing the public interest without catering to various instruments of ostensible public social controls, rules, and norms.

Much of the text deals with issues concerning criminal and civil case loads, the treatment of defendants, the importance of guilt, sincerity, and remorse in victim-victimizer relations, and the weaknesses of formal regulatory powers that administrators exercise in pursuit of their professional responsibilities. A major and provocative chapter titled "Hamlets and Hoodlums: The Social Impact of Law without Sanctions" continues the observation that those people in Japan who hold positions of authority and influence —the politicians, business leaders, and establishment types—are important by virtue of their abilities to secure group cooperation or collusion: law is used by these people to legitimize norms without resort to the weapons of coercion. Again, the reader may wish to reserve judgment. Perhaps this use of the law is true for many situations, but, in recent years, as Japan is beginning to become ever more aware of its need to join the world, the Western notions of law as policy and instrument for social justice are eroding the consensual basis of power wielding. Increasingly, public opinion polls in Japan reflect public cynicism of the exercise of consensual power. Women have won cases in courts on issues of sexual harassment, civil libertarians have been able to

challenge legal norms, public officials have had to sustain parliamentary inquiries about corrupt practices, and consumers have increasingly been able to organize group action designed to weaken the established consensus utilized by arbitrary public or elected officials. Authority without power is gradually being replaced in Japan by a cultural and political system quite different from the one described in this instructive and specialized text. Forms of genuine democracy are eroding the authoritarian social structures.

RENE PERITZ

Slippery Rock University
Pennsylvania

HODGES, DONALD C. *Argentina's "Dirty War": An Intellectual Biography*. Pp. xviii, 387. Austin: University of Texas Press, 1991. $37.50.

Once again, Donald Hodges has written an intriguing work of intellectual and political analysis, one that attempts to explain the foundations of the Argentine military's dirty war between 1975 and 1978, a barbaric episode in which as many as 30,000 civilians may have been killed.

Hodges defines the dirty war as a response to what he calls the "Argentine question," the crisis deriving from the interrelated impact of three major problem areas in the country's history since 1930: (1) the country's notorious economic decline (Hodges notes that in 1913 Argentina's per capita product was larger than that of France, twice that of Italy, and five times that of Japan); (2) chronic political instability and stalemate so severe that the transfer of power from Raúl Alfonsín to Carlos Menem in 1989 marked the first time in 61 years that one freely elected civilian president had succeeded another; and (3) the disintegration of Argentina into "a political inferno of social unrest and armed subversion bordering on civil war."

Using an immense variety of primary and secondary sources, including personal interviews, Hodges finds the intellectual roots of Argentine subversion and the dirty war in ideas deriving from Peronismo, the nineteenth- and twentieth-century Catholic Right, Cold War thinkers such as James Burnham, and numerous factions within the Argentine military and civil society. As with his two previous works, *Argentina, 1943-1987: The National Revolution and Resistance* and *Intellectual Foundations of the Nicaraguan Revolution*, Hodges's "intellectual biography" of Argentine political violence is bound to prove controversial. His detailed dissections of ideas are fascinating, yet they leave important questions about the causal linkages between ideas and patterns of historical events. Much can be debated about the absoluteness of many of his categorizations.

Hodges concludes that the dirty war did not result from the uncontrolled aberrant actions of extremist military sectors as argued by the imprisoned journalist Jacobo Timerman in *Prisoner without a Name, Cell without a Number*. Instead, Hodges maintains, the dirty war was "planned from the top" by "military moderates" as part of the "Military Process," a systematic program between 1976 and 1982 in which the Argentine armed forces sought to restore national greatness through liquidating the perceived sources of subversion, restructuring the economy, and cowing organized labor and the Peronist party. He forecasts that while there may be no recurrence of the dirty war, the persistence of the "Argentine question" will mean the continuance of militarism, popular resistance, and the potential for armed struggle in Argentine society.

ARTHUR SCHMIDT

Temple University
Philadelphia
Pennsylvania

KAMEN, CHARLES S. *Little Common Ground: Arab Agriculture and Jewish Settlement in Palestine, 1920-1948.* Pp. xi, 327. Pittsburgh, PA: University of Pittsburgh Press, 1991. $39.95.

HILTERMANN, JOOST. *Behind the Intifada.* Pp. xvii, 265. Princeton, NJ: Princeton University Press, 1991. $29.95.

A cloud of instability covers the Middle East. From Kuwait to Lebanon, these lands have become major areas of conflict in the late twentieth century. Nowhere have the lines been more sharply drawn than in the dispute between Israel and the Palestinians. Not surprisingly, the Israeli-Palestinian conflict has produced a rich body of literature. The two books reviewed here offer new perspectives that should be of interest to the generalist and the specialist alike.

Little Common Ground takes the position that the struggle over land is a major reason for the Israeli-Palestinian dispute. Kamen's study of agriculture during the thirty-year period of large Jewish settlement in Palestine demonstrates that, from the very beginning, Palestinians and Jews failed to understand each others' intentions. Furthermore, he calls into question the most popular theories concerning this period of history by pointing out that these theories were drawn almost entirely from British and Zionist sources. The exclusive use of this material misses the fact that Zionist and British agricultural policies largely coincided during this period. For most of these authors, the political importance of Palestinian agriculture was ignored. This omission has resulted in the creation of many of the myths associated with the impact of Israeli settlement on the Palestinians.

Kamen points out that the Zionists rationalized their activities by claiming that the establishment of their modern agricultural system would, by example, also benefit the Palestinians. In fact, Kamen demonstrates that the Zionists were interested only in encouraging the Palestinians to introduce vegetable and fruit production, which would require smaller plots, so that the land surplus created through this process could be made available for Jewish purchase. On the other hand, the popular Arab rationalization that their land was lost to the Zionists because absentee landlords sold it out from under tenant farmers is also not supported by the record. Kamen holds that traditional Arab agriculture was no longer economically viable. Control of the land was lost when inefficient farmers were forced to sell off their land to pay their debts to money lenders. This land was then purchased by the Jewish settlers. He states that misunderstandings such as these were common on both sides. He concludes that all of these issues became irrelevant with the Israeli military victory in 1948.

Charles Kamen's research on agriculture in Palestine between 1920 and 1948 brings new insights to a subject that often has been overlooked by other studies on the Israeli-Palestinian dispute. He brings to his study a number of years of experience working with Israelis and Palestinians. This is a thoroughly researched and well-written book. By exploring the history of land use in Palestine, Kamen has given us a fresh look at one of the major disputes of the twentieth century.

In *Behind the Intifada*, Joost Hiltermann paints a bleak picture of Palestinian life under Israeli occupation. He makes the point that the *intifada* includes far more than the struggle for the streets of the occupied territories. It also encompasses the political, economic, and social struggle against the Israeli military occupation. Using studies that focus on the political mobilization of the Palestinian labor and women's movements, Hiltermann shows how the *intifada* has

been sustained in the occupied territories. He argues that by successfully continuing the *intifada*, Palestinians have gained a victory because they have disproved the Israeli contention that the occupied territories can be successfully integrated into Israel proper. He asserts that the *intifada* has created a de facto green line between the State of Israel and the occupied territories.

Hiltermann holds that although there are similarities between Israeli colonial activity in the occupied territories and the European colonialism of an earlier age, certain fundamental differences exist. The support of the United States for Israel means that, unlike European retreat from their colonies, there is little chance that the Israelis can be pressured to withdraw in favor of a Palestinian state anytime soon. Even though Palestinians have successfully established a powerful resistance movement, Hiltermann believes that the best that they can hope for in the short term is to work for a situation where there can be a reduction of dependence on Israel.

Joost Hiltermann makes no secret that his sympathy lies with the Palestinians. He tends to discount the popular argument that the *intifada* represents a split between Palestinians living under occupation and Palestinians in the diaspora. Rather, he holds that the Palestinians in exile and those living under Israeli occupation have worked closely together since the beginning of the *intifada*. He believes that the unions and the women's movements have become some of the most important forces used by the Palestinians to successfully maintain the struggle against Israeli rule. His book includes original material on unions and the women's movements that he obtained during his long stay in the territories. This book is both interesting and important because it offers insights into the Palestinian movement that are seldom seen in Western literature.

These are valuable books that add to our knowledge on the complexities surrounding the dispute between Israel and Palestinians.

JOE N. WEATHERBY

California Polytechnic
  State University
San Luis Obispo

LEONARD, THOMAS M. *Central America and the United States: The Search for Stability*. Pp. xvi, 245. Athens: University of Georgia Press, 1991. $35.00. Paperbound, $15.00.

This well-organized, clearly written history tells us that the United States has frequently imposed its political, economic, and social institutions on Central America, often failing to comprehend the consequences of its actions. Sometimes the area's governments have appreciated U.S. protection, and often they have used it for their own purposes.

Thomas Leonard superbly synthesizes the 1820s and 1830s, when the United States endeavored to gain ascendancy over the British in the region. He shows how relations between the United States and Central America were basically established between 1865 and 1903 as the United States sought new markets and a canal across the isthmus. The United States believed that it could best achieve its goals through Central American unity but found that impossible in light of nationalist rivalries.

Once U.S. corporations established themselves on the isthmus and Panama was selected for a canal, Washington sought financial stability and discouraged competition in the region. The Roosevelt, Taft, and Wilson administrations wielded the "big stick" and intervened to prevent foreign intervention; Wilson endeavored to impose his Protestant morality on the Catholic region; and distrust of the United States caused the Central American states, except Costa Rica, to join the League of Nations to prevent U.S. incursions into their internal affairs.

During the 1920s and 1930s, when Salvadoran Augustín Farabundo Martí and Nicaragua's Augusto Sandino led struggles against the exploitation of the masses in their nations, the United States, misled by the mainstream press, blamed the insurgencies on socialism rather than on poverty, misery, and ignorance perpetuated by the governing elites. It also miscalculated that its Good Neighbor Policy of the 1930s would prevent the rise of dictatorships in Central America.

Leonard constantly touches on significant aspects of social, political, and economic history and brings forth considerable new information. He notes that the alliance against the Nazis enabled Central America's militaries to receive U.S. aid, which they used to stifle political opponents, and that U.S. military missions in each nation during World War II supervised the training of local forces, a practice that continued during the Cold War as the Mutual Security Acts tied the militaries to the United States in anticommunist pacts, which enabled Central America's armies to defend the status quo.

After World War II, Central America assumed a marginal position in the eyes of U.S. policymakers. Washington failed to differentiate between legitimate indigenous movements and international communism, and it often supported the region's oppressors. Leonard deals splendidly with the ideological conflicts in Costa Rica and Guatemala in the 1950s and notes that John Foster Dulles internationalized McCarthyism by exaggerating the role of Communists in Guatemala's reformist regimes of the 1940s and 1950s.

Leonard depicts the Kennedy administration as interested in social progress in Central America and claims that the

Johnson government de-emphasized social and economic reform in favor of restraining the Left. His analysis of the Reagan and Bush years suffers from the disinformation disseminated by the White House about the depth of Soviet penetration in Nicaragua. He contends that the U.S.-financed contra war against the legal government of Nicaragua failed and that elections ousted the Sandinista leadership in 1990, while I see the war as the primary factor that turned voters against the Sandinistas.

SHELDON B. LISS

University of Akron
Ohio

SYLVESTER, CHRISTINE. *Zimbabwe: The Terrain of Contradictory Development.* Pp. xii, 212. Boulder, CO: Westview Press, 1991. $34.95.

Readers familiar with Christine Sylvester's many articles on Zimbabwe will not be surprised at the theoretical approach employed in this book but will be pleased by the way in which this approach is presented with a minimum of jargon in order to make it easily intelligible to students. As the subtitle indicates, the primary focus is on the existence of contradictions and their potential resolution, but unities and disunities, continuities and discontinuities, types of revolution, and the search for hegemonic myths—the themes of Sylvester's earlier writings—all play their parts in the contradictions that she identifies. Yet Gramsci does not appear in the footnotes and the use of postmodernist terminology is, with occasional lapses, minimal. As Sylvester acknowledges in the conclusion, her framework is quite similar to the more widely accepted state-society relations approach, which I favor.

The format of the book is the one loosely followed by other titles in Westview's Profiles/Nations of Contemporary Africa series, starting with precolonial history and moving through settler-colonial Rhodesian history, postindependence state and political dynamics, political economy, state-society relations, and foreign policy, and concluding with the analysis of future possibilities. All of these topics are covered very competently, and much of the presentation is in accord with the conventional wisdom of the literature on Zimbabwe. The extensive treatments of gender and culture in the chapter on civil society and state-society relations, emphasizing their place in the contradictions of politics and society, are important additions to the conventional interpretations. They are part of Sylvester's consistent effort to include the people's view of politics, economy, and society. Zimbabwe's family planning program does not receive as high marks from Sylvester for either birthrate reduction or contribution to gender equality as it receives from some other commentators.

In her sophisticated conclusion, Sylvester points out that dichotomous questions about whether Zimbabwe is or is becoming socialist or capitalist, democratic or authoritarian, posed by analysts during the first few years after the country's independence in 1980, have been replaced by narrower questions that focus on contradictions, constraints, and opportunities. She describes her conclusions as ambivalent; others would describe them as balanced. Zimbabwe's future is uncertain because its state and society contain so many roughly evenly balanced contradictory tendencies.

JAMES R. SCARRITT

University of Colorado
Boulder

EUROPE

MACHADO, DIAMANTINO P. *The Structure of Portuguese Society: The Failure of Fascism.* Pp. xxii, 216. New York: Praeger, 1991. $47.95.

Although Samuel Huntington credits the Portuguese revolution with beginning the wave of democratization that has swept Latin America and Eastern Europe, study of Portugal has been largely neglected by English-speaking scholars. *The Structure of Portuguese Society: The Failure of Fascism* by Diamantino P. Machado is therefore a welcome contribution to a sparse field. In his book, Machado tries to explain the nature of the authoritarian regime that governed Portugal for almost fifty years and the circumstances that led to its swift demise on 25 April 1974. Machado attempts to understand the state's role by examining its institutional and ideological characteristics and by analyzing elite support for the regime after its creation in 1926. Moreover, to explain the coup in 1974, he looks at the purpose of Portugal's colonial empire, its role in the regime's collapse, and the professional and political changes in the armed forces as a result of Portugal's fight to retain its colonies—long after other imperial powers had relinquished theirs. In what is perhaps the most interesting part of the book, he explains how a left-wing faction of the armed forces orchestrated the coup in 1974 and why the revolution was really nothing more than a conflict between elites, not a mass movement from below.

Yet Machado's book does not advance the study of Portugal very far. He relies too heavily on dated, secondary sources in English and does not take advantage of the detailed research and numerous archival materials available in Portugal since the fall of the regime. Because Machado lacks primary as well as recent sources, he frequently reiterates old myths about Portugal and the Portuguese empire. For example, Machado argues that Portuguese colonialism was a case of "uneconomic imperialism," a view first introduced by R. J. Hammond in 1966. This view claimed that Portugal was too poor and backward to benefit from its colonies and that the Portuguese regime was unwilling or unable to invest in the empire. Both of these tenets have been convincingly challenged by W. G. Clarence-Smith in his 1986 book, *The Third Portuguese Empire, 1825-1975: A Study in Economic Imperialism*—sadly, a work not cited by Machado.

The activities of the previous regime were shrouded in secrecy, but since 1974, the archives in Portugal have offered rich material for research. It is hoped that these will afford scholars greater opportunities to tell interested readers why a regime that lasted so long collapsed so quickly.

M. ANNE PITCHER

Colgate University
Hamilton
New York

ROSE, SONYA O. *Limited Livelihoods: Gender and Class in Nineteenth-Century England.* Pp. xi, 291. Berkeley: University of California Press, 1992. $39.95.

Rose's book contains excellent definitions of gender written in remarkably clear prose with an admirable absence of jargon. Her thesis should make all historians rethink the way they write about men and women. Rose shows how cultural gender expectations shaped the relationship of women and men to their domestic worlds and their working worlds. Gender expectations trapped both sexes in the nineteenth-century industries that she examines. Instead of working together with women to improve wages and hours and working conditions, working-class men often agitated against their female counterparts as the cause of low wages for men or lack of employment.

In unions, women were usually unconsulted, nor were their needs confronted; their work was always merely supplementary. Rose shows vividly how the doctrines of working-class respectability underpinned by the necessity of male independence impelled men to make the workplace an unwelcome arena for women. An independent man supported his family on just his earnings while his wife stayed at home to care for children and keep the house. This manly rhetoric of independence was not merely a reflection of upper-class and middle-class values but had developed out of the experience of waged labor.

The problem, of course, as we all know, was that the wages of one man were usually inadequate to support a household. Rose documents many married women, who were in obvious agreement with the need for male independence, who left work when one of their children was old enough to go out to work. Many women, of course, did not have that choice and remained in the work force throughout their lives despite the disapproval of the males of their class.

On the whole, this is a worthwhile, clear book. It is an excellent example of the sort of women's history that is not peripheral but integrated with the whole human story. Strangely, though, the book is lacking in actual nineteenth-century people. Too often, Rose leaves her endnotes with the task of filling in the personal element and providing the examples. With so many and such long notes, it might have been a wiser choice to use footnotes, since many of the liveliest parts of the book would then have been more easily accessible to the reader.

MARY BETH EMMERICHS

University of Wisconsin
Milwaukee

ULLMAN, RICHARD H. *Securing Europe*. Pp. xv, 183. Princeton, NJ: Princeton University Press, 1991. $19.95.

HYDE-PRICE, ADRIAN. *European Security beyond the Cold War*. Pp. xv, 272. Newbury Park, CA: Sage, 1991. $60.00. Paperbound, $24.00.

At first glance, these two books appear very similar. Both are attempts to analyze a transformed European security environment in the aftermath of the Cold War. Both have, as their basic point of departure, the assumption that the Europe of the 1990s is qualitatively different from the pre-Cold War past, having been significantly transformed by the growth of economic interdependence, the proliferation of international institutions, democratic change, and processes of historical and social learning. As a result, both make strong and believable arguments that the European security order of the future will not be recognizable as the Hobbesian anarchy and balance-of-power struggle of the prewar past.

Beyond this basic similarity, however, the two books diverge. Ullman's is a smooth-flowing and highly readable essay written from an unabashedly liberal perspective. In many ways a response to Mearsheimer's pessimistic realist thesis, Ullman's book is extremely upbeat and optimistic about the prospects for peace and stability in the European future. Hyde-Price, on the other hand, has written a more academic and research-based work that, while also basically optimistic, is much more balanced and evenhanded in its conclusions.

Both books, after assessing the changed European security landscape, attempt the difficult task of predicting the future. Ullman's approach is much more normative. His central recommendation is the creation of a pan-European collective security regime. The institutional centerpiece of this new regime is a European Security Organization, which would build upon the bases of the Conference on Security and Cooperation in Europe (CSCE) and the Western European Union and would transcend and eventually replace the North Atlantic Treaty Organization (NATO). Hyde-Price, by contrast, chooses to outline four alternative scenarios for a future European security system, each based on projections from current institutions and trends. These are (1) a NATO-based system, (2) a supranational West European defense community, (3) a pan-European system based on the CSCE—which bears considerable resemblance to Ullman's recommendations, and (4) a modified balance-of-power system. Although he presents the arguments for and against each particular system, Hyde-Price is unwilling to indicate which he feels is preferable or more likely. Instead, he contents himself with enunciating 10 basic principles that, in his view, should guide the construction of a future European security order. These include avoidance of a unitary structure, the absence of institutional hierarchy, and room for regional differentiation. In the end, the eclectic, more evolutionary approach to European security suggested by Hyde-Price is less inspiring than the grand architectural schemes propounded by others, but it is also somehow more sensible and reassuring, if not realistic.

Both of these books share something else, and that is that they are already seriously dated. This is a matter, of course, that the authors could hardly be criticized for, writing as they were at a time of rapid and breathtaking change. Nevertheless, it must be mentioned that both books were published in early 1991, before such watershed events as the decisive conclusion of the Persian Gulf war, the Soviet coup and dissolution of the USSR, the Maastricht Treaty of European Union, and the civil war in Yugoslavia. Each of these events has had, in its own way, a significant impact on the evolving shape of the new European security order. It would be interesting to see if the conclusions of either of the authors, especially as they concern the future role of NATO and the United States, as well as the prospects of an integrated European security identity, would be any different in view of these developments. In any case, the more cautious and differentiated approach of Hyde-Price should enable his book to better stand the test of time.

MICHAEL BAUN

Georgia State University
Atlanta

UNITED STATES

ALLEN, ROBERT C. *Horrible Prettiness: Burlesque and American Culture.* Pp. xvi, 350. Chapel Hill: University of North Carolina Press, 1991. $34.95.

Burlesque, as described and analyzed by Robert C. Allen, is a dense and complex subject. Following its transformational and diffusive history in the United States, Allen begins with the arrival of Lydia Thompson and her "British Blondes" on the 1868 New York cultural scene. Noting that "no form of American commercial theatrical entertainment before or since has given the stage over to women to a greater degree," Allen traces the development and decline of this "thoroughly feminized" theatrical expression in this richly researched volume.

Thompson and her female troupe performed authentic burlesque, the parody of classical and legitimate plays. That these women did not obscure their sexuality while acting all the burlesque roles, both male and female, resulted in a dual transgression that left some observers squirming in their loges. Here was the female body displayed, and with it the disquieting spectacle of male impersonation and all that that implied: female insubordination breaching Victorian patriarchal standards. Burlesque posed a moral threat that severed it from bourgeois culture, a social construction that "defined itself in terms of what it had rejected, excluded, outlawed, or repressed." Writing for the *Atlantic Monthly*, William Dean Howells declared his simultaneous revulsion and attraction: "It was certainly a shocking thing to look at [the women] with their horrible prettiness, their archness in which was no charm, their grace which put to shame." He believed burlesque would lose its appeal quickly because it could not possibly fall to a lower level of transgression.

Howells was wrong. Burlesque flourished, albeit in new forms and under conditions resulting from bourgeois defensive strategies. These strategies represent Allen's most interesting arguments. By relegating all things burlesque to working-class realms—the saloon, the variety theater, the pages of the *Police Gazette*—middle-class culture effectively neutralized the potential power of female sexuality inherent in female performance art. As burlesque grew ever more sexually explicit, and therefore ever more transgressive, burlesque performers became associated not only with prostitutes but also with the freaks of boardwalk and circus sideshows.

Allen underscores that burlesque was a theatrical expression never authentically feminist. But as practiced by Lydia Thompson's troupe and other female performers, the form nevertheless subverted traditional gender representations. Still, during the period, burlesque existed as essentially antiauthoritarian and antipatriarchal, and after it was transformed, marginalized, and contained by bourgeois culture, burlesque remained within the continuum of the sexual exploitation of women.

While adding immensely to the scholarship on the American theater, this fascinating and well-written volume will number among the few that have cogently evaluated nineteenth- and early twentieth-century entertainment in the contexts of social relations and cultural history.

CATHERINE GOETZ

Montana State University
Bozeman

BLACK, EARL and MERLE BLACK. *The Vital South: How Presidents Are Elected*. Pp. x, 400. Cambridge, MA: Harvard University Press, 1992. $29.95.

The American South, consisting of the 11 states that made up the old Confederacy, has had a unique place in presidential politics. From 1880 through 1944, the South was solidly Democratic. The Republicans had to rely on winning a large proportion of the nonsouthern electoral vote.

Starting in 1952, this Democratic monopoly was broken, and since 1972 the Republicans have won practically all of the South's electoral vote, except for the Carter victory in 1976. This switch was due to a combination of factors, but the main factors were the racial upheavals and the domination of the Democratic Party by liberal candidates and liberal programs. This enabled the Republicans to play the race card with great success. Once George Wallace disappeared from the scene, the Republicans had the field to themselves. They established a firm base among the whites, who make up over 80 percent of the electorate in the South.

By gaining the South, the Republicans have obtained a great advantage in presidential politics. Beginning in 1992, the South controls 54 percent of the electoral votes. Thus the Republicans need obtain only 33 percent of the nonsouthern electoral vote. The Democrats, on the other hand, start with an enormous disadvantage; they must win between 60 and 69 percent of the nonsouthern electoral vote. In recent elections, they have not come close to that figure.

Winning back the South, or at least a portion of it, will be a daunting task for the Democrats. Yet they have no choice but to attempt to break the Republican monopoly. The Democratic task is to retain the black vote, to secure what remains of the white, core vote, and to make inroads into the swing vote, those whose vote is not committed to either party. This might be attained if the Democrats brought their program more in line with dominant southern values and interests. By nominating a southerner and with the help of a failed Republican presidency, the Democrats might succeed in recapturing some of the border states.

This book calls attention to what is undoubtedly an important aspect of presidential campaigns and the strategy and tactics that the political parties employ in them. But as this review is being written, it remains to be seen what effect the candidacy of Ross Perot will have on the Republican hold on the South.

EUGENE V. SCHNEIDER

Bryn Mawr College
Pennsylvania

[The preceding review was written in the spring of 1992.—Editor]

COOPER, PATRICIA A. *Once a Cigar Maker: Men, Women, and Work Culture in American Cigar Factories, 1900-1919.* Pp. xvi, 350. Urbana: University of Illinois Press, 1992. Paperbound, $15.95.

This book, newly available in paperback, has been justly hailed as one of the most successful research projects in American labor history in recent years. In a branch of social history that risks becoming a bit jaded, Patricia Cooper offers a readable and analytically useful study of work and workers in a classic nineteenth-century craft. Her story is a familiar one in some respects: an artisanal trade, though one involving workers of several racial and ethnic backgrounds and women as well as men, faces increasing pressure from new machines and profit-hungry employers. Work pride, a strong union—the cigar makers gave Samuel Gompers to American labor—and a willingness to fight back even outside union ranks all only delayed the inevitable. Close, but no cigar. After World War I, more fully mechanized procedures changed the face of the industry, and the old work culture faded away. Cigar making was not a major force in American economic life; Cooper makes no silly claims about massive numerical or political influence. Yet, despite modest importance and a familiar basic story, cigar making yields significant understanding.

The success of Cooper's study rests on several bases. The book reveals awareness of major conceptual issues, without belaboring them needlessly. It reflects wide research, including oral history, and an engaging sympathy with its subjects, a sympathy that Cooper, hostile to narrow craft unionism, did not expect to acquire. The book dynamically marries gender with labor history, dealing extensively with women cigar makers, the differences between their work culture and that of men, and the results of gender differences not only in male-exclusive unions but in the craft's larger struggles. The focus on work routines and values, and the way strikes and the union flowed from worker pride and loyalties, provides a welcome antidote to organizational accounts of labor movements without sacrificing real attention to the workers' struggle.

The book's flaws follow to some extent from its virtues in providing an in-depth look at a craft in a period of growing challenge. Everything is contained within the industry and the workplace; there is scant link to a wider history. Even the employers are shadowy figures for the most part. Workers themselves remain disembodied outside their shops; what the rest of their lives were like and whether these lives had any relationship to their labor struggles are not detailed. Perhaps most disturbingly, the actual transition away from the craft, while evoked, is scarcely treated, which means that the most dramatic change in cigar makers' history is prepared but not examined. While its contours may be entirely predictable, the reader cannot quite be sure whether all the drama was leeched out during the pre-1919 decades, when the workers had managed to hold the course.

This is a study of workers, divided to be sure, as they successfully maintained a sense of pride and comradeship even amid a rising tide of industrial capitalism. The portrait is immensely engaging.

PETER N. STEARNS

Carnegie Mellon University
Pittsburgh
Pennsylvania

DIONNE, E. J., JR. *Why Americans Hate Politics.* Pp. 430. New York: Simon & Schuster, 1991. $22.95.

Prepublicity concerning this book proclaims it addresses "why Americans hate politics." A reading of it touches on, sometimes at length, what have become familiar themes in this conventional anxiety—race relations, feminism and its critics, and the evolution of religious conservatism, especially among Protestant evangelicals and fundamentalists. In the 1990s, E. J. Dionne avers, the nation's politics will likely be dominated primarily by three considerations: the

Vietnam war's real meaning, feminism and its ramifications—especially abortion and how it plays out—and the continuing struggle to digest the civil rights upheavals of recent decades. For all its prospective impact, Dionne does not deal much with the war and its aftermath. The most conspicuous impression emerging from reading this book, however, leaves me with two paramount conclusions—what Dionne identifies as the primary forces shaping the politics of the 1990s is not systematically or coherently examined so that it explains how those forces are really going to likely shape national politics, nor does his analysis provide a very insightful case concerning why all of this should make Americans hate politics.

There does not seem to be any serious question that Americans remain uninspired by the political process as it currently functions. Voter turnout has regularly moved downward since the Nixon-Kennedy race of 1960; state and local turnouts among the electorate are even less encouraging. Are Vietnam, feminism, and civil rights necessarily the entire—or even the major—explanations for this state of affairs, however? Dionne disregards, quite strikingly in my judgment, other important considerations in the political process of the past two decades that are turning voters away from participation in politics for one reason or another—the policy stalemates attributable to voters' desires to separate partisan control of the executive and legislative branches of government, nationally and in most states, during this time frame, with attendant operational gridlocks; and the pervasive cynicism among voters arising from political action committees and the persistent disclosures of how they corrupt public agencies and those responsible for managing them.

The chapters treating feminism, race, values, and the rise in religious conservativism during the past three decades are, in and of themselves, quite informative treatments of how these respective changes in recent political phenomena have wrought variations in party and voters' behavior. The treatment of how such changes have had a bearing on the nominating of presidential candidates and the reasons behind the quality of their performance in office—be it adjudged successful, mediocre, or somewhere in between—is less satisfactory, largely because the connections are not seriously pursued or their effects are not seriously examined in relation to the obvious phenomenon they identify as the crucial variable: declining political participation and its consequences. The "so what?" of Dionne's analysis of pertinent materials still remains unconnected by and large. He could have done better; the topic deserves better treatment.

HARRY W. REYNOLDS, JR.

University of Nebraska
Omaha

GRABBE, CROCKETT L. *Space Weapons and the Strategic Defense Initiative.* Pp. xii, 252. Ames: Iowa State University Press, 1991. $27.95.

One problem with discussions of the Strategic Defense Initiative (SDI) is that scientists and policy analysts do not communicate well. As a result, policy arguments often slight the science behind SDI, and many hard scientists are on unfamiliar territory when writing about politics. This book, written by a physicist, attempts to bridge that gap.

Bridging the gap is an admirable goal, but the book fails to deliver on its promise. Neither the policy nor the scientific discussions are detailed enough to offer a full treatment of the controversial political and technological issues surrounding SDI. The technical analysis does intro-

duce readers to the many physical constraints on missile defenses—which, Grabbe points out, cannot be eluded—such as the geometry of attacking missiles above the atmosphere, time-critical targeting and battle management requirements, and the physics of high-acceleration rocket boosters. Yet most readers will find the scientific descriptions hard to decipher: critical terms are left undefined, and formulae and technical concepts are offered without the necessary context or explanation.

Grabbe is on shakier ground when he examines the policy implications of SDI (aside from the problem, beyond an author's control, that any book on nuclear policy written in the last few years has been overtaken by events). He does not cite the substantial literature on the subject, and he is frustrated that those who support SDI for political reasons are less than objective in their evaluation of the scientific data. Unfortunately, here Grabbe does not succeed at what could have been the major contribution of the volume: explaining what happens when scientific data and political realities collide.

Grabbe has included a useful section on the arms control implications of SDI, and appendices contain the text of the relevant agreements. He directly confronts the Reagan administration's effort to reinterpret the Anti-Ballistic Missile Treaty to permit SDI development.

The book contains a number of rather minor, but nonetheless distracting, faults. Some of the references are peculiar. For example, Grabbe quite reasonably argues that SDI could increase the probability of accidental nuclear war, and points to the September 1983 downing of KAL-007 as an example of the dangers of misperception; but to support the contention that the Soviets did not know they were attacking a civilian airliner, he cites a movie, *Tailspin (The Korean Airline Di-*

saster), broadcast on HBO in 1988. The arms control section contains some important inaccuracies: Grabbe claims that no arms control treaty has "led to a halt or decrease in nuclear arms buildup," ignoring the Intermediate-Range Nuclear Forces Treaty, which required both superpowers to withdraw and destroy hundreds of weapons.

The author is to be commended for his attempt to provide general readers with information about the technology of space weapons and their applications to missile defense systems. Yet the book is a frustrating read and is of only limited utility in informing debate on space-based defenses.

KENNETH R. MAYER

University of Wisconsin
Madison

GRAHAM, OTIS L., JR. *Losing Time: The Industrial Policy Debate.* Pp. xiii, 370. Cambridge, MA: Harvard University Press, 1992. $29.95.

This book is both a timely and a provocative contribution to the continuing debate about America's economic competitiveness and policy alternatives: timely in the sense that its focus, industrial policy or, more generally, competitiveness, recently was again, as in 1984 and 1988, at the center of a presidential election year debate, and provocative in the sense that it ends up calling for a more "strategic state" just as many industrial countries and the former Communist and developing world are reducing statist interventions in domestic markets.

Graham is a historian who practices his craft deftly. Establishing that industrial policy is an old phenomenon in the United States particularly at the state and local level, he chronicles the attempts to rationalize the myriad micro-

economic interventions of government from the planning pretensions of the New Deal era to the emerging industrial policy of the Carter administration and the competitiveness preoccupations of the Reagan-Bush years. Throughout, he laments the abuse of history, marshaled to prove that microeconomic interventions do or do not work. Instead, he notes, success has been mixed and depended on particular circumstances. Even successful cases of industrial policy in the past, of which he suggests there have been many, may not work in the future.

Graham tries to rescue the industrial policy debate from historical and political abuse by calling for a minimalist approach to institutionalize and make explicit the industrial policy that already exists. Expert units in the executive branch would invite more conscious, technocratic, and purposeful analysis and decision making about microeconomic intervention. Although this approach may yield little in the short run, it could, he believes, become a "beachhead" for wider coordination of government policies in macroeconomic and trade policy areas, both at home and abroad.

The argument may be disputed. At times in this account, industrial policy appears to be a solution in search of a problem. Graham accepts the orthodoxy that America is in decline and that world markets have become more oligopolistic and therefore require more "strategic" direction and trade. Another view would highlight the resurgence of American growth, manufacturing productivity, and exports in the 1980s and judge U.S. fiscal policy to be a bigger problem than the lack of industrial policy. If the U.S. government has trouble running a sensible macroeconomic policy, why should we think it can shape a coherent microeconomic policy? Much of the world has learned that "strategic" government may mean being selective, stimulating instead private sector initiatives to do the lion's share of the job.

HENRY R. NAU

George Washington University
Washington, D.C.

HELLWEG, SUSAN A., MICHAEL PFAU, and STEVER R. BRYDON. *Televised Presidential Debates*. Pp. xxiii, 168. New York: Praeger, 1992. $45.00. Paperbound, $15.95.

ALEXANDER, HERBERT E. and MONICA BAUER. *Financing the 1988 Election*. Pp. xvi, 160. Boulder, CO: Westview Press, 1991. $49.95. Paperbound, $15.95.

We have come a long way since the first broadcast debate on radio occurred in 1948. At that time, Thomas Dewey and Harold Stassen locked horns over the question of whether or not communism should be outlawed in the United States. Since then, television has replaced radio, with some claiming that television would educate us, transform the world into a global village, and provide for a better-educated electorate. One way that the electorate may become more educated on the path toward "teledemocracy" is through watching aspiring presidential candidates debate one another. Hellweg, Pfau, and Brydon's volume chronicles the evolution of this process.

Television is presented as having more of an interpersonal component to it than radio or print media. When radio was a primary media source, it forced listeners to visualize. Television sends its own images into the home and reduces the need to imagine. That change coupled with the fact that most people obtain their political cues and information from television has resulted in enormous changes in the way we select our leaders and the qualities that they need in order to be selected.

Today, it is probably true that a good sound bite or snappy zinger in a debate—for example, "I knew Jack Kennedy, Jack Kennedy was a friend of mine. Senator, you are no Jack Kennedy"—is more important in winning elections than a well-thought-out presentation of a policy position.

This volume analyzes the evolution of televised debates, their structure, their format, and the importance of both verbal and visual dimensions to the impacts of debates. Some of the more interesting conclusions are that intraparty primary debates are more informal than bipartisan debates. Opening statements have been used rarely, but closing statements are standard fare. The majority of panelists have been print-media journalists, but almost without exception moderators have come from the broadcast media. In most elections, character issues are more important than specific policy positions. The Democrats stress party identification in their debates, and the Republicans attempt to target independents and ticket splitters. Debates place a premium on ambiguity: it is not devastating not to win a debate, but it is crucial that the candidate avoid the perception of having lost such a contest. Television awards photogenic candidates with a casual yet expressive style of communication. Debates were found to socialize the young and to set the political agenda.

Alexander and Bauer's volume is more focused in that it is concerned primarily with 1988, but it loses much of the strength of the longitudinal appeal found in *Televised Presidential Debates*. The authors attempt to examine the role that money played in both national and congressional elections. They review spending patterns by categories—presidential, congressional, and state, local, and national party races—where donations originate, and the regulations involved with such donations. They also examine financing the national conventions and make recommendations for improving the system. General election campaign expenditures are analyzed as are media expenditures (the Bush-Quayle campaign spent about $31.5 million on the media, and Dukakis-Bentsen, $23.5 million). Alexander and Bauer address the topics of broadcast regulations and reasonable access. Funding innovations such as the use of soft money are also covered.

The book closes with recommended reforms that were supported by at least 75 percent or more of those who participated in a conference held under the auspices of the Citizens Research Foundation. Recommendations included raising individual contribution limits to $5000, eliminating state limitations because they are too difficult to enforce, restructuring the Federal Election Commission audit procedures, and attempting to achieve greater electoral participation (about 50 percent of the people register; only half of this group actually votes, which results in about 13 percent of the electorate actually selecting the winning candidate).

It would be impossible for candidates to achieve the name recognition necessary for victory without the media; however, access to the media is extremely expensive. For better or worse, our process has come to be dominated by the media and by money. Both of the books reviewed here highlight this fact, and it is at this juncture that they most complement each other. They are timely volumes, having been published during an election year. Both are well written and researched and present valuable insights into the electoral process. They should be of interest to those concerned with the electoral process, communications, or American politics.

JOHN S. ROBEY

University of Texas
Austin

MAYER, KENNETH R. *The Political Economy of Defense Contracting*. Pp. xviii, 232. New Haven, CT: Yale University Press, 1991. $28.50.

The Political Economy of Defense Contracting is an excellent book. A significant scholarly contribution and yet accessible to nonspecialists, Mayer's book could and should be read by a wide audience.

Mayer seeks to untangle a long-standing paradox in the study of American defense policy. While journalists—and even many politicians and bureaucrats!—see politics everywhere in the defense policy process, scholars seem unable to find politics anywhere. Who is correct? Neither and both. That is, Mayer finds that while politics pervade the defense policy process, it explains very few outcomes or legislative decisions. Here, politics are defined as economic parochialism: legislative behavior motivated by the economic costs and benefits to a member's district or state. Typically, some members of Congress are motivated by parochial concerns, but the institution as a whole is not.

The politics in the process are largely symbolic and rarely decisive. For legislators, the goal is to claim credit for a positive outcome, such as a contract for their districts, and to be able to cry politics when their districts lose. Contractors use political action committee donations and subcontracts to influence the process, but Mayer's data tend to show that these strategies do not buy votes as much as attention and access. The other area where politics play a major role is in the timing—not the size—of procurement contract awards. That is, the Pentagon has considerable discretion over when it awards a contract. The award has immediate economic effects as the contractor gears up for production. Mayer shows that procurement contract awards increase significantly in the two months prior to national elections. This helps maintain good relations between the Pentagon and many legislators.

Mayer makes his argument through a series of case studies and some quantitative analysis. Although Mayer uses some complicated regression techniques to analyze some of the data, he explains all the results in plain English. This is not to say that the argument is airtight. Some claims are more supported than proven. For example, Mayer argues but does not prove that the lobbying of parochial legislators did not provide the margin to save the F-14 in 1989. Also, now that the defense budget is being cut, new dynamics are at work. It is difficult to find anything but parochial politics and logrolling behind the recent congressional action to save the Seawolf submarine.

Nevertheless, this subtle and important book is the best work on the subject to date. It should serve as a benchmark for the journalists and scholars who will continue to delve into the complicated world of the politics of national security policy.

DANIEL WIRLS

University of California
Santa Cruz

STANILAND, MARTIN. *American Intellectuals and African Nationalists, 1955-1970.* Pp. ix, 310. New Haven, CT: Yale University Press, 1991. $30.00.

Martin Staniland's judicious and useful book is more focused on American than African ideas. His discussion of the American response to African nationalism is timely, as Americans currently are engaged in a debate over the merits of European nationalist uprisings.

Instead of proceeding chronologically, Staniland has structured his study thematically around the writings of four groups of American writers: liberals, radicals, African Americans, and conservatives. By examining the reactions of these groups to this period of African decolonization and nationalism, he shows us the beliefs and inconsistencies that lace their four value systems.

Liberals, Staniland finds, were committed to an Enlightenment rationality that rejected African dependence on superstition. Liberals supported modernization and nationalism, with echoes of 1776, instead of the African tradition of tribalism. Conservatives, however, while they believed that Western societies were better and more advanced than those in Africa, were yet willing to endorse tribalism as a source of tradition and community and shared Africans' suspicions about the benefit of a community devoted to liberal reason alone. As a consequence, liberals lobbied for larger political units —nations—in Africa, while conservatives wanted to keep smaller tribal units.

This work is less revealing about the positions and dilemmas of radicals and African Americans, who receive less attention than the liberals and conservatives.

As a work of intellectual history, there is a striking lack of context for the American ideas that Staniland traces. Even an occasional mention of how Americans' opinions toward Africa paralleled their other ideas in this period would have made the book far more complete and resonant.

For example, Staniland points out that liberals were faced with several contradictions. Liberals valued the right of African self-determination yet also believed in the correctness of universal liberal principles—including large nations— which they wanted Africans to adopt. Liberals were faced with believing that peoples were unique, yet similar.

Clearly, those contradictions underlay the New Frontier and the Great Society and helped propel the United States into the Vietnam war and other conflicts in the period after World War II. Yet we hear none of this from Staniland. He tells us that liberals' interactions with Africa provide clues to the unraveling of the American liberal consensus, but he then fails to identify these parallels even in passing. This lack of context characterizes most of the book, so that the reader is in danger of seeing the American reaction to Africa as unique rather than as part of a larger intellectual framework.

NEIL JUMONVILLE

Florida State University
Tallahassee

SOCIOLOGY

DAY, ALICE T. *Remarkable Survivors: Insights into Successful Aging among Women.* Pp. xxv, 314. Washington, DC: Urban Institute Press, 1991. $42.75. Paperbound, $24.50.

FINEMAN, MARTHA ALBERTSON. *The Illusion of Equality: The Rhetoric and Reality of Divorce Reform.* Pp. 252. Chicago: University of Chicago Press, 1991. $27.50.

These two books analyze two significant changes affecting women's lives at the end of the twentieth century: longer lives and an increased likelihood of divorce.

Alice Day has studied the quality of life today for women born between 1900 and 1910. Her data set includes information from a survey of 1049 women carried out in 1978, with 589 reinterviewed in 1987. In 1989, she chose 20 individuals from the sample for qualitative interviews. The two surveys provide broad data over time, and the qualitative data reveal information hidden in the survey. For example, in reporting friendships and social supports, the more reticent respondents enumerated fewer relationships in the survey than they did in the context of the conversational interview. Another strength of the study is the balancing of individual and environmental factors in assessing successful aging.

Day's findings are rarely surprising, but they do have a depth that goes beyond common knowledge. Maintaining control of one's life is the priority for these women. Day finds that being able to stay in one's own home is a stronger predictor of satisfaction than either income or number of children. Sharing a house with a child was viewed as a last resort, and these women preferred having kin move in with them to moving in with kin. In addition, while this study underlines the importance of social supports, it also suggests that kin are not the only source of such support; these elderly women report reciprocal relationships with friends and neighbors. Finally, the presence of a spouse is not necessarily a social support given that having to care for a dependent husband can increase the dependence of the older woman herself.

Despite the fact that women in the oldest ages have less capacity for independent living and "thinner reserves of social support," these old women showed high levels of satisfaction with their lives. Day suggests that such findings show the value of including a subjective element in estimations of people's well-being. Although, objectively, the very old experience losses, many report continuing satisfaction in the fact of survival.

Martha Fineman, a professor of law, gives us a critical study of divorce law reforms. Although liberal feminists, among others, advocated instituting the reforms, Fineman argues that the new laws presume an equality between husbands and wives that rarely exists and places women at a disadvantage.

The ideology of gender neutrality backfired also for women who want custody of their children. For young children, "the best interest of the child" used to be interpreted to mean the mother, but, as the ideology of gender neutrality took over, evidence supporting mothers was ignored in court. Fineman argues, "The nurturing ideal is being read out of custody policy or minimized in favor of more biologically centered goals which recognize both parents' rights to control of the children after divorce." Current judgments lean toward awarding custody to the "most generous parent"—the one who is more likely to share the children with the other parent. In an ironic twist, data that show fathers are less involved in the care of the children are used to argue for joint custody. Fineman sees this as an ideologically driven position that assumes that fathers will become more involved in child care if awarded legal responsibility.

Fineman also contends that the reformed laws mandate continued state intervention in the lives of family members. She characterizes the old divorce laws as "emancipatory"—after a divorce, the relationship was over. Joint custody arrangements mandate continuing relations between the parents and often involve lawyers and social workers, with their differing approaches to custody issues.

While Day provides a statistical analysis, Fineman documents the ideological assumptions of the various parties. She offers a discourse analysis attuned to the rhetoric and narrative used by different parties—liberal feminists, legal reformers, social workers—in a struggle to define the situation. Fineman also criticizes social science and the uses that have been made of it in this struggle.

Both Fineman and Day treat important issues and analyze the experiences of the first cohort of women to have to deal with the new circumstances. Although policy is not the main focus of either book, both consider policy questions to some extent. Day offers concrete suggestions to improve the lives of old women. Fineman's contention that in the reforms we should strive for "equality of results" rather than "equality of treatment" raises major questions about current family law policy.

MARY JO NEITZ

Missouri University
Columbia

FINE, MICHELLE. *Framing Dropouts: Notes on the Politics of an Urban High School.* Pp. xiii, 299. Albany: State University of New York Press, 1991. Paperbound, $19.95.

The American public high school system boasts of having achieved equal opportunity of access. What this educational system has not accomplished, however, as Michelle Fine's ethnographic research highlights, is the provision of "equitable educational outcomes." Educational decisions based on bureaucratic requirements only guarantee the status quo; they do not meet the continuum of needs of a vast majority of adolescents, especially those of color and low socioeconomic status.

Fine explores a primary tactic, labeled "silencing," that affects students and teachers. Silencing, she found, when not successful with dissenters, too often results in banishment by discharge. Criticism is seen as insubordination, a cause for suspension if not discharge.

Fine's research is based on a study of a cohort of ninth graders at a comprehensive high school (CHS) in New York City, where only a shocking 20 percent of the cohort ever graduated.

Patterns of dropping-out differ, depending on such factors as "social class, race, ethnicity, gender and disability." Fine reviews the economic and social consequences of leaving school without a high school diploma. Students who do not dissent but overly "conform" are shown to be more likely to remain in school and graduate. The complaints of students labeled troublemakers, who end up leaving the system involuntarily, eventually are turned in upon themselves, resulting in self-blame and depression.

Fine's commentary on the complex "politics of discharge" is most revealing. Although she found many discharge practices at the CHS to be illegal and infringements of civil rights, the students and their parents tended not to be aware of the law and their right to due process. Being "left back" a grade was found to be another factor causing low-skilled students to "give up" academically and served to confirm their personal sense of inadequacy.

Fine's interviews with dropouts and their own autobiographical vignettes reveal a chilling social critique. The urban markers of failure that Fine articulates are "unemployment, poverty, crime, homelessness, drugs, and burned out apartment buildings." Receipt of welfare is seen as a sign of personal failure.

The need for structural remedies is made clear. Fine calls for a transformation of the educational system. Ways must be found to encourage retention of "difficult" students. She envisions this as requiring broader empowerment. Potential remedies suggested include organizing parents to be respected "partners" in the educational process and developing coordinated social services to meet the needs of at-risk students.

A wealth of quantitative data derived from Fine's cohort study is available, as listed in the book's index. Her bibliography is comprehensive and impressive. Her scholarly and sensitive research affords the reader stunning documentation of problem areas heretofore not as fully or courageously explored. She provides

the reader with a heightened awareness of the politics surrounding the social problem of school dropouts.

FLORENCE P. ENGELHARDT

Arizona State University
Tempe

RAKOW, LANA F. *Gender on the Line: Women, the Telephone, and Community Life*. Pp. xiii, 165. Champaign: University of Illinois Press, 1992. $23.50.

In *Gender on the Line*, Lana Rakow calls attention to one of the least-studied forms of modern communication: the telephone. Debunking the technoenthusiasts' dream that telephone technology could cut across old social hierarchies, Rakow argues that telephone use is deeply embedded with gendered meanings and gendered structures of power. As she puts it, "use of the telephone by women is both gendered work—work delegated to women—and gender work—work that confirms the community's beliefs about what are women's natural tendencies and abilities."

As *Gender on the Line* demonstrates, telephone behavior does reflect persistent gender hierarchies. In the small town Rakow studied, women used the telephone to maintain kin and friendship networks, while men prided themselves on not using the telephone and urged women to make calls for them. Men and women fought over the seriousness, length, and expense of phone calls; both men and women disparaged callers who engaged in mere gossip. It is in such fine, seemingly personal distinctions that gender hierarchies are located and reproduced, and Rakow deserves credit for showing how much we can learn by studying them.

Yet, to get at this highly personalized interaction, Rakow selected a case study

method that sharply limits the significance of her research. Following the well-
worn path established by Helen and
Robert Lynd in *Middletown*, Rakow chose
to do her research in a rural midwestern
town she calls "Prospect." Prospect's
major advantage as a research site is its
manageable size: it boasts less than 1000
residents, a fact that allowed Rakow to
conduct 43 personal interviews and to act
(for six weeks) as a visiting member of the
community. Prospect's major disadvantage is that its claims to representative-
ness are shaky at best. To take the most
obvious example, a town with only one
African American family and no other
people of color is an inadequate paradigm
for a community study in modern multicultural America. Prospect is the kind of
town where it is possible for Rakow to
assert that there is a sharp split between
public activity—labeled male—and private activity—labeled female—though
feminist scholars have criticized this di-
chotomy for more than a decade. Prospect
is also—or was, in 1985, when Rakow's
research was conducted—the kind of
town where the newer telephone technologies like call waiting and answering machines seem not to have been in use. For
all these reasons, Rakow's research
seems curiously dated.

Rakow is well aware that *Gender on
the Line* is "only one of many possible
stories yet to be told." My hope is that it
will, as it should, inspire new and more
broadly based research on this fascinating topic.

PEGGY PASCOE

University of Utah
Salt Lake City

ECONOMICS

BALKIN, STEVEN. *Self-Employment for
Low-Income People*. Pp. xviii, 240.
New York: Praeger, 1989. $40.00.

GUERON, JUDITH M. and EDWARD
PAULY. *From Welfare to Work*. Pp. xvi,
316. New York: Russell Sage Foundation, 1991. $34.95. Paperbound, $12.95.

These two books catalogue and critically review the evaluation research literature on the question of providing the
poor with decent jobs and income. Steven
Balkin reviews the literature on state-
based or community-run self-employment training programs and entrepreneurship models for improving the income of the poor. In light of the 1988
Family Support Act goal of making Aid to
Families with Dependent Children a
"temporary" support program, Judith M.
Gueron and Edward Pauly examine what
they call "the knowledge base" on welfare-to-work programs sponsored by
state and local governments.

Both books provide a wealth of information and aim at comprehensive biblio-
graphic treatment of these issues. They
describe existing and planned programs,
discuss the success or failure of various
policies in particular contexts, and evaluate the costs incurred and benefits derived from these programs for taxpayers,
investors, and low-income clients. Both
books also call for more research into and
discuss the requirements for rigorous
evaluation of the success of a particular
program, from the perspective of all the
different parties who have an interest in
the process.

It turns out that many of the programs
work from the perspective of increasing
client income and lowering welfare expenditures but do not generally increase
income enough to eliminate poverty.
There are several reasons for this. First,
welfare-to-work programs are not funded
well enough to serve all the poor adequately. Thus policymakers face tremendous pressure to use limited resources to
serve people who could become self-suffi-
cient—even if still poor or near poor—
most quickly and easily. Second, providing welfare-to-work services to people

who are not likely to become self-suffi-cient quickly is a tremendous revenue drain on strapped state and local govern-ments. In the absence of structural im-provements on the demand side of the job market, policymakers fight an uphill battle.

It is in light of these constraints that Balkin proposes self-employment and en-trepreneurship models as an alternative to welfare-to-work programs. He encour-ages policymakers and investors to think of self-employment and small business formation as solutions to welfare depen-dency. He suggests setting up specific programs to encourage entrepreneurship and removing from the welfare system regulations that discourage entrepre-neurship. Current policy too frequently takes away a family's welfare and Medic-aid benefit if a member earns too much or begins to accumulate capital. He sug-gests that the current cost of such forms of jobs creation—between "$3,000 and $10,000 per job"—would be less than the cost of welfare-to-work programs. More critically, if such programs really could generate some entrepreneurial human capital and self-confidence in the poor, they would also provide something of an immunization against a return to welfare dependency.

In short, both books permit the reader to think and talk intelligently about the problem of poverty and the responsibili-ties of the citizens, government, and the private sector in alleviating it.

MARGO ANDERSON

University of Wisconsin
Milwaukee

SHOSTAK, ARTHUR B. *Robust Union-ism: Innovations in the Labor Move-ment.* Pp. xi, 384. Ithaca, NY: ILR Press, 1991. $42.00. Paperbound, $18.95.

In the midst of the most important crisis to face the American labor move-ment since the 1920s, endless analyses of its problems and solutions have been published. From cooperation with busi-ness and corporate campaigns to a more intensified focus on picket line solidar-ity—based on contradictory assumptions that unions are too complacent and too hostile—scattershot strategies for labor's rebirth are discussed in an economic and political atmosphere as given to despair as the years that preceded the Great De-pression. For those in a fighting mood, Arthur Shostak's new book, *Robust Unionism*, is a guide to some of the more "robust" union efforts for survival and growth. Almost like a gazetteer, Shostak explores the terrain of efforts to reorgan-ize workers, recapture moral, economic, and political ground for the labor move-ment, and reinvest in labor in the future.

Shostak's book emphasizes efforts to revitalize connections between labor unions, workers, and communities through new organizing and reorganiz-ing campaigns, union service to the com-munity, public relations, political work, and overtures to business. Case studies such as those of the campaign to reorgan-ize the air traffic controllers, worker safety organizations, and the Harvard clerical workers' union affirm what a new generation of labor scholars and activists have argued—that a labor movement which seeks to rebuild its base must extend beyond the specific workplace and indus-try, to engage simultaneously in commu-nity-based and work-oriented politics.

Robust Unionism has a very practical, how-to feel; it is a book of ideas for union-ists trying to find their way in the tem-pestuous seas of the postindustrial era. In the same light, Shostak provides the reader with some powerful quotations, statistics, and stories. To understand the crisis of labor union membership, for ex-ample, we need only George Meany's words:

"Why should we worry about organizing groups of people who do not want to be organized? . . . Frankly, I used to worry about the size of membership. But quite a few years ago, I just stopped worrying about it, because to me, it doesn't make any difference." (p. 59)

Throughout, Shostak gathers the good quote, the appropriate example, the telling illustration.

If there is one weakness in the volume, it is that, despite the proliferation of analyses of labor's crisis and the chosen focus on strategies, no volume such as the present one can refuse to provide the analysis that gives coherence to the strategies offered. We need to know why the "robust" strategies are robust, how they help address fundamental problems, and where they might lead. Aside from this quibble —ultimately an academic one—*Robust Unionism* is a fine study of labor's current efforts at revival.

ELIZABETH FAUE

Wayne State University
Detroit
Michigan

OTHER BOOKS

ACKELSBERG, MARTHA A. *Free Women of Spain: Anarchism and the Struggle for the Emancipation of Women*. Pp. xvi, 229. Bloomington: Indiana University Press, 1991. $39.95. Paperbound, $14.95.

ALMQUIST, PETER. *Red Forge: Soviet Military Industry since 1965*. Pp. xi, 227. New York: Columbia University Press, 1990. $35.00.

ANDERSON, MALCOLM. *Policing the World: Interpol and the Politics of International Police Cooperation*. Pp. x, 211. New York: Oxford University Press, 1989. $42.50.

BALL, HOWARD. *"We Have a Duty": The Supreme Court and the Watergate Tapes Litigation*. Pp. xiii, 164. Westport, CT: Greenwood Press, 1990. $39.95.

BARTLEY, W. W., III and STEPHEN KRESGE, eds. *The Trend of Economic Thinking: Essays on Political Economists and Economic History*. Vol. 3. Pp. xi, 388. Chicago: University of Chicago Press, 1991. $40.00.

BERGER, BRIGITTE, ed. *The Culture of Entrepreneurship*. Pp. viii, 242. San Francisco, CA: ICS Press, 1992. $29.95.

BETTS, RICHARD K. *Soldiers, Statesmen, and Cold War Crises*. Pp. xvii, 326. New York: Columbia University Press, 1991. $45.00. Paperbound, $16.50.

BIENEN, HENRY S. *Armed Forces, Conflict, and Change in Africa*. Pp. viii, 211. Boulder, CO: Westview Press, 1989. $42.50.

BLAU, JUDITH R. and NORMAN GOODMAN, eds. *Social Roles and Social Institutions: Essays in Honor of Rose Laub Coser*. Pp. xxix, 288. Boulder, CO: Westview Press, 1991. $45.00.

BOIA, LUCIAN, ed. *Great Historians of the Modern Age: An International Dictionary*. Pp. xxiv, 841. Westport, CT: Greenwood Press, 1991. $95.00.

BOWMAN, LARRY W. *Mauritius: Democracy and Development in the Indian Ocean*. Pp. xiv, 208. Boulder, CO: Westview Press, 1991. $36.50.

BRAINARD, WILLIAM C., WILLIAM D. NORDHAUS, and HAROLD W. WATTS, eds. *Money, Macroeconomics, and Economic Policy*. Pp. xii, 357. Cambridge, MA: MIT Press, 1991. $40.00.

BROWN, J. F. *Surge to Freedom: The End of Communist Rule in Eastern Europe*. Pp. x, 338. Durham, NC: Duke University Press, 1991. $45.00. Paperbound, $19.95.

BROWN, JUDITH M. *Gandhi: Prisoner of Hope*. Pp. xii, 440. New Haven, CT: Yale University Press, 1991. $35.00. Paperbound, $17.00.

CEASER, JAMES W. *Liberal Democracy and Political Science*. Pp. 242. Baltimore, MD: Johns Hopkins University Press, 1990. $29.95.

CERNEA, MICHAEL M., ed. *Putting People First: Sociological Variables in Rural Development*. Pp. xxi, 575. New York: Oxford University Press, 1991. Paperbound, $19.95.

CHRISTENSON, RON. *Political Trials in History: From Antiquity to the Present*. Pp. xxiv, 528. New Brunswick, NJ: Transaction, 1991. $49.95.

CODE, LORRAINE. *What Can She Know? Feminist Theory and the Construction of Knowledge*. Pp. xiv, 349. Ithaca, NY: Cornell University Press, 1991. $42.50. Paperbound, $14.95.

CRANE, GEORGE T. and ABLA AMAWI, eds. *The Theoretical Evolution of International Political Economy*. Pp. ix, 302. New York: Oxford University Press, 1991. Paperbound, $18.95.

CRIBB, ROBERT. *Gangsters and Revolutionaries: The Jakarta People's Militia and the Indonesian Revolution 1945-1949*. Pp. xiii, 222. Honolulu: University of Hawaii Press, 1991. $32.00.

CUFF, DANA. *Architecture: The Story of Practice*. Pp. xi, 306. Cambridge: MIT Press, 1991. $24.95.

CUNNINGHAM, NOBLE E., JR. *Popular Images of the Presidency: From Washington to Lincoln*. Pp. xi, 312. Columbia: University of Missouri Press, 1991. $44.95.

DALBY, SIMON. *Creating the Second Cold War: The Discourse of Politics*. Pp. x, 211. New York: Guilford Press, 1990. $35.00.

DAVIS, BERNARD D., ed. *The Genetic Revolution: Scientific Prospects and Public Perceptions*. Pp. xvi, 295. Baltimore, MD: Johns Hopkins University Press, 1991. $45.00. Paperbound, $15.95.

DEAN, HARTLEY. *Social Security and Social Control*. Pp. x, 221. New York: Routledge, Chapman & Hall, 1991. $74.50.

DEBARDELEBEN, JOAN, ed. *To Breathe Free: Eastern Europe's Environmental Crisis*. Pp. xiv, 266. Baltimore, MD: Johns Hopkins University Press, 1991. $34.50. Paperbound, $12.95.

DEVINE, F. E. *Commercial Bail Bonding: A Comparison of Common Law Alternatives*. Pp. xii, 216. New York: Praeger, 1991. $49.95.

ENCARNATION, DENNIS J. *Dislodging Multi-Nationals: India's Strategy in Comparative Perspective*. Pp. xiii, 237. Ithaca, NY: Cornell University Press, 1989. $29.95.

FELDMAN, ALLEN. *Formations of Violence: The Narrative of the Body and Political Terror in Northern Ireland*. Pp. vii, 319. Chicago: University of Chicago Press, 1991. $48.00. Paperbound, $17.95.

FISHER, JOSEY G., ed. *The Persistence of Youth: Oral Testimonies of the Holocaust*. Pp. xxi, 171. Westport, CT: Greenwood Press, 1991. $45.00.

FIX, MICHAEL, ed. *The Paper Curtain: Employer Sanctions' Implementation, Impact, and Reform*. Pp. xx, 334. Washington, DC: Urban Institute Press, 1991. $56.00. Paperbound, $28.50.

FONER, ERIC and JOHN A. GARRATY, eds. *The Reader's Companion to American History*. Pp. xxii, 1226. Boston: Houghton Mifflin, 1991. $35.00.

FRANKLIN, MICHAEL with MARC WILKE. *Britain: In the European Community*. Pp. viii, 133. New York: Council on Foreign Relations Press, 1990. Paperbound, $14.95.

FROST, GERALD, ed. *Europe in Turmoil: The Struggle for Pluralism*. Pp. vi, 377. New York: Praeger, 1991. $59.95.

GENTRY, CURT. *J. Edgar Hoover: The Man and the Secrets*. Pp. 846. New York: Norton, 1991. $29.95.

GEORGE, ALEXANDER L., ed. *Avoiding War: Problems of Crisis Management*. Pp. xvii, 590. Boulder, CO: Westview Press, 1991. $59.95. Paperbound, $24.95.

GIBSON, JOHN S. *International Organizations, Constitutional Law, and Human Rights*. Pp. xvii, 265. New York: Praeger, 1991. $45.00.

GOODMAN, LISL MARBURG and LEE ANN HOFF. *Omnicide: The Nuclear Dilemma*. Pp. xx, 153. New York: Praeger, 1990. $35.00.

GRAFF, HARVEY J. *The Literacy Myth: Cultural Integration and Social Structure in the Nineteenth Century*. Pp. xliv, 352. New Brunswick, NJ: Transaction, 1991. Paperbound, $19.95.

GRAUBARD, STEPHEN R., ed. *Eastern Europe . . . Central Europe . . . Europe*. Pp. xiv, 365. Boulder, CO: Westview Press, 1991. $49.95. Paperbound, $15.95.

GRAY, RICHARD. *Black Christians and White Missionaries*. Pp. viii, 134. New Haven, CT: Yale University Press, 1991. $20.00.

GRELE, RONALD J. *Envelopes of Sound: The Art of Oral History*. 2d ed. Pp. xxiv, 283. New York: Praeger, 1991. $32.50. Paperbound, $19.95.

GURIN, PATRICIA et al. *Hope and Independence: Blacks' Response to Electoral and Party Politics*. Pp. xii, 356. New York: Russell Sage Foundation, 1990. $37.50.

HENKIN, LOUIS et al. *Right v. Might: International Law and the Use of Force.* Pp. xii, 200. New York: Council on Foreign Relations Press, 1991. Paperbound, $14.95.

HERZFELD, MICHAEL. *A Place in History: Social and Monumental Time in a Cretan Town.* Pp. xvi, 305. Princeton, NJ: Princeton University Press, 1991. $45.00. Paperbound, $16.95.

HERZIK, ERIC B. and BRENT W. BROWN, eds. *Gubernatorial Leadership and State Policy.* Pp. x, 201. Westport, CT: Greenwood Press, 1991. $45.00.

HOCHSCHILD, ADAM. *The Mirror at Midnight: A South African Journey.* Pp. xii, 308. New York: Penguin, 1991. Paperbound, $10.95.

HOFFMANN, SAUL D. and LAURENCE S. SEIDMAN. *The Earned Income Tax Credit: Antipoverty Effectiveness and Labor Market Effects.* Pp. ix, 91. Kalamazoo, MI: W. E. Upjohn Institute, 1990. Paperbound, $8.95.

HONDERICH, TED. *Conservatism.* Pp. 255. Boulder, CO: Westview Press, 1991. $45.00.

INGHAM, KENNETH. *Politics in Modern Africa: The Uneven Tribal Dimension.* Pp. viii, 248. New York: Routledge, Chapman & Hall, 1991. $57.50.

ISAAK, ROBERT A. *International Political Economy: Managing World Economic Change.* Pp. xv, 316. Englewood Cliffs, NJ: Prentice-Hall, 1991. Paperbound, no price.

ISRAELI, RAPHAEL. *Palestinians between Israel and Jordan: Squaring the Triangle.* Pp. viii, 206. New York: Praeger, 1991. $45.00.

JASPER, JAMES M. *Nuclear Politics: Energy and the State in the United States, Sweden, and France.* Pp. xix, 327. Princeton, NJ: Princeton University Press, 1990. $39.50.

JONES, ANTHONY and DAVID E. POWELL, eds. *Soviet Update, 1989-1990.* Pp. vii, 152. Boulder, CO: Westview Press, 1991. $39.95. Paperbound, $14.95.

KHAN, AMAN, ed. *Budgeting in Texas: Process, Problems, Prospects.* Pp. 225. Lanham, MD: University Press of America, 1991. $43.50.

KIRBY, ANDREW, ed. *The Pentagon and the Cities.* Pp. x, 207. Newbury Park, CA: Sage, 1991. $43.95. Paperbound, $19.95.

LANGLEY, LESTER D. *Mexico and the United States: The Fragile Relationship.* Pp. xvi, 138. Boston: G. K. Hall, 1991. $27.95. Paperbound, $13.95.

LIN, JING. *The Red Guards' Path to Violence: Political, Educational, and Psychological Factors.* Pp. x, 187. New York: Praeger, 1991. $45.00.

LONGLEY, LAWRENCE D. and DAVID M. OLSON, eds. *Two into One: The Politics and Processes of National Legislative Cameral Change.* Pp. xvi, 240. Boulder, CO: Westview Press, 1991. $39.95.

MACKINTOSH, MAUREEN. *Gender, Class and Rural Transition: Agribusiness and the Food Crisis in Senegal.* Pp. xvii, 218. Atlantic Highlands, NJ: Humanities Press, 1989. $55.00. Paperbound, $17.50.

MAIDMENT, RICHARD and ANTHONY McGREW. *The American Political Process.* 2d ed. Pp. 224. Newbury Park, CA: Sage, 1991. Paperbound, $19.95.

MALIYAMKONO, T. L. and M.S.D. BAGACHWA. *The Second Economy in Tanzania.* Pp. xix, 197. Athens: Ohio University Press, 1990. $29.95.

MARRIOTT, McKIM, ed. *India through Hindu Categories.* Pp. 209. Newbury Park, CA: Sage, 1990. $32.00.

MASSARO, JOHN. *Supremely Political: The Role of Ideology and Presidential Management in Unsuccessful Supreme Court Nominations.* Pp. xiii, 272. Albany: State University of New York Press, 1990. $57.50. Paperbound, $18.95.

MASTERSON, DANIEL M. *Militarism and Politics in Latin America: Peru from Sanchez Cerro to Sendero Luminoso*. Pp. xiii, 345. Westport, CT: Greenwood Press, 1991. $47.95.

McDERMOTT, JOHN. *Corporate Society: Class, Property, and Contemporary Capitalism*. Pp. xvi, 208. Boulder, CO: Westview Press, 1991. $48.50.

McLEOD, MARK W. *The Vietnamese Response to French Intervention, 1862-1874*. Pp. xvii, 171. New York: Praeger, 1991. $39.95.

MIDDLE EAST WATCH. *Syria Unmasked: The Suppression of Human Rights by the Asad Regime*. Pp. xx, 215. New Haven, CT: Yale University Press, 1991. $25.00.

MILLER, KENNETH E. *Denmark: A Troubled Welfare State*. Pp. xiii, 224. Boulder, CO: Westview Press, 1991. $38.50.

MORE, HARRY W. and PETER CHARLES UNSINGER, eds. *Managerial Control of the Police: Internal Affairs and Audits*. Pp. xiii, 194. Springfield, IL: Charles C Thomas, 1991. $35.75.

MORMINO, GARY R. and GEORGE E. POZZETTA. *The Immigrant World of Ybor City: Indians and Their Latin Neighbors in Tampa, 1885-1985*. Pp. xiii, 368. Champaign: University of Illinois Press, 1990. Paperbound, $14.95.

MORRISON, JOHN. *Boris Yeltsin: From Bolshevik to Democrat*. Pp. xii, 303. New York: Dutton, 1991. $20.00.

NORDHOLT, JAN WILLEM SCHULTE. *Woodrow Wilson: A Life for World Peace*. Pp. 495. Berkeley: University of California Press, 1991. No price.

PARKER, JAMES G. *Lord Curzon 1859-1925: A Bibliography*. Pp. viii, 124. Westport, CT: Greenwood Press, 1991. $49.50.

PASCAL, ROBERT ANTHONY et al., eds. *The Nature of the Law and Related Legal Writings: The Collected Works of Eric Voegelin*. Vol. 27. Pp. xxiv, 119. Baton Rouge: Louisiana State University Press, 1991. $16.95.

PENN, ROGER. *Class, Power and Technology: Skilled Workers in Britain and America*. Pp. x, 196. New York: St. Martin's Press, 1990. $45.00.

PERSICO, JOSEPH E. *Casey: From the OSS to the CIA*. Pp. xix, 601. New York: Penguin, 1991. Paperbound, $14.95.

PIERSON, CHRISTOPHER. *Beyond the Welfare State?* Pp. vii, 248. University Park: Pennsylvania State Press, 1991. $32.50. Paperbound, $14.95.

PRATKANIS, ANTHONY and ELLIOT ARONSON. *Age of Propaganda: The Everyday Use and Abuse of Persuasion*. Pp. xiii, 299. New York: Freeman, 1991. Paperbound, $11.95.

RICH, P. J. *Chains of Empire: English Public Schools, Masonic Cabalism, Historical Causality, and Imperial Clubdom*. Pp. 266. New York: Regency Press, 1991. No price.

RITTNER, CAROL and JOHN K. ROTH, eds. *Memory Offended: The Auschwitz Convent Controversy*. Pp. xiv, 289. New York: Praeger, 1991. $49.95. Paperbound, $17.95.

ROTFELD, ADAM DANIEL and WALTHER STUTZLE, eds. *Germany and Europe in Transition*. Pp. x, 236. New York: Oxford University Press, 1991. $48.00.

ROY, SUMIT. *Agriculture and Technology in Developing Countries: India and Nigeria*. Pp. 223. Newbury Park, CA: Sage, 1991. $27.50.

SEARS, STEPHEN W. *Eyewitness to World War II: The Best of American Heritage*. Pp. ix, 308. Boston: Houghton Mifflin, 1991. $19.95.

SMITH, CHRISTOPHER E. *United States Magistrates in the Federal Courts: Subordinate Judges*. Pp. x, 198. New York: Praeger, 1990. $45.00.

SMITH, LACEY BALDWIN. *The Elizabethan World*. Pp. 332. Boston: Houghton Mifflin, 1991. Paperbound, $10.95.

STEPHENS, MICHAEL D. *Japan and Education*. Pp. x, 166. New York: St. Martin's Press, 1991. $35.00.

STOLL, RICHARD J. *U.S. National Security Policy and the Soviet Union: Persistent Regularities and Extreme Contingencies*. Pp. xvi, 263. Columbia: University of South Carolina Press, 1990. $39.95. Paperbound, $21.95.

SULLIVAN, MICHAEL J., III. *Measuring Global Values: The Ranking of 162 Countries*. Pp. xvi, 423. Westport, CT: Greenwood Press, 1991. $65.00.

THALER, RICHARD H. *Quasi-Rational Economics*. Pp. xxii, 367. New York: Russell Sage Foundation, 1991. $42.50.

THORP, ROSEMARY. *Economic Management and Economic Development in Peru and Colombia*. Pp. xviii, 238. Pittsburgh, PA: University of Pittsburgh Press, 1991. $44.95. Paperbound, $19.95.

TROLLINGER, WILLIAM VANCE, JR. *God's Empire: William Bell Riley and Midwestern Fundamentalism*. Pp. x, 233. Madison: University of Wisconsin Press, 1991. $37.50. Paperbound, $14.95.

TROTTER, JOE WILLIAM, JR. *Coal, Class, and Color: Blacks in Southern West Virginia, 1915-32*. Pp. xvi, 290. Champaign: University of Illinois Press, 1990. $44.95. Paperbound, $14.95.

VAUBEL, ROLAND and THOMAS D. WILLETT, eds. *The Political Economy of International Organizations: A Public Choice Approach*. Pp. viii, 311. Boulder, CO: Westview Press, 1991. $59.95.

VAYRYNEN, RAIMO, ed. *New Directions in Conflict Theory: Conflict Resolution and Conflict Transformation*. Pp. viii, 232. Newbury Park, CA: Sage, 1991. $55.00. Paperbound, $22.50.

VITAL, DAVID. *The Future of the Jews: A People at the Crossroads?* Pp. ix, 161. Cambridge, MA: Harvard University Press, 1990. $18.95.

VOLL, JOHN O., ed. *Sudan: State and Society in Crisis*. Pp. xi, 170. Bloomington: Indiana University Press, 1991. $29.95. Paperbound, $10.95.

WESCHLER, LAWRENCE. *A Miracle, A Universe: Settling Accounts with Torturers*. Pp. ix, 293. New York: Penguin, 1991. Paperbound, $9.95.

WILLS, GARRY. *Under God: Religion and American Politics*. Pp. 445. New York: Touchstone, 1991. Paperbound, $12.00.

WOODBY, SYLVIA and MARTHA L. COTTAM. *The Changing Agenda: World Politics since 1945*. 2d ed. Pp. xi, 242. Boulder, CO: Westview Press, 1991. $45.00. Paperbound, $14.95.

INDEX

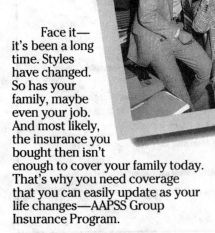

Explore ...

Published annually by the Carnegie Council on Ethics and International Affairs, ETHICS & INTERNATIONAL AFFAIRS discusses the moral foundations of international relations and the ethics of decision making.

Purchase Volume 7 for $10 (U.S.); $12 outside U.S. and Canada.

the ethical traditions affecting global change in

Ethics & International Affairs

 VOLUME 7

The Changing Terms of Sovereignty and Intervention

[ ] Please send me _____ copies of the 1993 edition of ETHICS & INTERNATIONAL AFFAIRS (Volume 7) for $10 per copy ($12 outside U.S. and Canada). Enclosed is $_____. (Make check payable to Carnegie Council. Payment must accompany order. Shipping included.)

Name _____

Address _____

City, State, Zip _____

Telephone _____

Publications Fulfillment Department
Carnegie Council on Ethics and International Affairs
170 East 64th Street, New York, NY 10021-7478
(212) 838-4120